The Supreme Knowledge

A Divine Plan's Companion

Compiled from the works of

Sri Aurobindo

by Divine Plan Publications

With the Invitation By

The Mother

Published By

Divine Plan

ISBN 978-0-9680768-4-2

15th August © 2011

Invitation

There are, in the history of the earth, moments of transition when things that have existed for thousands of years must give way to those that are about to manifest. A special concentration of the world consciousness, one might almost say, an intensification of its effort, occurs at such times, varying according to the kind of progress to be made, the quality of the transformation to be realised. We are at precisely such a turning-point in the world's history.

Just as Nature has already created upon earth a mental being, man, so too there is now a concentrated activity in this mentality to bring forth a supramental consciousness and individuality. Sri Aurobindo, incarnating the supramental consciousness in a human body, has not only revealed to us the nature of the path to follow and the way to follow it in order to reach the goal, but has also by his own personal realisation given us the example; he has provided us, so to say, with the proof that the thing can be done and the time has come to do it.

His yoga is especially intended for those who have realised in themselves all that man can realise and yet are not satisfied, for they demand from life what it cannot give. Those who yearn for the unknown and aspire for perfection, who ask themselves agonising questions and have not found any definite answers to them, they are the ones who are ready for this yoga. Certain beings who, I might say, are in the secret of the gods, are aware of the importance of this moment in the life of the world, and they have taken birth on earth to play their part in whatever way they can.

The Mother

All the world's possibilities in man are waiting as the tree waits in its seed,

Welcome

O thou who com'st to me out of Time's silences,
Yet thy voice has wakened my heart to an unknown bliss,
Immortal or mortal only in thy frame,
For more than earth speaks to me from thy soul
And more than earth surrounds me in thy gaze,
How art thou named among the sons of men?

Aim

Our aim is to live in the Divine, the Infinite, in God and not in any mere egoism and temporality, but at the same time not apart from Nature, from our fellow-beings, from earth and the mundane existence, any more than the Divine lives aloof from us and the world. He exists also in relation to the world and Nature and all these beings, but with an absolute and unalienable power, freedom and self-knowledge. Our liberation and perfection is to transcend ignorance, bondage and weakness and live in Him in relation to the world and Nature with the divine power, freedom and self-knowledge.

To know, be and posses the Divine is the one thing needful and it includes or leads up to all the rest; towards this sole good we have to drive and this attained, all the rest that the divine Will chooses for us, all necessary form and manifestation, will be added.

> Late will he know, opening the mystic script,
> Whether to a blank port of the Unseen
> He goes or, armed with her fiat, to discover
> A new mind and body in the city of God
> And enshrine the Immortal in his glory's house
> And make the finite one with Infinity.

Aspiration

It is this zeal for the Lord, — utsaha, the zeal of the whole nature for its divine results, vyakulata, the heart's eagerness for the attainment of the Divine, — that devours the ego and breaks up the limitations of its petty and narrow mould for the full and wide reception of that which it seeks, that which, being universal, exceeds and, being transcendent, surpasses even the largest and highest individual self and nature.

The power of aspiration of the heart, the force of the will, the concentration of the mind, the perseverance and determination of the applied energy are the measure of that intensity.

The sadhana of this yoga does not proceed through any set mental teaching or prescribed forms of meditation, Mantras or others, but by aspiration, by a self-concentration inwards or upwards, by self-opening to an Influence, to the Divine Power above us and its workings, to the Divine Presence in the heart and by rejection of all that is foreign to these things. It is only by faith, aspiration and surrender that this self-opening can come.

Even there shall come as a high crown of all
The end of Death, the death of Ignorance.
But first high Truth must set her feet on earth
And man aspire to the Eternal's light
And all his members feel the Spirit's touch
And all his life obey an inner Force.

6

Awareness

In the course of our Yoga or as the result of a free return of our realised Self upon the world and a free repossession of its Prakriti by the Purusha in us, we become conscious not only of the bodies and outward self-expression of others, but intimately of their inner being, their minds, their souls and that in them of which their own surface minds are not aware, then we see the real Being in them also and we see them as selves of our Self and not as mere names and forms. They become to us realities of the Eternal.

At last there wakes in us a witness Soul
That looks at truths unseen and scans the Unknown,
Then all assumes a new and marvellous face.
The world quivers with a God-light at its core,
In Time's deep heart high purposes move and live,
Life's borders crumble and join infinity.

Base

It is necessary that advancing Knowledge should base herself on a clear, pure and disciplined intellect. It is necessary, too, that she should correct her error sometimes by a return to the restraint of sensible fact, the concrete realities of the physical world. The touch of Earth is always reinvigorating to the son of Earth, even when he seeks a supraphysical Knowledge. It may even be said that the supraphysical can only be really mastered in its fullness — to its heights we can always reach — when we keep our feet firmly on the physical. "Earth is His footing", says the Upanishad whenever it images the Self that manifests in the universe. And it is certainly the fact that the wider we extend and the surer we make our knowledge of the physical world, the wider and surer becomes our foundation for the higher knowledge even for the highest, even for the *Brahmavidya*.

This world is a beginning and a base
Where Life and Mind erect their structured dreams;
An unborn Power must built reality.
A deathbound littleness is not all we are:
Immortal our forgotten vastnesses
Await discovery in our summit selves;
Unmeasured breadths and depths of being are ours.

Basic Requirement

This yoga can only be done to the end by those who are in total earnest about it and ready to abolish their little human ego and its demands in order to find themselves in the Divine. It cannot be done in a spirit of levity or laxity; the work is too high and difficult, the adverse powers in the lower Nature too ready to take advantage of the least sanction or the smallest opening, the aspiration and tapasya needed too constant and intense. It cannot be done if there is a petulant self-assertion of the ideas of the human mind or wilful indulgence of the demands and instincts and pretensions of the lowest part of the being, commonly justified under the name of human nature. It cannot be done if you insist on identifying these lowest things of the Ignorance with the divine Truth or even the lesser truth permissible on the way. It cannot be done if you cling to your past self and its old mental, vital and physical formations and habits; one has continually to leave behind his past selves and to see, act and live from an always higher and higher conscious level. It cannot be done if you insist on "freedom" for your human mind and vital ego. All the parts of the human being are entitled to express and satisfy themselves in their own way at their own risk and peril, if he so chooses, as long as he leads the ordinary life. But to enter into a path of yoga whose whole object is to substitute for these human things the law and power of a greater Truth and the whole heart of whose method is surrender to the Divine Shakti, and yet to go on claiming this so-called freedom, which is no more than a subjection to certain ignorant cosmic Forces, is to indulge in a blind contradiction and to claim the right to lead a double life.

Least of all can this yoga be done if those who profess to be its sadhaks continue always to make themselves centres, instruments or spokesmen of the forces of the Ignorance which oppose, deny and ridicule its very principle and object.

> An unshaped consciousness desired light
> And a blank prescience yearned towards distant change.
> As if a childlike finger laid on a cheek
> Reminded of the endless need in things
> The heedless Mother of the universe,
> An infant longing clutched the sombre Vast.

Battle

This pilgrimage of ascension and this descent for the labour of transformation must be inevitably a battle, a long war with ourselves and with opposing forces around us which, while it lasts, may well seem interminable. For all our old obscure and ignorant nature will contend repeatedly and obstinately with the transforming Influence, supported in its lagging unwillingness or its stark resistance by most of the established forces of environing universal Nature; the powers and principalities and the ruling beings of the Ignorance will not easily give up their empire.

The battle and conquest and empire in the shape of a victorious conflict with the Powers of Darkness, an entire spiritual self-rule and mastery over inward and outward Nature, a conquest by Knowledge, Love and Divine Will over the domains of the Ignorance is life's true object.

> Great titan beings and demoniac powers,
> World-egos racked with lust and thought and will,
> Vast minds and lives without a spirit within:
> Impatient architects of error's house,
> Leaders of cosmic ignorance and unrest
> And sponsors of sorrow and mortality
> Embodied the dark Ideas of the Abyss.

Being Conscious

The psychical consciousness, as it develops, makes us aware of the great mass of thoughts, feelings, suggestions, wills, impacts, influences of all kinds that we are receiving from others or sending to others or imbibing from and throwing into the general mind atmosphere around us. As it evolves in power, precision and clearness, we are able to trace these to their source or feel immediately their origin and transit to us and direct consciously and with an intelligent will our own messages. It becomes possible to be aware, more or less accurately and discerningly, of the activities of minds whether near to us physically or at a distance, to understand, feel or identify ourselves with their temperament, character, thoughts, feelings, reactions, whether by a psychic sense or a direct mental perception or by a very sensible and often intensely concrete reception of them into our mind or on its recording surface. At the same time, we can consciously make at least the inner selves and, if they are sufficiently sensitive, the surface minds of others aware of our own inner mental or psychic self and plastic to its thoughts, suggestions, influences or even cast it or its active image in influence into their subjective, even into their vital and physical being to work there as a helping or moulding or dominating power and presence.

> In beings it knew what lurked to them unknown;
> It seized the idea in the mind, the wish in the heart;
> It plucked out from grey folds of secrecy
> The motives which from their own sight men hide.

Birth

The soul takes birth each time, and each time a mind, life and body are formed out of the materials of universal nature according to the soul's past evolution and its need for the future.

The soul gathers the essential elements of its experiences in life and makes that its basis of growth in the evolution; when it returns to birth it takes up with its mental, vital, physical sheaths so much of its Karma as is useful to it in the new life for further experience.

As regards the stage at which the soul returning for rebirth enters the new body no rule can be laid down, for the circumstances vary with the individual. Some psychic beings get into relation with the birth-environment and the parents from the time of conception and determine the preparation of the personality and future in the embryo, others join only at the time of delivery, others even later on in the life and in these cases it is some emanation of the psychic being which upholds the life. It should be noted that the conditions of the future birth are determined fundamentally not during the stay in the psychic world but at the time of death — the psychic being then chooses what it should work out in the next terrestrial appearance and the conditions arrange themselves accordingly.

My hidden presence led thee unknowing on
From thy beginning in earth's voiceless bosom
Through life and pain and time and will and death,
Through outer shocks and inner silences
Along the mystic roads of Space and Time.

Body

The gross body of man is not like the stone or the earth; it is a combination of two sheaths, the vital and the "food" sheath and its life is a constant interaction of these two. Still the life-energy and the physical frame are two different things and in the withdrawal of the mind from the absorbing sense of the body we become increasingly sensible of the Prana and its action in the corporeal instrument and can observe and more and more control its operations. Practically, in drawing back from the body we draw back from the physical life-energy also, even while we distinguish the two and feel the latter nearer to us than the mere physical instrument. The entire conquest of the body comes in fact by the conquest of the physical life-energy.

Sadhana has to be done in the body, it cannot be done by the soul without the body. When the body drops, the soul goes wandering in other worlds — and finally it comes back to another life and another body. Then all the difficulties it had not solved meet it again in the new life. Moreover, if one throws away the body wilfully, one suffers much in the other worlds and when one is born again, it is in worse, not in better conditions. The only sensible thing is to face the difficulties in this life and this body and conquer them.

The darkness failed and slipped like a falling cloak
From the reclining body of a god.
Then through the pallid rift that seemed at first
Hardly enough for a trickle from the suns,
Outpoured the revelations and the flame.

Body - Nature

Our physical part has to give up its instincts, needs, blind conservative attachments, settled grooves of nature, its doubt and disbelief in all that is beyond itself, its faith in the inevitability of the fixed functionings of the physical mind, the physical life and the body, that they may be replaced by a new power which establishes its own greater law and functioning in form and force of Matter...

The supramental creation, since it is to be a creation upon earth, must be not only an inner change but a physical and external manifestation also. And it is precisely for this part of the work, the most difficult of all, that surrender is most needful; for this reason, that it is the actual descent of the supramental Divine into Matter and the working of the Divine Presence and Power there that can alone make the physical and external change possible. Even the most powerful self-assertion of human will and endeavour is impotent to bring it about; as for egoistic insistence and vital revolt, they are, so long as they last, insuperable obstacles to the descent. Only a calm, pure and surrendered physical consciousness, full of the psychic aspiration, can be its field; this alone can make the effective opening of the material being to the Light and Power and the supramental change a thing actual and practicable.

In the world's contacts meet his single touch;
All things shall fold thee into his embrace.
Conquer thy heart's throbs, let thy heart beat in God.

Bondage

Our renunciation must obviously be an inward renunciation; especially and above all, a renunciation of attachment and the craving of desire in the senses and the heart, of self-will in the thought and action and of egoism in the centre of the consciousness. For these things are the three knots by which we are bound to our lower nature and if we can renounce these utterly, there is nothing else that can bind us. Therefore attachment and desire must be utterly cast out; there is nothing in the world to which we must be attached, not wealth nor poverty, nor joy nor suffering, nor life nor death, nor greatness nor littleness, nor vice nor virtue, nor friend, nor wife, nor children, nor country, nor our work and mission, nor heaven nor earth, nor all that is within them or beyond them. And this does not mean that there is nothing at all that we shall love, nothing in which we shall take delight; for attachment is egoism in love and not love itself, desire is limitation and insecurity in a hunger for pleasure and satisfaction and not the seeking after the divine delight in things.

Our nature acts on a basis of confusion and restless compulsion to action, the Divine acts freely out of a fathomless calm. Into that abyss of tranquillity we must plunge and become that, if we are to annul the hold of this lower nature upon the soul. Therefore the universalised Jiva first ascends into the Silence; it becomes vast, tranquil, actionless. What action takes place, whether of body and these organs or any working whatever, the Jiva sees but does not take part in, authorise or in any way associate itself with it. There is action, but no personal actor, no bondage, no responsibility.

On Nature's gift to man a curse was laid.
All walks inarmed by its own opposites,
Error is the comrade of our mortal thought,
And falsehood lurks in the deep bosom of truth,
Sin poisons with its vivid flowers of joy
Or leaves a red scar burnt across the soul;
Virtue is a grey bondage and a goal.
At every step is laid for us a snare.

Business

The true business of man upon earth is to express in the type of humanity a growing image of the Divine; whether knowingly or unknowingly, it is to this end that Nature is working in him under the thick veil of her inner and outer processes.

To fulfil God in life is man's manhood. He starts from the animal vitality and its activities, but a divine existence is his objective.

To clear the vital, (of the spirit of vital falsehood, dramatic and romantic spirit obscuring the reason and shutting out common sense and simple truth) you must get out of its all compromise with falsehood — no matter how specious the reason it advances — and get the habit of simple straightforward psychic truth engraved in it so that nothing may have a chance to enter. Put the Mother's notice henceforth at the door of your vital being, "No falsehood hereafter shall ever enter here", and station a sentry there to see that it is put into execution.

> As a sculptor chisels a deity out of stone
> He slowly chipped off the dark envelope,
> Line of defence of Nature's ignorance,
> The illusion and mystery of the Inconscient
> In whose black pall the Eternal wraps his head
> That he may act unknown in cosmic Time.

Central Vital

Is the seat of stronger vital longings and reactions, e.g. ambition, pride, fear, love of fame, attractions and repulsions, desires and passions of various kinds and the field of many vital energies.

At the centre we meet a stronger Will of life with a greater gusto, but it is a blinded Demon, a perverted spirit and exults in the very elements that make of life a striving turmoil and an unhappy imbroglio. It is a soul of human or Titanic desire clinging to the garish colour, disordered poetry, violent tragedy or stirring melodrama of the mixed flux of good and evil, joy and sorrow, light and darkness, heady rapture and bitter torture. It loves these things and would have more and more of them or, even when it suffers and cries out against them, can accept or joy in nothing else; it hates and revolts against higher things and in its fury would trample, tear or crucify any diviner Power that has the presumption to offer to make life pure, luminous and happy and snatch from its lips the fiery brew of that exciting mixture.

> Its heart was drunk with a dire hunger's wine
> In others' suffering felt a thrilled delight
> And of death and ruin the grandiose music heard.
> To have power, to be master, was sole virtue and good:
> It claimed the whole world for Evil's living room.

Chakras – Our Inner Centres

Each of these lotuses is the centre and the storing-house of its own particular system of psychological powers, energies and operations, — each system corresponding to a plane of our psychological existence, — and these flow out and return in the stream of the pranic energies as they course through the Nadis.

This movement as it proceeds opens up the six centres of the subtle nervous system and by the opening one escapes from the limitations of the surface consciousness bound to the gross body and great ranges of experience proper to the subliminal self, mental, vital, subtle physical are shown to the sadhak.

The two most important things here are the opening of the heart centre and the opening of the mind centres to all that is behind and above them. For the heart opens to the psychic being and the mind centres open to the higher consciousness and the nexus between the psychic being and the higher consciousness is the principle means of siddhi.

The psychic opening through the heart puts us primarily into connection with the individual Divine, the Divine in his inner relation with us; it is especially the source of love and bhakti. This upward opening puts us into direct relation with the whole Divine and can create in us the divine consciousness and a new birth or births of the spirit.

Our hidden centres of celestial force
Open like flowers to a heavenly atmosphere;
Mind pauses thrilled with the supernal Ray,
And even the transient body then can feel
Ideal love and flawless happiness.

18

Chakras – The Kundalini

This arrangement of the psychic body is reproduced in the physical with the spinal column as a rod and the ganglionic centres as the Chakras which rise up from the bottom of the column, where the lowest is attached, to the brain and find their summit in the brahmarandhra at the top of the skull. These Chakras or lotuses, however, are in physical man closed or only partly open, with the consequence that only such powers and only so much of them are active in him as are sufficient for his ordinary physical life, and so much mind and soul only is at play as will accord with its needs. This is the real reason, looked at from the mechanical point of view, why the embodied soul seems so dependent on the bodily and nervous life, — though the dependence is neither so complete nor so real as it seems. The whole energy of the soul is not at play in the physical body and life, the secret powers of mind are not awake in it, the bodily and nervous energies predominate. But all the while the supreme energy is there, asleep; it is said to be coiled up and slumbering like a snake, — therefore it is called the kundalinï sakti, — in the lowest of the Chakras, in the mūlādhāra. When by Pranayama the division between the upper and lower prana currents in the body is dissolved, this Kundalini is struck and awakened, it uncoils itself and begins to rise upward like a fiery serpent breaking open each lotus as it ascends until the Shakti meets the Purusha in the brahmarandhra in a deep samadhi of union.

Put less symbolically, in more philosophical though perhaps less profound language, this means that the real energy of our being is lying asleep and inconscient in the depths of our vital system, and is awakened by the practice of Pranayama. In its expansion it opens up all the centres of our psychological being in which reside the powers and the consciousness of what would now be called perhaps our subliminal self; therefore as each centre of power and consciousness is opened up, we get access to successive psychological planes and are able to put ourselves in communication with the worlds or cosmic states of being which correspond to them; all the psychic powers abnormal to physical man, but natural to the soul develop in us. Finally, at the summit of the ascension, this arising and expanding energy meets with the superconscient self which sits concealed behind and above our physical and mental existence; this meeting leads to a profound Samadhi of union in which our waking consciousness loses itself in the superconscient. Thus by the thorough and unremitting practice of Pranayama the Hathayogin attains in his own way the psychic and spiritual results which are pursued through more directly psychical and spiritual methods in other Yogas.

A flaming serpent rose released from sleep.
It rose billowing its coils and stood erect
And climbing mightily stormily on its way
It touched her centres with flaming mouth:
As if a fiery kiss had broken their sleep,
They bloomed and laughed surcharged with light and bliss;
Then at the crown it joined the Eternal's space.

The Opening of the Centres

In our yoga there is no willed opening of the chakras, they open of themselves by the descent of the Force.

The ordinary method is the opening up of the chakras by the physical processes of Hathayoga (of which something is also included in the Rajayoga) or by the methods of the Tantric discipline. But while these may be optionally used at certain stages by the integral Yoga, they are not indispensable; for here the reliance is on the power of the higher being to change the lower existence, a working is chosen mainly from above downward and not the opposite way, and therefore the development of the superior power of the gnosis will be awaited as the instrumentative change in this part of the Yoga.

The first opening is effected by a concentration in the heart, a call to the Divine to manifest within us and through the psychic to take up and lead the whole nature. Aspiration, prayer, bhakti, love, surrender are the main supports of this part of the sadhana — accompanied by a rejection of all that stands in the way of what we aspire for. The second opening is effected by a concentration of the consciousness in the head (afterwards, above it) and an aspiration and call and a sustained will for the descent of the divine Peace, Power, Light, Knowledge, Ananda into the being ... Whatever comes has to be welcomed — for there is no absolute rule for all — but if the peace has not come first, care must be taken not to swell oneself in exultation or lose the balance. The capital movement however is when the Divine Force or Shakti, the power of the Mother comes down and takes hold, for then the organization of the consciousness begins and the larger foundation of the yoga.

All underwent a high celestial change:
Breaking the black Inconscient's blind mute wall,
Effacing the circles of the Ignorance,
Powers and divinities burst flaming forth;
Each part of the being trembling with delight
Lay overwhelmed with tides of happiness
And saw her hand in every circumstance
And felt her touch in every limb and cell.
In the country of the lotus of the head

Which thinking mind has made its busy space,
In the castle of the lotus twixt the brows
Whence it shoots the arrows of its sight and will,
In the passage of the lotus of the throat
Where speech must rise and the expressing mind
And the heart's impulse run towards word and act,
A glad uplift and a new working came

Circumconscient

Around us too is a circumconscient Universal of which we are a portion. This circumconscience is pouring its forces, suggestions, stimuli, compulsions into us at every moment of our existence.

Around us is a universal Mind of which our mind is a formation and our thoughts, feelings, will, impulses are continually little more than a personally modified reception and transcription of its thought-waves, its force-currents, its foam of emotion and sensation, its billows of impulse.

Around us is a permanent universal Life of which our petty flow of life-formation that begins and ceases is only a small dynamic wave.

So must the dim being grow in light and force
And rise to his higher destiny at last,
Look up to God and round at the universe,
And learn by failure and progress by fall
And battle with environment and doom,
By suffering discover his deep soul
And by possession grow to his own vasts.

Complex Personality

The most disconcerting discovery is to find that every part of us — intellect, will, sense-mind, nervous or desire-self, the heart, the body — has each, as it were, its own complex individuality and natural formation independent of the rest; it neither agrees with itself nor with the others nor with the representative ego which is the shadow cast by some central and centralising self on our superficial ignorance. We find that we are composed not of one but many personalities and each has its own demands and differing nature. Our being is a roughly constituted chaos into which we have to introduce the principle of a divine order. Moreover, we find that inwardly too, no less than outwardly, we are not alone in the world; the sharp separateness of our ego was no more than a strong imposition and delusion; we do not exist in ourselves, we do not really live apart in an inner privacy or solitude. Our mind is a receiving, developing and modifying machine into which there is being constantly passed from moment to moment a ceaseless foreign flux, a streaming mass of disparate materials from above, from below, from outside. Much more than half our thoughts and feelings are not our own in the sense that they take form out of ourselves; of hardly anything can it be said that it is truly original to our nature.

Whatever the appearance we must bear,
Whatever our strong ills and present fate,
When nothing we can see but drift and bale,
A mighty Guidance leads us still through all.
After we have served this divided world
God's bliss and oneness are our inborn right.

Concentration

Ordinarily the consciousness is spread out everywhere, dispersed, running in this or that direction, after this subject and that object in multitude. When anything has to be done of a sustained nature the first thing one does is to draw back all this dispersed consciousness and concentrate. It is then, if one looks closely, bound to be concentrated in one place and on one occupation, subject or object — as when you are composing a poem or a botanist is studying a flower. The place is usually somewhere in the brain if it is the thought, in the heart if it is the feeling in which one is concentrated. The yogic concentration is simply an extension and intensification of the same thing.

Concentration is a gathering together of the consciousness and either centralising at one point or turning on a single object, e.g., the Divine; there can also be a gathered condition throughout the whole being, not at a point. In meditation it is not indispensable to gather like this, one can simply remain with a quiet mind thinking of one subject or observing what comes in the consciousness and dealing with it.

One can concentrate in any of the three centres which is easiest to the sadhak or gives most result. The power of the concentration in the heart-centre is to open that centre and by the power of aspiration, love, bhakti, surrender, remove the veil which covers and conceals the soul and bring forward the soul or psychic being to govern the mind, life and body and turn and open them all fully to the Divine, removing all that is opposed to that turning and opening.

The power of concentration above the head is to bring peace, silence, liberation from the body sense, the identification with mind and life and open the way for the lower (mental, vital, physical) consciousness to rise up to meet the higher consciousness above and for the powers of the higher (spiritual nature) consciousness to descend into mind, life and body.

The power and concentration in the eyebrows is to open the centre there, liberate the inner mind, and vision and the inner or yogic consciousness and its experiences and powers.

They lived in the mind and knew truth from within;
A sight withdrawn in the concentrated heart
Could pierce behind the screen of Time's results
And the rigid cast and shape of visible things.

Conditions for Higher Life

The first process of the yoga is to make the determination of self-consecration. Put yourself with all your heart and all your strength into God's hands. Make no conditions ask for nothing, not even a spiritual realisation in the yoga, for nothing at all except that in you and through you his will may be directly performed.

To those who demand from him, God gives what they demand, but to those who give themselves and demand nothing, he gives everything that they might otherwise have asked or needed and in addition he gives himself and the spontaneous boons of his love.

All ambition, pride and vanity must disappear from the thoughts and the feelings... All falsehood must be rejected from the speech, thought and action and all ostentation, arrogance and insolence. A simple, quiet and unpretending aspiration to the Truth and reception of it for its own sake and not for any profit it may bring you, a straightforward acceptance of the Mother's will whatever it may be, a complete casting away of all pretensions and pretences, a readiness to obey completely and without reserve and to accept any position and any discipline given are the only conditions on which a divine change can be effected in you.

By heavy toil and slow aeonic steps
Reaching the bright miraculous fringe of God,
Into the glory of the Oversoul.
My will, my call is there in men and things.

Consciousness

Consciousness is a fundamental thing, the fundamental thing in existence — it is the energy, the motion, the movement of consciousness that creates the universe and all that is in it — not only the macrocosm but the microcosm is nothing but consciousness arranging itself. For instance, when consciousness in its movement or rather a certain stress of movement forgets itself in the action it becomes an apparently "unconscious" energy; when it forgets itself in the form it becomes the electron, the atom, the material object. In reality it is still consciousness that works in the energy and determines the form and the evolution of form. When it wants to liberate itself, slowly, evolutionarily, out of Matter, but still in the form, it emerges as life, as animal, as man and it can go on evolving itself still farther out of its involution and become something more than mere man.

All can be rendered into terms of consciousness because all is either a creation of consciousness or else one of its forms. All exists in an infinite conscious existence and is a part or a form of it. In proportion as one can share directly or indirectly, completely or incompletely in the eternal awareness of this Infinite, or momentarily contact or enter into it, or formulate some superior or inferior power of its consciousness or knowledge, one can know what it knows in part or whole, by a direct knowing or an indirect coming to knowledge. A conscious, half conscious or subconscious participation in the awareness of the Infinite is the basis of all knowledge.

It can subjectively formulate itself as a physical, a vital, a mental, a psychic consciousness.

If it chooses to work in you through the sense of ego, you think that it is the clear-cut individual "I" that does everything — if it begins to release itself from the limited working, you begin to expand your sense of "I" till it bursts into infinity and no longer exists or you shed it and flower into spiritual wideness. Of course, this is not what is spoken of in modern materialistic thought as consciousness, because that thought is governed by science and sees consciousness only as a phenomenon that emerges out of inconscient Matter and consists of certain reactions of the system to outward things. But that is a phenomenon of consciousness, it is not consciousness itself, it is even only a very small part of the possible phenomenon of consciousness and can give no clue to Consciousness the Reality which is of the very essence of existence.

Out of the Inconscient I build consciousness
And lead through death to reach immortal life.
Many are God's forms by which he grows in man;
They stamp his thoughts and deeds with divinity,
Uplift the stature of the human clay
Or slowly transmute it into heaven's gold.

Cosmic Consciousness

Is that in which the limits of ego, personal mind and body disappear and one becomes aware of a cosmic vastness which is or filled by a cosmic spirit and aware also of the direct play of cosmic forces, universal mind forces, universal life forces, universal energies of Matter, universal overmind forces. But one does not become aware of all these together; the opening of the cosmic consciousness is usually progressive.

All the attempt of man to arrive at universal sympathy, universal love and the understanding and knowledge of the inner soul of other existences is an attempt to beat thin, breach and eventually break down by the power of the enlarging mind and heart the walls of the ego and arrive nearer to a cosmic oneness.

The cosmic consciousness has many levels — the cosmic physical, the cosmic vital, the cosmic mind, Intuition, Overmind and Supermind where the Transcendental begins.

By entering into the cosmic consciousness we participate in that all-vision and see everything in the values of the Infinite and the One. Limitation itself, ignorance itself changes their meaning for us. Ignorance changes into a particular action of divine knowledge, strength and weakness and incapacity into a free putting forth and holding back various measures of divine Force, joy and grief, pleasure and pain into a mastering and a suffering of divine delight, struggle into a balancing of forces and values in the divine harmony.

> The circle of the little self was gone;
> The separate being could no more be felt;
> It disappeared and knew itself no more,

Creation

This inevitable evolution first develops, as it is bound to develop, Matter and a material universe; in Matter, Life appears and living physical beings; in Life, Mind manifests and embodied thinking and living beings; in Mind, ever increasing its powers and activities in forms of Matter, the Supermind or Truth-Consciousness must appear, inevitably, by the very force of what is contained in the Inconscience and the necessity in Nature to bring it into manifestation. Supermind appearing manifests the Spirit's self-knowledge and whole-knowledge in a supramental living being and must bring about by the same law, by an inherent necessity and inevitability, the dynamic manifestation here of the divine Existence, Consciousness and Delight of existence. It is this that is the significance of the plan and order of the terrestrial evolution; it is this necessity that must determine all its steps and degrees, its principle and its process. Mind, Life and Matter are the realised powers of the evolution and well-known to us; Supermind and the triune aspects of Sachchidananda are the secret principles which are not yet put in front and have still to be realised in the forms of the manifestation, and we know them only by hints and a partial and fragmentary action still not disengaged from the lower movement and therefore not easily recognisable. But their evolution too is part of the destiny of the soul in the Becoming, — there must be a realisation and dynamisation in earth-life and in Matter not only of Mind but of all that is above it, all that has descended indeed but is still concealed in earth-life and Matter.

> A slow reversal's movement then took place:
> A gas belched out from some invisible Fire,
> Of its dense rings were formed these million stars;
> Upon earth's new-born soil God's tread was heard.

Dangers

It often happens too that some power or powers undivine in their nature present themselves as the Supreme Lord or as the Divine Mother and claim the being's services and surrender. If these things are accepted, there will be an extremely disastrous consequences. If indeed there is the assent of the sadhak to the Divine working alone and the submission or surrender to that guidance, then all can go smoothly. This assent to the Divine and a rejection of all egoistic forces or forces that appeal to the ego are the safeguard throughout the sadhana. But the ways of nature are full of snares, the disguises of the ego are innumerable, the illusions of the Powers of Darkness Rakshasi Maya, are extraordinary skilful; the reason is an insufficient guide and often turns traitor; vital desire is always with us tempting to follow any alluring call.

What they (Hostile Forces) do is press with all their force upon some weak point of our nature and if we are vigilant, we can see and throw away that weakness. Only the attack method of these Forces is too violent and upheaving and endangers the good things in one also, faith and peace etc. - so one has to be careful to keep these against all attacks.

The hostiles when they cannot break the yoga by positive means, by positive temptations or vital outbreaks, are quite willing to do it negatively; first by depression, then by refusal at once of ordinary life and of sadhana.

The first thing is for the mental being to stand back, refuse to accept, say "This is no longer mine." Then, even if the vital being responds to the attack, one part of the nature can be free and observe and discourage it.

The Fiend was visible, but cloaked in light;
He seemed a helping angel from the skies:
He armed untruth with Scripture and the Law;
He deceived with wisdom, with virtue slew the soul
And led to perdition by the heavenward path.

32

Dangers of the Inner Ranges

There is a more outer and confused activity of the awakening subliminal mind and life which is clogged with and subject to the grosser desires and illusions of the mind and vital being and vitiated in spite of its wider range of experience and power and capacities by an enormous mass of error and deformations of the will and knowledge, full of false suggestions and images, false and distorted intuitions and inspirations and impulses. This is an inferior activity to which clairvoyants, psychists, spiritists, occultists, seekers of power and Siddhi are very liable and to which all the warnings against the dangers and errors of this kind of seeking are more especially applicable. The seeker of spiritual perfection has to pass as quickly as possible, if he cannot altogether avoid, this zone of danger, and the safe rule here is to be attached to none of these things, but to make spiritual progress one's sole real objective.

Incalculable are her strength and ruse,
Her touch is a fascination and a death;
She kills her victim with his own delight;
Even Good she makes a hook to drag to Hell.

Death

The soul after it leaves the body travels through several states or planes until the psychic being has shed its temporary sheaths, then it reaches the psychic world where it rests in a kind of sleep till it is ready for reincarnation. What it keeps with it of the human experience in the end is only the essence of all that it has gone through, what it can use for its development. This is the general rule, but it does not apply to exceptional cases or to very developed beings who have achieved a greater consciousness than the ordinary human level.

When the body is dissolved, the vital goes into the vital plane and remains there for a time, but after a time the vital sheath disappears. The last to dissolve is the mental sheath. Finally the soul or psychic being retires into the psychic world to rest there till a new birth is close.

The departed soul retains the memory of its past experiences only in their essence, not in their form of detail. It is only if the soul brings back some past personality or personalities as part of its present manifestation that it is likely to remember the details of the past life. Otherwise, it is only by Yogadrishti that the memory comes.

The evolution has to be done in the body, it cannot be done by the soul without the body. When the body drops, the soul goes wandering in other worlds — and finally it comes back to another life and another body. Then all the difficulties it had not solved meet it again in the new life. Moreover, if one throws away the body wilfully, one suffers much in the other worlds and when one is born again, it is in worse, not in better conditions. The only sensible thing is to face the difficulties in this life and this body and conquer them.

Our life' repose is in the Infinite:
It cannot end, its end is Life supreme.
Death is a passage, not a goal of our walk:
Some ancient deep impulsion labours on:
Our souls are dragged as with a hidden leash,
Carried from birth to birth, from world to world,
Our acts prolong after the body's fall
The old perpetual journey without pause.

Delight of Existence

When the divine conscious-force working secretly in us has devoured these growths of desire, when in the image of Rig Veda the fire of God has burnt up the shoots of earth, that which is concealed at the roots of these pains and pleasures, their cause and secret being, the sap of delight in them, will emerge in new forms not of desire, but of self-existent satisfaction which will replace mortal pleasure by the Immortal's ecstasy. And this transformation is possible because these growths of sensation and emotion are in their essential being, the pains no less than the pleasures, that delight of existence which they seek but fail to reveal, — fail because of division, ignorance of self and egoism.

Thy mind's light hides from thee the Eternal's thought,
Thy heart's hopes hide from thee the Eternal's will,
Earth's joys shut from thee the Immortal's bliss.
Thence rose the need of a dark intruding god,
The world's dread teacher, the creator, pain.

Depression

The constant recurrence of depression and despair or of doubt and revolt is due to a mental or vital formation which takes hold of the vital mind and makes it run round always in the same circle at the slightest provoking cause or even without cause. It is like an illness to which the body consents from habit and from belief in the illness even though it suffers from it, and once started the illness runs its habitual course unless it is cut short by some strong counteracting force. If once the body can withdraw its consent, the illness immediately or quickly ceases. So too, if the vital mind withdraws its consent, refuse to be dominated by the habitual suggestions and the habitual movements, these recurrences of depression and despair can be made soon to cease. This can be done easily only when the mind refuses any longer to believe in the suggestions or accepts the ideas or feelings that start the circle.

Free yourself from all exaggerated self-depreciation and the habit of getting depressed by the sense of sin, difficulty or failure. These feelings do not really help, on the contrary, they are an immense obstacle and hamper the progress. They belong to the religious, not to the yogic mentality. The yogin should look on all the defects of the nature as movements of the lower Prakriti common to all and reject them calmly, firmly and persistently with full confidence in the Divine Power — without weakness or depression or negligence and without excitement, impatience or violence.

When some weakness comes up you should take it as an opportunity to know what is still to be done and call down the strength into that part. Whatever you see, don't get disturbed or depressed. If one sees a defect one must look at it with utmost quietude and call down more force and light to get rid of it.

A Will, a hope immense now seized his heart,
And to discern the superhuman's form
He raised his eyes to unseen spiritual heights,
Aspiring to bring down a greater world.

Desire

Desire is a psychological movement, and it can attach itself to a "true need" as well as to things that are not true needs. One must approach even true needs without desire. If one does not get them, one must feel nothing.

The lower vital has its place, it is not to be crushed or killed; but it has to be changed, "caught hold of by both ends," at the upper end a mastery and control, at the lower end a right use.

The rejection of desire is essentially the rejection of the element of craving, putting that out from the consciousness itself as a foreign element not belonging to the true self and the inner nature... It is only when this done in a wrong way, by a mental ascetic principle or hard moral rule, that it can be called suppression...

It is quite true that ''in our path the attitude is not one of forceful suppression, nigraha''; it is not coercion according to a mental rule or principle on an unpersuaded vital being. But that does not mean either that the vital has to go its own way and do according to its fancy. It is not coercion that is the way, but an inner change in which the lower vital is led, enlightened and transformed by a higher consciousness which is detached from the objects of vital desire.

The spiritual life will draw its sustenance not from desire but from a pure and selfless spiritual delight of essential existence.

> Then lest a human cry should spoil the Truth
> He tore desire up from its bleeding roots
> And offered to the gods the vacant place.
> Thus could he bear the touch immaculate.

Desire and Action

It is a common error to suppose that action is impossible or at least meaningless without desire. If desire ceases, we are told, action also must cease. But this, like other too simply comprehensive generalisations, is more attractive to the cutting and defining mind than true. The major part of the work done in the universe is accomplished without any interference of desire; it proceeds by the calm necessity and spontaneous law of Nature. Even man constantly does work of various kinds by a spontaneous impulse, intuition, instinct or acts in obedience to a natural necessity and law of forces without either mental planning or the urge of a conscious vital volition or emotional desire. Often enough his act is contrary to his intention or his desire; it proceeds out of him in subjection to a need or compulsion, in submission to an impulse, in obedience to a force in him that pushes for self-expression or in conscious pursuance of a higher principle.

Impervious to desire and doom and hope,
Their station of inviolable might
Moveless upholds the world's enormous task,
Its ignorance is by their knowledge lit,
Its yearning lasts by their indifference.

Desire and Tamas

Desire is an additional lure to which Nature has given a great part in the life of animated beings in order to produce a certain kind of rajasic action necessary for her intermediate ends; but it is not her sole or even her chief engine. It has its great use while it endures: it helps us to rise out of inertia, it contradicts many tamasic forces which would otherwise inhabit action. But the seeker who has advanced far on the way of works has passed beyond this intermediate stage in which desire is a helpful engine. Its push is no longer indispensable for his action, but is rather a terrible hindrance and source of stumbling, inefficiency and failure.

Wherever desire and ego harbour, passion and disturbance harbour with them and share their life.

This constant change spells progress to her eyes;
Her thought is an endless march without a goal.
There is no summit on which she can stand
And see in a single glance the Infinite's whole.

Desire Soul

All the difficulty in dealing spiritually with the works of life arises because the Will-in-Life for its purposes in the Ignorance has created a false kind of desire-soul and substituted it for that spark of the Divine which is the true psyche. All or most of the works of life are at present or seem to be actuated and vitiated by this soul of desire; even those that are ethical or religious, even those that wear the guise of altruism, philanthropy, self-sacrifice, self-denial, are shot through and through with the threads of its making. This soul of desire is a separative soul of ego and all its instincts are for a separative self-affirmation; it pushes always, openly or under more or less shining masks, for its own growth, for possession, for enjoyment, for conquest and empire. If the curse of disquiet and disharmony and perversion is to be lifted from Life, the true soul, the psychic being, must be given its leading place and there must be a dissolution of the false soul of desire and ego. But this does not mean that life itself must be coerced and denied its native line of fulfilment; for behind this outer life soul of desire there is in us an inner and true vital being which has not to be dissolved but brought out into prominence and released to its true working as a power of the Divine Nature. The prominence of this true vital being under the lead of the true inmost soul within us is the condition for the divine fulfilment of the objects of the Life-Force. Those objects will even remain the same in essence, but transformed in their inner motive and their outer character.

At every moment the sadhak must proceed with a vigilant eye upon the deceits of the ego and the ambushes of the misleading Powers of Darkness who ever present themselves as the one source of Light and Truth and joy, a triple disguise,

Attire of the rapturous Dancer in the ways,
Withhold from thee the body of God's bliss.

Desire World

In this world forms do not determine the conditions of the life, but it is life which determines the form, and therefore forms are there much more free, fluid, largely to our conceptions strangely variable than in the material world. Desire and the satisfaction of impulse are the first law of this world, it may be called the desire-world, for that is its principal characteristic.

This world contains not only the possibility of large or intense or continuous enjoyments almost inconceivable to the limited physical mind, but also the possibility of equally enormous sufferings. It is here therefore that there are situated the lowest heavens and all the hells with the tradition and imagination of which the human mind has lured and terrified itself since the earliest ages.

To fling delight down like a net of gold.
Earth is a chosen place of mightiest souls;
Earth is the heroic spirit's battlefield,
The forge where the Arch-mason shapes his works.

Destiny

What we call destiny is only in fact the result of the present condition of the being and the nature and energies it has accumulated in the past acting on each other and determining the present attempts and their future results. But as soon as one enters the path of spiritual, this old predetermined destiny begins to recede. There comes in a new factor, the Divine Grace, the help of a higher Divine Force other than the force of Karma, which can lift the sadhak beyond the present possibilities of his nature. One's spiritual destiny is then the divine election which ensures the future.

Those who fall, fall not because of the attack of the vital forces, but because they put themselves on the side of the hostile Force and prefer a vital ambition or desire (ambition, vanity, lust, etc.) to the spiritual siddhi.

> Here Matter seems to mould the body's life
> And the soul follows where its nature drives:
> Nature and Fate compel his free-will's choice.
> But greater spirits this balance can reverse
> And make the soul the artist of its fate.

Discrimination

There is the true psychic which is always good and there is the psychic opening to mental, vital and other worlds which contain all kinds of things good, bad and indifferent, true, false and half true, thought-suggestions which are of all kinds, and messages also which are of all kinds. What is needed is not to give yourself impartially to all of them but to develop both a sufficient knowledge and experience and a sufficient discrimination to be able to keep your balance and eliminate falsehood, half-truths and mixtures. It will not do to dismiss impatiently the necessity for discrimination on the ground that that is mere intellectualism. The discrimination need not be intellectual, although that also is a thing not to be despised. But it may be psychic discrimination or one that comes from the higher supra-intellectual mind and from the higher being. If you have not this, then you have need of constant protection and guidance from those who have it, and who have also long psychic experience, and it may be disastrous for you to rely entirely on yourself and to reject such guidance.

In the meantime there are three rules of the sadhana which are very necessary in an earlier stage which you should remember. First, open yourself to experience but do not take the bhoga of the experiences. Do not attach yourself to any particular kind of experience. Do not take all ideas and suggestions as true and do not take any knowledge, voice or thought-message as absolutely final and definitive. Truth itself is only true when complete and it changes its meaning as one rises and sees it from a higher level.

> The middle path is made for thinking man.
> To choose his steps by reason's vigilant light,
> To choose his path among many paths
> Is given him, for each his difficult goal
> Hewn out of infinite possibility.

Divine

The Divine has three aspects for us:

1. It is the Cosmic Self and Spirit that is in and behind all things and beings, from which and in which all is manifested in the universe – although it is now a manifestation in the Ignorance.

2. It is the Spirit and Master of our own being within us whom we have to serve and learn to express his will in all our movements so that we may grow out of the Ignorance into the Light.

3. The Divine is transcendent Being and Spirit, all bliss and light and divine knowledge and power, and towards that highest divine existence and its Light we have to rise and bring down the reality of it more and more into our consciousness and life.

In the ordinary Nature we live in the Ignorance and do not know the Divine. The forces of the ordinary Nature are undivine forces because they weave a veil of ego and desire and unconsciousness which conceals the Divine from us. To get into the higher and deeper consciousness which knows and lives luminously in the Divine, we have to get rid of the forces of the lower nature and open to the action of the Divine Shakti which will transform our consciousness into that of the Divine Nature.

Most people live in their ordinary outer ignorant personality which does not easily open to the Divine; but there is an inner being within them of which they do not know, which can easily open to the Truth and the Light. But there is a wall which divides them from it, a wall of obscurity and unconsciousness. When it breaks down, then there is the release; the feeling of calm, Ananda, joy...

This is the conception of the Divine from which we have to start — the realisation of its truth can only come with the opening of the consciousness and its change.

In the one task for which our lives were born,
To raise the world to God in deathless Light,
To bring God down to the world on earth we came,
To change the earthly life to life divine.

Divine Consciousness

That which creates in itself all things by a movement of its conscious-force and governs their development through a self-evolution by inherent knowledge-will of the truth of existence or real-idea which has formed them. The Being that is thus conscient is what we call God; and He must obviously be omnipresent, omniscient, omnipotent. Omnipresent, for all forms are forms of His conscious being created by its force of movement in its own extension as Space and Time; omniscient, for all things exist in His conscious-being, are formed by it and possessed by it; omnipotent, for this all-possessing consciousness is also an all-possessing Force and all-informing Will. And this Will and Knowledge are not at war with each other as our will and knowledge are capable of being at war with each other, because they are not different but are one movement of the same being.

The divine consciousness might in the end, increasing its conquests, remould mind, life and body themselves into a more perfect image of its eternal Truth and realise not only in soul but in substance its kingdom of heaven upon earth. The first of these victories, the internal, has certainly been achieved in a greater or less degree by some, perhaps by many, upon earth; the other, the external, even if never more or less realised in past aeons as a first type for future cycles and still held in the subconscious memory of the earth-nature, may yet be intended as a coming victorious achievement of God in humanity.

> One who could love without return for love,
> Meeting and turning to the best the worst,
> It healed the bitter cruelties of earth
> Transforming all experience to delight.

Divine Gnosis

Supermind is the divine Gnosis which creates, governs and upholds the worlds: it is the secret Wisdom which upholds both our Knowledge and our Ignorance.

This creation is inspired by the divine delight, the eternal Ananda; it is full of the joy of its own truth and power, it creates in bliss, creates out of bliss, creates that which is blissful. Therefore the world of the gnosis, the supramental world is the true and the happy creation, rtam, bhadram, since all in it shares in the perfect joy that made it. A divine radiance of deviating knowledge, a divine power of unfaltering will and a divine ease of unstumbling bliss are the nature or Prakriti of the soul in supermind... Supermind or gnosis is the supreme Truth, the supreme Thought, the supreme Word, the supreme Light, the supreme Will-Idea; it is the inner and outer extension of the Infinite who is beyond Space, the unfettered Time of the Eternal who is timeless, the supernal harmony of all absolutes of the Absolute.

The fount of the creation and its works
It is the originer of all truth here,
The sun-orb of mind's fragmentary rays,
Infinity's heaven that spills the rain of God.

Divine Love

The Divine Love which is at the heart of all creation and the most powerful of all redeeming and creative forces has yet been the least frontally present in earthly life, the least successfully redemptive, the least creative.

Love is that by which we can enter directly into possession of the self-existent delight of the divine Being. Divine love is indeed itself that possession and, as it were, the body of the Ananda.

The true divine Ananda in the physical has a different quality and movement and substance; self-existent in its essence, its manifestation is dependent only on an inner union with the Divine. You have spoken of Divine Love; but Divine Love, when it touches the physical, does not awaken the gross lower vital propensities; indulgence of them would only repel it and make it withdraw again to the heights from which it is already difficult enough to draw it down into the coarseness of the material creation which it alone can transform. Seek the Divine Love through the only gate through which it will consent to enter, the gate of the psychic being, and cast away the lower vital error.

To bring the Divine Love and Beauty and Ananda into the world is, indeed, the whole crown and essence of our yoga. But it has always seemed to me impossible unless there comes as its support and foundation and guard the Divine Truth - what I call the supramental - and its Divine Power.

My love is not a hunger of the heart,
My love is not a craving of the flesh;
It came to me from God, to God returns.

Divine Presence

After we have entered the path, he envelops us with his wide and mighty liberating Impersonality or moves near to us with the face and form of a personal Godhead. In and around us we feel a Power that upholds and protects and cherishes; we hear a Voice that guides; a conscious Will greater than ourselves rules us; an imperative Force moves our thought and actions and our very body; an ever-widening Consciousness assimilates ours, a living Light of Knowledge lights all within, or a Beatitude invades us; a Mightiness presses from above, concrete, massive and overpowering, and penetrates and pours itself into the very stuff of our nature; a Peace sits there, a Light, a Bliss, a Strength, a Greatness. Or there are relations, personal, intimate as life itself, sweet as love, encompassing like the sky, deep like deep waters. A Friend walks at our side; a Lover is with us in our heart's secrecy; a Master of the Work and the Ordeal points our way; a Creator of things uses us as his instrument; we are in the arms of the eternal Mother. All these more seizable aspects in which the Ineffable meets us are truths and not mere helpful symbols or useful imaginations; but as we progress, their first imperfect formulations in our experience yield to a larger vision of the one Truth that is behind them. At each step their mere mental masks are shed and they acquire a larger, a profounder, a more intimate significance.

A fire has come and touched men's hearts and gone;
A few have caught flame and risen to greater life.

48

Divine Will

There is a secret divine Will, eternal and infinite, omniscient and omnipotent, that expresses itself in the universality and in each particular of all these apparently temporal and finite, inconscient or half-conscient things.

Only, it is not our conscious mental will; it rejects often enough what our conscious will accepts and accepts what our conscious will rejects. For while this secret One knows all and every whole and each detail, our surface mind knows only a little part of things. Our will is conscious in the mind, and what it knows, it knows by the thought only; the divine Will is superconscious to us because it is in its essence supramental, and it knows all because it is all. This divine Will is not an alien Power or Presence; it is intimate to us and we ourselves are part of it: for it is our own highest Self that possesses and supports it. If we surrender our conscious will and allow it to be made one with the will of the Eternal, then and then only shall we attain to a true freedom; living in the divine liberty, we shall no longer cling to this shackled so-called free will, a puppet freedom ignorant, illusory, bound to the error of its own inadequate vital motives and mental figures.

> Then miracle is made the common rule,
> One mighty deed can change the course of things;
> A lonely thought becomes omnipotent.

Divinisation

Means taking up of the human elements, showing them the way to their own perfection, raising them by purification and perfection to their full power and Ananda and that means the raising of the whole of the earthly life to its full power and Ananda.

He who seeks the Divine must consecrate himself to God and to God only. Our whole being soul, mind, sense, heart, will, life, body must consecrate all its energies so entirely and in such a way that it shall become a fit vehicle for the Divine. The secret of success in Yoga is to regard it not as one of the aims to be pursued in life, but as the whole of life. This is not an easy task; for everything in the world follows the fixed habit which is to it a law and resists a radical change. And no change can be more radical than the revolution attempted in the integral Yoga.

All grace and glory and all divinity
Were here collected in a single form;
All worshipped eyes looked through his from one face;
He bore all godheads in his grandiose limbs.

Dynamic Mind

Dynamic mind is concerned with the putting out of mental forces for realisation of the idea.

The true inner consciousness is a silent consciousness which has not to think out things, but gets the right perception, understanding and knowledge in a spontaneous way from within and speaks or acts according to that. It is the outer consciousness which has to depend on outside things and to think about them because it has not this spontaneous guidance.

Intellect, will, etc. are intermediaries which try to catch something of the hidden higher truths and bring them into life or else raise life to them so that the possibilities of life here may become the complete realities that are already there above.

An essential movement of the Yoga is to draw back from the outward ego sense by which we are identified with the action of mind, life and body and live inwardly in the soul. The liberation from an externalised ego sense is the first step towards the soul's freedom and mastery.

When we thus draw back into the soul, we find ourselves to be not the mind, but a mental being who stands behind the action of the embodied mind, not a mental and vital personality, — personality is a composition of Nature, — but a mental Person, manomaya purusa. We become aware of a being within who takes his stand upon mind for self-knowledge and world-knowledge and thinks of himself as an individual for self-experience and world-experience, for an inward action and an outward-going action, but is yet different from mind, life and body.

But now he walks in Nature's doubtful ray.
Yet can the mind of man receive God's light,
The force of man can be driven by God's force,
Then is he a miracle doing miracles.

Earth's Boon

The boon that we have asked from the Supreme is the greatest that the Earth can ask from the Highest, the change that is most difficult to realise, the most exacting in its conditions. It is nothing less than the descent of the supreme Truth and Power into Matter, the supramental established in the material plane and consciousness and the material world and an integral transformation down to the very principle of Matter. Only a supreme Grace can effect this miracle.

The supreme Power has descended into the most material consciousness but it has stood there behind the density of the physical veil, demanding before manifestation, before its great open workings can begin, that the conditions of the supreme Grace shall be there, real and effective.

A total surrender, an exclusive self-opening to the divine influence, a constant and integral choice of the Truth and rejection of the falsehood, these are the only conditions made. But these must be fulfilled entirely, without reserve, without any evasion or pretence, simply and sincerely down to the most physical consciousness and its workings.

Only one boon, to greaten thy spirit, demand;
Only one joy, to raise thy kind, desire.
Above blind fate and the antagonist powers
Moveless there stands a high unchanging Will;
To its omnipotence leave thy work's result.
All things shall change in God's transfiguring hour.

Education

The First Principle

The first principle of true teaching is that nothing can be taught. The teacher is not an instructor or task-master, he is a helper and a guide. His business is to suggest and not to impose. He does not actually train the pupil's mind, he only shows him how to perfect his instruments of knowledge and helps and encourages him in the process. He does not impart knowledge to him, he shows him how to acquire knowledge for himself. He does not call forth the knowledge that is within; he only shows where it lies and how it can be habituated to rise to the surface. The distinction that reserves this principle for the teaching of adolescent and adult minds and denies its application to the child, is a conservative and unintelligent doctrine. Child or man, boy or girl, there is only one sound principle of good teaching. Difference of age only serves to diminish or increase the amount of help and guidance necessary; it does not change its nature.

> Communicates without means the unspoken thought;
> It moves events by its bare silent will,
> Acts at a distance without hands or feet.
> This giant Ignorance, this dwarfish Life
> It can illumine with a prophet sight.

Education

The Second Principle

The second principle is that the mind has to be consulted in its growth. The idea of hammering the child into the shape desired by the parent or teacher is a barbarous and ignorant superstition. It is he himself who must be induced to expand in accordance with his own nature. There can be no greater error than for the parent to arrange beforehand that his son shall develop particular qualities, capacities, ideas, virtues, or be prepared for a prearranged career. Every one has in him something divine, something his own, a chance of perfection and strength in however small a sphere which God offers him to take or refuse. The task is to find it, develop it and use it. The chief aim of education should be to help the growing soul to draw out that in itself which is best and make it a noble use.

> The infant soul in his small nursery school
> Mid objects meant for a lesson hardly learned
> Outgrow its early grammar of intellect
> And its imitation of Earth-Nature's art,
> Its earthly dialect to God-language change,
> In living symbols study Reality
> And learn the logic of the Infinite.

Education

The Third Principle

The third principle of education is to work from the near to the far, from that which is to that which shall be. The basis of a man's nature is almost always, in addition to his soul's past, his heredity, his surroundings, his nationality, his country, the soil from which he draws sustenance, the air which he breathes, the sights, sounds, habits to which he is accustomed. They mould him not the less powerfully because insensibly, and from that then we must begin. We must not take up the nature by the roots from the earth in which it must grow or surround the mind with images and ideas of a life which is alien to that in which it must physically move. If anything has to be brought in from outside, it must be offered, not forced on the mind. A free and natural growth is the condition of genuine development. There are souls which naturally revolt from their surroundings and seem to belong to another age and clime. Let them be free to follow their bent; but the majority languish, become empty, become artificial, if artificially moulded into an alien form. It is God's arrangement that they should belong to a particular nation, age, society, that they should be children of the past, possessors of the present, creators of the future. The past is our foundation, the present our material, the future our aim and summit. Each must have its due and natural place in a national system of education.

In this investiture of fleshly life
A soul that is spark of God survives
And sometimes it breaks through the sordid screen
And kindles a fire that makes us half-divine.

Ego

Nature invented the ego that the individual might disengage himself from the inconscience or subconscience of the mass and become an independent living mind, life-power, soul, spirit, co-ordinating himself with the world around him but not drowned in it and separately inexistent and ineffective. For the individual is indeed part of the cosmic being, but he is also something more, he is a soul that has descended from the Transcendence. This he cannot manifest at once, because he is too near to the cosmic Inconscience, not near enough to the original Super-conscience; he has to find himself as the mental and vital ego before he can find himself as the soul or spirit.

As long as the ego is at work in us, our personal action is and must always be in its nature a part of the lower grades of existence; it is obscure or enlightened, limited in its field, very partially effective in its power.

Throughout the Yoga this figure of the ego is the enemy against whom we have always to be on guard with an unsleeping vigilance. "Not for myself, but for the Divine" should grow to be the law of the whole consciousness and thought and action.

A greater Personality sometimes
Possesses us which yet we know is ours:
Or we adore the Master of our souls.
Then the small bodily ego thins and falls;
No more insisting on its separate self,
Losing the punctilio of its separate birth,
It leaves us one with Nature and with God.

Ego and its Nature

The nature of the ego is a self-limitation of consciousness by a willed ignorance of the rest of its play and its exclusive absorption in one form, one combination of tendencies, one field of the movement of energies. Ego is the factor which determines the reactions of error, sorrow, pain, evil, death; for it gives these values to movements which would otherwise be represented in their right relation to the one Existence, Bliss, Truth, Good. By recovering the right relation we may eliminate the ego-determined reactions, reducing them eventually to their true values; and this recovery can be effected by the right participation of the individual in the consciousness of the totality and in the consciousness of the transcendent which the totality represents.

> An animal in the instinctive herd
> Pushed by life impulses, forced by common needs,
> Each in his own kind saw his ego's glass;
> All served the aim and action of the pack.
> Those like himself, by blood or custom kin,
> To him were parts of his life, his adjunct selves,
> His personal nebula's constituent stars,
> Satellite companions of his solar I.

Ego's False Freedom

The apparent freedom and self-assertion of our personal being to which we are so profoundly attached, conceal a most pitiable subjection to a thousand suggestions, impulsions, forces which we have made extraneous to our little person. Our ego, boasting of freedom, is at every moment the slave, toy and puppet of countless beings, powers, forces, influences in universal Nature. This self-abnegation of the ego in the Divine is its self-fulfilment; its surrender to that which transcends it is its liberation from bonds and limits and its perfect freedom.

However insistent the ego may be, one has to keep one's eye on it and say no to all its suggestions so that each position it takes up proves to be fruitless move. Treated in that way, it becomes ready for the moment when the psychic has only to give a slight push for it to fall away in each field of its activity from its loosened roots.

> It's knowledge was the body's instrument
> Absorbed in the little works of its prison-house
> It turned around the same unchanging points
> In the same circle of interest and desire,
> But thought itself the master of its jail.

Egoism

Egoism is part of the machinery — chief part — of universal Nature, first to develop individuality out of indiscriminate force and substance of Nature and, secondly, to make the individual (through the machinery of egoistic thought, feeling, will and desire) a tool of the universal forces. It is only when one gets into touch with a higher Nature that it is possible to get free of this rule of ego and subjection to these forces.

In the world we act with the sense of egoism; we claim the universal forces that work in us as our own; we claim as the effect of our personal will, wisdom, force, virtue the selective, formative, progressive action of the Transcendent in this frame of mind, life and body. Enlightenment brings to us the knowledge that the ego is only an instrument; we begin to perceive and feel that these things are our own in the sense that they belong to our supreme and integral Self, one with the Transcendent, not to the instrumental ego. Our limitations and distortions are our contribution to the working; the true power in it is the Divine's. When the human ego realises that its will is a tool, its wisdom ignorance and childishness, its power an infant's groping, its virtue a pretentious impurity, and learns to trust itself to that which transcends it, that is its salvation.

> When naked of ego and mind it hears the voice;
> It looks through light to ever greater light
> And sees Eternity ensphering Life.

Egoism - Its Understanding

We see in the teaching of the Gita how subtle a thing is the freedom from egoism which is demanded. Arjuna is driven to fight by the egoism of strength, the egoism of the Kshatriya; he is turned from the battle by the contrary egoism of weakness, the shrinking, the spirit of disgust, the false pity that overcomes the mind, the nervous being and the senses, — not that divine compassion which strengthens the arm and clarifies the knowledge. But this weakness comes garbed as renunciation, as virtue: "Better the life of the beggar than to taste these blood-stained enjoyments; I desire not the rule of all the earth, no, nor the kingdom of the gods." How foolish of the Teacher, we might say, not to confirm this mood, to lose this sublime chance of adding one more great soul to the army of Sannyasins, one more shining example before the world of a holy renunciation. But the Guide sees otherwise, the Guide who is not to be deceived by words; "This is weakness and delusion and egoism that speak in thee. Behold the Self, open thy eyes to the knowledge, purify thy soul of egoism." And afterwards? "Fight, conquer, enjoy a wealthy kingdom." Or to take another example from ancient Indian tradition. It was egoism, it would seem, that drove Rama, the Avatara, to raise an army and destroy a nation in order to recover his wife from the King of Lanka. But would it have been a lesser egoism to drape himself in indifference and misusing the formal terms of the knowledge to say, "I have no wife, no enemy, no desire; these are illusions of the senses; let me cultivate the Brahman-knowledge and let Ravana do what he will with the daughter of Janaka"?

> The immortal sees not as we vainly see.
> He looks on hidden aspects and screened powers,
> He knows the law and natural line of things.
> Undriven by a brief life's will to act,
> Unharassed by the spur of pity and fear,
> He makes no haste to untie the cosmic knot
> Or the world's torn jarring heart to reconcile.

Egoistic Action of Mind, Life and Body

The members of our being, mind, life-force, physical or body consciousness, are too much under the control of the Ignorance to be a sure instrumentation and much less can they be a guide or the source of an unerring impulse. Always the greater part of the motive and action of these powers clings to the old law, the deceiving tablets, the cherished inferior movements of Nature and they meet with reluctance, alarm or revolt or obstructing inertia the voices and the forces that call and impel us to exceed and transform ourselves into a greater being and a wider Nature. In their major part the response is either a resistance or a qualified or temporising acquiescence; for even if they follow the call, they yet tend — when not consciously, then by automatic habit — to bring into the spiritual action their own natural disabilities and errors. At every moment they are moved to take egoistic advantage of the psychic and spiritual influences and can be detected using the power, joy or light these bring into us for a lower life-motive. Afterwards too, even when the seeker has opened to the Divine Love transcendental, universal or immanent, yet if he tries to pour it into life, he meets the power of obscuration and perversion of these lower Nature-forces. Always they draw away towards pitfalls, pour into that higher intensity their diminishing elements, seek to capture the descending Power for themselves and their interests and degrade it into an aggrandised mental, vital or physical instrumentation for desire and ego. Instead of a Divine Love creator of a new heaven and a new earth of Truth and Light, they would hold it here prisoner as a tremendous sanction and glorifying force of sublimation to gild the mud of the old earth and colour with its rose and sapphire the old turbid unreal skies of sentimentalising vital imagination and mental idealised chimera. If that falsification is permitted, the higher Light and Power and Bliss withdraw, there is a fall back to a lower status; or else the realisation remains tied to an insecure half-way and mixture or is covered and even submerged by an inferior exaltation that is not the true Ananda.

Amid a tedious crawl of drab desires
She writhed, a worm mid worms in Nature's mud,
Then, Titan-statured, took all earth for food,
Ambitioned the seas for robe, for crown the stars
And shouting strode from peak to peak,
Clamouring for worlds to conquer and to rule.

Ego's Disappearance

As our consciousness changes into the height and depth and wideness of the spirit, the ego can no longer survive there: it is too small and feeble to subsist in that vastness and dissolves into it; for it exists by its limits and perishes by the loss of its limits. The being breaks out of its imprisonment in a separated individuality, becomes universal, assumes a cosmic consciousness in which it identifies itself with the self and spirit, the life, the mind, the body of all beings. Or it breaks out upward into a supreme pinnacle and infinity and eternity of self-existence independent of its cosmic or its individual existence. The ego collapses, losing its wall of separation, into the cosmic immensity; or it falls into nothingness, unable to breathe in the heights of the spiritual ether. If something of its movements remains by habit of Nature, yet these also fall away and are replaced by a new impersonal-personal seeing, feeling, action. This disappearance of the ego does not bring with it the destruction of our true individuality, our spiritual existence, for that was always universal and one with the Transcendence; but there is a transformation which replaces the separative ego by the Purusha, a conscious face and figure of the universal being and a self and power of the transcendent Divine in cosmic Nature.

The attitude of our mind must not be ''This is my strength'' or ''Behold God's power in me'', but rather ''A Divine Power works in this mind and body and it is the same that works in all men and in the animal, in the plant and in the metal, in conscious and living things and in things appearing to be inconscient and inanimate.'' This large view of the One working in all and of the whole world as the equal instrument of a divine action and gradual self-expression, if it becomes our entire experience, will help to eliminate all rajasic egoism out of us and even the sattwic ego-sense will begin to pass away from our nature.

The island ego joined its continent:
Overpassed was this world of rigid limiting forms:
Life's barriers opened to the Unknown.

Emotional Vital

Emotional vital is the seat of various feelings, such as love, joy, sorrow, hatred and the rest.

There is in front in men a heart of vital emotion similar to the animal's, if more variously developed; its emotions are governed by egoistic passion, blind instinctive affections and all the play of the life-impulses with their imperfections, perversions, often sordid degradations, — heart besieged and given over to the lusts, desires, wraths, intense or fierce demands or little greeds and mean pettinesses of an obscure and fallen life-force and debased by its slavery to any and every impulse. This mixture of the emotive heart and the sensational hungering vital creates in man a false soul of desire; it is this that is the crude and dangerous element which the reason rightly distrusts and feels a need to control, even though the actual control or rather coercion it succeeds in establishing over our raw and insistent vital nature remains always very uncertain and deceptive.

When one leaves the outer consciousness and goes inside, it is here that one enters — some or most entering into the inner vital first, others into the inner mental or inner physical; the emotional vital is the most direct road, for the seat of the psychic is just behind the emotional in the heart-centre. It is absolutely necessary for our purpose that one should become conscious in these inner regions, for if they are not awake, then the psychic being has no proper and sufficient instrumentation for its activities; it has then only the outer mind, outer vital and body for its means and these are too small and narrow and obscure.

Hard is to persuade earth-nature's change;
Mortality bears ill the eternal's touch:
It fears the pure divine intolerance
Of that assault of ether and of fire.

Equality

No doubt, hatred and cursing are not the proper attitude. It is true also that to look upon all things and all people with a calm and clear vision, to be uninvolved and impartial in one's judgments is a quite proper yogic attitude. A condition of perfect samata can be established in which one sees all as equal, friends and enemies included, and is not disturbed by what men do or by what happens. The question is whether this is all that is demanded from us. If so, then the general attitude will be of a neutral indifference to everything. But the Gita, which strongly insists on a perfect and absolute samata, goes on to say, "Fight, destroy the adversary, conquer." If there is no kind of general action wanted, no loyalty to Truth as against Falsehood except for one's personal sadhana, no will for the Truth to conquer, then the samata of indifference will suffice. But here there is a work to be done, a Truth to be established against which immense forces are arranged, invisible forces which can use visible things and persons and actions for their instruments. If one is among the disciples, the seekers of this Truth, one has to take sides for the Truth, to stand against the forces that attack it and seek to stifle it. Arjuna wanted not to stand for either side, to refuse any action of hostility even against assailants; Sri Krishna, who insisted so much on samata, strongly rebuked his attitude and insisted equally on his fighting the adversary. "Have samata," he said, "and seeing clearly the Truth, fight." Therefore to take sides with the Truth and to refuse to concede anything to the Falsehood that attacks, to be unflinchingly loyal and against the hostiles and the attackers, is not inconsistent with equality. It is personal and egoistic feeling that has to be thrown away; hatred and vital ill-will have to be rejected. But loyalty and refusal to compromise with the assailants and the hostiles or to dally with their ideas and demands and say, "After all, we can compromise with what they ask from us", or to accept them as companions and our own people - these things have a great importance. If the attack were a physical menace to the work and the leaders and doers of the work, one would see this at once. But because the attack is of a subtler kind, can a passive attitude be right? It is a spiritual battle inward and outward; by neutrality and compromise or even passivity one may allow the enemy forces to pass and crush down the Truth and its children. If you look at it from this point, you will see that if the inner spiritual equality is right, the active loyalty and firm taking of sides is as right, and the two cannot be incompatible.

One-souled to all and free from narrowing bonds,
Large like a continent of warm sunshine
In wide equality's impartial joy,
These sages breathed for God's delight in things.

Evolution

The earth is a material field of evolution. Mind, life, supermind, Sachchidananda are in principle involved there in the earth consciousness; but only Matter is at first organized; then life descends from the life plane and gives shape and organisation and activity to the life principle in Matter, creates the plant and animal; then mind descends from the mind plane, creating man. Now supermind is to descend so as to create a supramental race.

The earth is the place of evolution in which all these forces meet and try to manifest and out of their working something has to develop. On the other planes (the mental, vital etc.) there is not the evolution — there each acts separately according to its own law.

The psychic is the support of the individual evolution; it is connected with the universal both by direct contact and through the mind, vital and body.

Our evolution has brought the being up out of inconscient Matter into the Ignorance of mind, life and body tempered by an imperfect knowledge and is trying to lead us into the light of the Spirit, to lift us into that light and to bring the light down into us, into body and life as well as mind and heart and to fill with it all that we are. This and its consequences, of which the greatest is the union with the Divine and life in the divine consciousness, is the meaning of the integral transformation.

There is no end to the world's stupendous march,
There is no rest for the embodied soul.
It must live on, describe all Time's huge curve.
An influx presses from the closed Beyond
Forbidding to him rest and earthly ease,
Till he has found himself he cannot pause.

Existence

Each thing in Nature, whether animate or inanimate, mentally self-conscious or not self-conscious, is governed in its being and in its operations by an indwelling Vision and Power, to us subconscient or inconscient because we are not conscious of it, but not inconscient to itself, rather profoundly and universally conscient. Therefore each thing seems to do the work of intelligence, even without possessing intelligence, because it obeys, whether subconsciously as in the plant and animal or half-consciously as in man, the real-idea of the divine Supermind within it. But it is not a mental Intelligence that informs and governs all things; it is a self-aware Truth of being in which self-knowledge is inseparable from self-existence: it is this Truth-Consciousness which has not to think out things but works them out with knowledge according to the impeccable self-vision and the inevitable force of a sole and self-fulfilling Existence. Mental intelligence thinks out because it is merely a reflecting force of consciousness which does not know, but seeks to know; it follows in Time step by step the working of a knowledge higher than itself, a knowledge that exists always, one and whole, that holds Time in its grasp, that sees past, present and future in a single regard.

All the world's values changed heightening life's aim;
A wiser word, a larger thought came in
Than what the slow labour of human mind can bring,
A secret sense awoke that could perceive
A Presence and a Greatness everywhere.

External Nature

This little mind, vital and body which we call ourselves is only a surface movement and not our "self" at all. It is an external bit of personality put forward for one brief life, for the play of the Ignorance. It is equipped with an ignorant mind stumbling about in search of fragments of truth, an ignorant vital rushing about in search of fragments of pleasure, an obscure and mostly subconscious physical receiving the impacts of things and suffering rather than possessing a resultant pain or pleasure. All that is accepted until the mind gets disgusted and starts looking about for the real Truth of itself and things, the vital gets disgusted and begins wondering whether there is not such a thing as real bliss and the physical gets tired and wants liberation from itself and its pains and pleasures. Then it is possible for the little ignorant bit of personality to get back to its real Self and with it to these greater things — or else to extinction of itself, Nirvana.

A power is in thee that thou knowest not;
Thou art a vessel of the imprisoned spark.
It seeks relief from Time's envelopment,
And while thou shutst it in, the seal is pain:
Bliss is the Godhead's crown, eternal, free.

Externalising Mind

The mind proper is divided into three parts — thinking Mind, dynamic Mind, externalising Mind — the former concerned with ideas and knowledge in their own right, the second with the putting out of mental forces for realisation of the idea, the third with the expression of them in life (not only by speech, but by any form it can give).

The throat is the centre of the externalising mind, that which deals with outer and physical things and responds to them.

Even those who have a strong inner life, take a long time before they can connect it with the outer speech and action. Outer speech belongs to the externalising mind — that is why it is so difficult to connect it with the inner life.

People take no trouble to see whether their mind is giving them right thoughts, right conclusions, right view on things and persons, right indications about their conduct or course of action. They have their idea and accept it as truth or follow it simply because it is their idea. Even when they recognise that they have made mistakes of the mind, they do not consider it of any importance nor they try to be more careful mentally than before.

In the vital field people know that they must not follow their desires or impulses without check or control, they know that they ought to have a conscience or a moral sense which discriminates what they can or should do or what they cannot or should not do; in the field of intellect no such care is taken.

The little Mind is tied to little things:
Its sense is but the spirit's outward touch
Half-waked in a world of dark Inconscience;
It feels out for its beings and its forms
Like one left fumbling in the ignorant Night.

Faith

Faith is an occult light and power from the soul amidst the mind's ignorance, doubts, weakness and incertitude. Faith is indispensable to man, for without it he could not proceed forward in his journey through the Unknown; but it ought not to be imposed, it should come as a free perception or an imperative direction from the inner spirit.

It is therefore necessary from the beginning to understand and accept the arduous difficulty of the path and to feel the need of a faith which to the intellect may seem blind, but yet is wiser than our reasoning intelligence. For this faith is a support from above, it is the brilliant shadow thrown by a secret light that exceeds the intellect and its data; it is the heart of hidden knowledge that is not at the mercy of immediate appearances. Our faith, persevering, will be justified in its works and will be lifted and transfigured at last into the self-revelation of a divine knowledge.

In all doubt and depression, to say, "I belong to the Divine, I cannot fail"; to all suggestions of impurity and unfitness, to reply, "I am a child of Immortality chosen by the Divine; I have but to be true to myself and to Him — the victory is sure; even if I fell, I would rise again"; to all impulses to depart and serve some smaller ideal, to reply, "This is the greatest, this is the Truth that alone can satisfy the soul within me; I will endure through all tests and tribulations to the very end of the divine journey". This is what I mean by faithfulness to the Light and the Call.

> I am charged by God to do his mighty work,
> Uncaring I serve his will who sent me forth,
> Reckless of peril and earthly consequence.
> I reason not of virtue and of sin
> But do the deed he has put into my heart.

Fall

The fall of man is his deviation from the full and pure acceptance of God and himself, or rather of God in himself, into a dividing consciousness which brings with it all the train of the dualities, life and death, good and evil, joy and pain, completeness and want, the fruit of the divided being. This is the fruit which Adam and Eve, Purusha and Prakriti, the soul tempted by Nature, have eaten. The redemption comes by the recovery of the universal in the individual and of the spiritual term in the physical consciousness. Then alone the soul in Nature can be allowed to partake of the fruit of the tree of life and be as the Divine and live for ever.

Then by the Angel of the Vigil Tower
A name is struck from the recording book;
A flame that sang in Heaven sinks quenched and mute,
In ruin ends the epic of a soul.
This is the tragedy of the inner death
When forfeited is the divine element
And only a mind and body live to die.

Fear

Fear calls the thing feared; the adverse forces take advantage of any perturbation of that kind, for it opens, as it were, a passage to their action. Fear is one thing that one must never feel in face of them, for it makes them bold and aggressive — it must therefore be thrown out altogether.

Fear, desire and sorrow are diseases of the mind; born of its sense of division and limitation, they cease with the falsehood that begot them.

The Divine even as the Master does not punish anybody, does not threaten, does not force obedience. It is the human soul that has freely to come to the Divine and offer itself to his overpowering force that he may seize and uplift it towards his own divine levels, and give it the joy of mastery of the finite nature by the Infinite and of service to the Highest by which there comes freedom from the ego and the lower nature. Love is the key of this relation and this service.

All that represses our fallen consciousness
Was taken from him like a forgotten load:
A fire that seemed the body of a god
Consumed the limiting figures of the past
And made large room for a new self to live.
Eternity's contact broke the moulds of sense.

First Step

It is the emptiness inward and outward that often in yoga becomes the first step towards a new consciousness. Man's nature is like a cup of dirty water — the water has to be thrown out, the cup left clean and empty for the divine liquor to be poured into it. The difficulty is the human physical consciousness feels it difficult to bear this emptiness — it is accustomed to be occupied by all sorts of mental and vital movements which keep it interested and amused or even if in trouble and sorrow still active. The cessation of these things is hard to bear for it. It begins to feel dull and restless and eager for the old interests and movements. But by this restlessness it disturbs the quietude and brings back the things that had been thrown out. If you can accept emptiness as a passage to the true consciousness and true movements, then it will be easier to get rid of the obstacle. To have neither vital joy nor vital grief is considered by the yogins to be a very desirable release, — it makes it possible from the ordinary human vital feelings to the true and constant inner peace, joy or happiness.

Aware of his occult omnipotent Source,
Allured by the omniscient Ecstasy,
A living centre of the Illimitable
Widened to equate with the world's circumference,
He turned to his immense spiritual fate.

Forces

The play of forces is very complex and one has to be conscious of them, and as it were, see and watch how they work before one can really understand why things happen as they do. All action is surrounded by a complexity of forces. Each man is himself a field of many forces — some are working for his sadhana, some are working for his ego and desire. There are besides powers which seek to make a man an instrument for purposes not his own without his knowing it. All of these may combine to bring about a particular result. The forces work each for the fulfilment of its own drive - they need not be at all what we call hostile forces, — they are simply forces of Nature.

The Divine is there, but He does not ignore the conditions, the laws, the circumstances of Nature; it is under these conditions that He does all His work, His work in the world and in man and consequently also in the sadhak, the aspirant, even in the God-knower and God-lover. The miracle can and does happen but only when there is the full call and complete self-giving of the soul and the entire widest opening of the nature.

For Nature walks upon her mighty way
Unheeding when she breaks a soul, a life;
Leaving her slain behind she travels on:
Man only marks and God's all-seeing eyes.

Forces of Darkness

These are the forces and beings that are interested in maintaining the falsehoods they have created in the world of the Ignorance and in putting them forward as the Truth which men must follow. In India they are termed Asuras, Rakshasas, Pishachas who are in opposition to the Gods, the Powers of Light. These too are Powers, for they too have their cosmic field in which they exercise their function and authority and some of them were once divine Powers who have fallen towards the darkness by revolt against the divine Will behind the cosmos.

Their main characteristic is egoistic strength and struggle, which refuses the higher law. The Asura has self control, intelligence, but all that for the sake of his ego.

Be it well noted, with the error of the Asura, the Titan, who lives in his own inordinately magnified shadow, mistakes ego for the self and spirit and tries to impose his fragmentary personality as the one dominant existence upon all his surroundings.

Some kinds of Asuras are very religious, very fanatical about their religion, very strict about rules of ethical conduct. Others of course are just the opposite. There are others who use spiritual ideas without believing in them...

The Asura and Rakshasa hold this evolving earthly nature and have to be met and conquered on their own terms in their own long-conquered fief and province. They are powerful in a world of ignorance for they have only to persuade people to follow the established bent of their lower nature, while the Divine always calls for a change of nature.

No wandering ray of heaven can enter there.
Armoured, protected by their lethal masks,
As in a studio of creative Death
The giant sons of Darkness sit and plan
The drama of the earth, their tragic stage.
All who would raise the fallen world must come
Under the dangerous arches of their power.
None can reach heaven who has not passed through hell.

Foundation

What you have to aspire for most is the improved quality of the recipient consciousness in you, discrimination in the mind, the unattached impersonal Witness look on all that goes on in you and around you, purity in the vital, calm equanimity, enduring patience, absence of pride and the sense of greatness — and more especially, the development of the psychic being in you — surrender, self-giving, psychic humility, devotion. It is a consciousness made up of these things, cast in this mould, that can bear without breaking, stumbling or deviation into error the rush of lights, power and experiences from the supraphysical planes.

The things that have to be established are — complete sex purity; quiet and harmony in the being, its forces maintained but controlled, harmonised, disciplined; truth and sincerity in the whole nature; a general state of peace and calm; the power and habit to control whatever needs control in the movements of the nature. When these are fairly established, one has laid a foundation on which one can develop the yogic consciousness and with the yogic consciousness there comes an easy opening to realisation and experience.

I am thy portion here charged with thy work,
As thou myself seated for ever above,
Speak to my depths, O great and deathless Voice,
Command, for I am here to do thy will.

Free Heart

A free heart is a heart delivered from the gusts and storms of the affections and the passions; the assailing touch of grief, wrath, hatred, fear, inequality of love, trouble of joy, pain of sorrow fall away from the equal heart, and leave it a thing large, calm, equal, luminous, divine.

To the free spirit wrath and hatred are impossible, but not the strong Rudra energy of the Divine which can battle without hatred and destroy without wrath.

Around him shone a great felicitous Day.
A lustre of some rapturous Infinite,
It held in the splendour of its golden laugh
Regions of the heart's happiness set free,
Intoxicated with the wine of God,
Immersed in light, perpetually divine

Freedom

For even before complete purification, if the strings of the egoistic heart and mind are already sufficiently frayed and loosened, the Jiva can by a sudden snapping of the main cords escape, ascending like a bird freed into the spaces or widening like a liberated flood into the One and Infinite. There is first a sudden sense of a cosmic consciousness, a casting of oneself into the universal; from that universality one can aspire more easily to the Transcendent. There is a pushing back and rending or a rushing down of the walls that imprisoned our conscious being; there is a loss of all sense of individuality and personality, of all placement in Space or Time or action and law of Nature; there is no longer an ego, a person definite and definable, but only consciousness, only existence, only peace and bliss; one becomes immortality, becomes eternity, becomes infinity. All that is left of the personal soul is a hymn of peace and freedom and bliss vibrating somewhere in the Eternal.

> Wisdom upraised him to her master craft
> And made him an arch-mason of the soul,
> A builder of the Immortal's secret house,
> An aspirant to supernal Timelessness:
> Freedom and empire called to him from on high;
> Above mind's twilight and life's star-led night
> There gleamed the dawn of a spiritual day.

Glimpses

As an inner equality increases and with it the sense of the true vital being waiting for the greater direction it has to serve, as the psychic call increases in all the members of our nature, That to which the call is addressed begins to reveal itself, descends to take possession of the life and its energies and fills them with the height, intimacy, vastness of its presence and its purpose. In many, if not most, it manifests something of itself even before the equality and the open psychic urge or guidance are there. A call of the veiled psychic element oppressed by the mass of the outer ignorance and crying for deliverance, a stress of eager meditation and seeking for knowledge, a longing of the heart, a passionate will ignorant yet but sincere may break the lid that shuts off the Higher from this Lower Nature and open the floodgates. A little of the Divine Person may reveal itself or some Light, Power, Bliss, Love out of the Infinite. This may be a momentary revelation, a flash or a brief-lived gleam that soon withdraws and waits for the preparation of the nature, but also it may repeat itself, grow, endure. A long and large and comprehensive working will then have begun, sometimes luminous or intense, sometimes slow and obscure. A Divine Power comes in front at times and leads and compels or instructs and enlightens; at others it withdraws into the background and seems to leave the being to its own resources. All that is ignorant, obscure, perverted or simply imperfect and inferior in the being is raised up, perhaps brought to its acme, dealt with, corrected, exhausted, shown its own disastrous results, compelled to call for its own cessation or transformation or expelled as worthless or incorrigible from the nature. This cannot be a smooth and even process; alternations there are of day and night, illumination and darkness, calm and construction or battle and upheaval, the presence of the growing Divine Consciousness and its absence, heights of hope and abysses of despair, the clasp of the Beloved and the anguish of its absence, the overwhelming invasion, the compelling deceit, the fierce opposition, the disabling mockery of hostile Powers or the help and comfort and communion of the gods and the Divine Messengers.

Our aim is to bring the secret forces out and unwalled into the open, so that instead of getting some shadows or lightnings of themselves out through the veil or being wholly obstructed, they may pour down and flow in rivers. But to expect that all at once is a presumptuous demand which shows an impatient ignorance and inexperience. If they begin to trickle at first, that is enough to justify the faith in a future downpour.

His soul steps back and sees the Light supreme.
A Godhead stands behind the brute machine.
This truth broke in in a triumph of fire;
A victory was won for God in man,
The deity revealed its hidden face.

Gods and Goddesses

The Gods are in origin and essence permanent Emanations of the Divine put forth from the Supreme by the Transcendent Mother, the Adya Shakti; in their cosmic action they are Powers and Personalities of the Divine each with his independent cosmic standing, function and work in the universe.

The personal God of popular religions is a being limited by his qualities, individual and separate from all others; for all such personal Gods are only limited representations or names and divine personalities of the One.

The Sadhaka of the integral Yoga makes use of all these aids according to his nature; but it is necessary that he should shun their limitations and cast from himself that exclusive tendency of egoistic mind which cries, "My God, my Incarnation, my Prophet, my Guru," and opposes it to all other realisation in a sectarian or a fanatical spirit.

The aim of these external aids is to awaken his soul to the Divine within him. Nothing has been finally accomplished if that has not been accomplished. It is not sufficient to worship Krishna, Christ or Buddha without, if there is not the revealing and the formation of the Buddha, the Christ or Krishna in ourselves.

It is necessary for man to conceive God in his own image or in some form that is beyond himself but consonant with his highest tendencies and seizable by his feelings or his intelligence. Otherwise it would be difficult for him to come into contact and communion with the Divine.

This call is satisfied by the Divine manifest in a human appearance, the Incarnation, the Avatar — Krishna, Christ, Buddha.

A might is with her that makes wonders true;
The incredible is her stuff of common fact.
Her purposes, her workings riddles prove;
Examined, they grow other than they were,
Explained, they seem yet more inexplicable.

The Golden Age

If by some miracle of divine intervention all mankind at once could be raised to this level, we should have something on earth like the Golden Age of the traditions, Satya Yuga, the Age of Truth or true existence. For the sign of the Satya Yuga is that the Law is spontaneous and conscious in each creature and does its own works in a perfect harmony and freedom. Unity and universality, not separative division, would be the foundation of the consciousness of the race; love would be absolute; equality would be consistent with hierarchy and perfect in difference; absolute justice would be secured by the spontaneous action of the being in harmony with the truth of things and the truth of himself and others and therefore sure of true and right result; right reason, no longer mental but supramental, would be satisfied not by the observation of artificial standards but by the free automatic perception of right relations and their inevitable execution in the act. The quarrel between the individual and society or disastrous struggle between one community and another could not exist: the cosmic consciousness imbedded in embodied beings would assure a harmonious diversity in oneness.

> All heavenly light shall visit the earth's thoughts,
> The might of heaven shall fortify earthly hearts;
> Earth's deeds shall touch the superhuman's height,
> Earth's seeing widen into the infinite.

Good and Evil

For good is all that helps the individual and the world towards their divine fullness, and evil is all that retards or breaks up that increasing perfection. But since the perfection is progressive, evolutive in Time, good and evil are also shifting quantities and change from time to time their meaning and value.

If we are to be free in the spirit, if we are to be subject only to the supreme Truth, we must discard the idea that our mental or moral laws are binding on the Infinite or that there can be anything sacrosanct, absolute or eternal even in the highest of our existing standards of conduct. To form higher and higher temporary standards as long as they are needed is to serve the Divine in his world march; to erect rigidly an absolute standard is to attempt the erection of a barrier against the eternal waters in their outflow. Once the nature-bound soul realises this truth, it is delivered from the duality of good and evil.

> In the anomalies of the human heart
> Where Good and Evil are close bed-fellows
> And Light is by Darkness dogged at every step,
> Where his largest knowledge is an ignorance,
> I am the Power that labours towards the best
> And works for God and looks up towards the heights.

Guidance

As the crust of the outer nature cracks, as the walls of inner separation break down, the inner light gets through, the inner fire burns in the heart, the substance of the nature and the stuff of consciousness refine to a greater subtlety and purity, and the deeper psychic experiences, those which are not solely of an inner mental or inner vital character, become possible in this subtler, purer, finer substance; the soul begins to unveil itself, the psychic personality reaches its full stature. The soul, the psychic entity, then manifests itself as the central being which upholds mind and life and body and supports all the other powers and functions of the Spirit; it takes up its greater function as the guide and ruler of the nature. A guidance, a governance begins from within which exposes every movement to the light of Truth, repels what is false, obscure, opposed to the divine realisation: every region of the being, every nook and corner of it, every movement, formation, direction, inclination of thought, will, emotion, sensation, action, reaction, motive, disposition, propensity, desire, habit of the conscious or subconscious physical, even the most concealed, camouflaged, mute, recondite, is lighted up with the unerring psychic light, their confusions dissipated, their tangles disentangled, their obscurities, deceptions, self-deceptions precisely indicated and removed; all is purified, set right, the whole nature harmonised, modulated in the psychic key, put in spiritual order... As a final result the whole conscious being is made perfectly apt for spiritual experience of every kind, turned towards spiritual truth of thought, feeling, sense, action...

A breath comes down from a supernal air,
A presence is borne, a guiding Light awakes,
A stillness falls upon the instruments:
Fixed sometimes like a marble monument,
Stone-calm, the body is a pedestal
Supporting a figure of eternal Peace.

Guide

The full recognition of this inner Guide, the eternal secret in the heart of every man, Master of the Yoga, lord, light, enjoyer and goal of all sacrifice and effort, is of the utmost importance in the path of integral perfection.

It is he who destroys our darkness by the resplendent light of his knowledge; that light becomes within us the increasing glory of his own self-revelation. He discloses progressively in us his own nature of freedom, bliss, love, power, immortal being. He sets above us his divine example as our ideal and transforms the lower existence into a reflection of that which it contemplates. By the inpouring of his influence and presence into us he enables the individual being to attain to identity with the universal and transcendent.

A Light there is that leads, a Power that aids;
Unmarked, unfelt it sees in him and acts:
Ignorant, he forms the All-conscient in his depths,
Human, looks up to superhuman peaks:
A borrower of Supernature's gold,
He paves his road to Immortality.

Happiness

Happiness in the ordinary sense is a sunlit state of the vital with or without cause. Contentment is less than happiness — joy of peace or being free from difficulty is rather a state of joyful sãnti. Happiness ought not to be a status of self-satisfaction or inertia, and need not be, for one can combine happiness and aspiration. Of course there can be a state of happy inertia, but most people don't remain satisfied with that long, they begin to want something else. There are yogins who are satisfied with a happy calm immobility, but that is because the happiness is a form of Ananda and in the immobility they feel the Self and its eternal calm and want nothing more.

There is no happiness in smallness of the being, says the Scripture, it is with the large being that happiness comes. The ego is by its nature a smallness of being; it brings contraction of the consciousness and with the contraction limitation of knowledge, disabling ignorance, — confinement and a diminution of power and by that diminution incapacity and weakness, — scission of oneness and by that scission disharmony and failure of sympathy and love and understanding, — inhibition or fragmentation of delight of being and by that fragmentation pain and sorrow. To recover what is lost we must break out of the worlds of ego.

Experience shows that, in proportion as we deliver ourselves from the limiting mental and vital ego, we command a wider life, a larger existence, a higher consciousness, a happier soul-state, even a greater knowledge, power and scope.

My light shall be in thee, my strength thy force.
Let not the impatient Titan drive thy heart,
Ask not the imperfect fruit, the partial prize.
Only one boon, to greaten thy spirit, demand;
Only one joy, to raise thy kind, desire.

Hathayoga

Hathayoga is a powerful, but difficult and onerous system whose whole principle of action is founded on an intimate connection between the body and the soul. The body is the key, the body the secret both of bondage and of release, of animal weakness and of divine power, of the obscuration of the mind and soul and of their illumination, of subjection to pain and limitation and of self-mastery, of death and of immortality. The body is not to the Hathayogin a mere mass of living matter, but a mystic bridge between the spiritual and the physical being; one has even seen an ingenious exegete of the Hathayogic discipline explain the Vedantic symbol OM as a figure of this mystic human body.

In fact the whole aim of the Hathayogin may be summarised from our point of view, though he would not himself put it in that language, as an attempt by fixed scientific processes to give to the soul in the physical body the power, the light, the purity, the freedom, the ascending scales of spiritual experience which would naturally be open to it, if it dwelt here in the subtle and the developed causal vehicle.

Man, still a child in Nature's mighty hands,
In the succession of the moment lives;
To a changing present is his narrow right;
His memory stares back at a phantom past,
The future flees before him as he moves;
He sees imagined garments, not a face.
Armed with a limited precarious strength,
He saves his fruits of work from adverse chance.

Harmony in Progress

A cosmos or universe is always a harmony, otherwise it could not exist, it would fly to pieces. But as there are musical harmonies which are built out of discords partly or even predominantly, so this universe (the material) is disharmonious in its separate elements — the individual elements are at discord with each other to a large extent; it is only owing to the sustaining Divine Will behind that the whole is still a harmony to those who look at it with the cosmic vision. But it is a harmony in evolution in progress — that is, all is combined to strive towards a goal which is not yet reached, and the object of our yoga is to hasten the arrival to this goal. When it is reached, there will be a harmony of harmonies substituted for the present harmony built up on discords. This is the explanation of the present appearance of things.

> The Immanent lives in man as in his house;
> He has made the universe his pastime's field,
> A vast gymnasium of his works of might.
> All-knowing he accepts our darkened state,
> Divine, wears shapes of animal and man;
> Eternal, he assents to Fate and Time,
> Immortal, dallies with mortality.

Hatred

All is our self, one self that has taken many shapes. Hatred and dislike and scorn and repulsion, clinging and attachment and preference are natural, necessary, inevitable at a certain stage: they attend upon or they help to make and maintain Nature's choice in us. But to a Yogi they are a survival, a stumbling-block, a process of the Ignorance and, as he progresses, they fall away from his nature. The child-soul needs them for its growth; but they drop from an adult in the divine culture. In the God-nature to which we have to rise there can be an adamantine, even a destructive severity but not hatred, a divine irony but not scorn, a calm, clear-seeing and forceful rejection but not repulsion and dislike. Even what we have to destroy, we do not abhor or fail to recognise as a disguised and temporary movement of the Eternal.

Out of earth's heavy smallness we must break,
We must search our nature with spiritual fire:
An insect crawl preludes our glorious flight.

Heart Lotus and Above the Head The Thousand Petalled Lotus

Within us there are two centres of the Purusha, the inner Soul through which God touches us to our awakening. There is the Purusha in the lotus of the heart which opens upwards all our powers and the Purusha in the thousand-petalled lotus whence descend through the thought and will, opening the third eye in us, the lightnings of vision and the fire of the divine energy. The bliss existence may come to us through either one of these centres. When the lotus of the heart breaks open, we feel a divine joy, love and peace expanding in us like a flower of Light which irradiates the whole being.

When the other upper lotus opens, the whole mind becomes full of a divine light, joy and power, behind which is the Divine, the Lord of our being on his throne with our soul beside him or drawn inward into his rays; all the thought and will become then a luminosity, power and ecstasy; in communication with the Transcendent, this can pour down towards our mortal members and flow by them outwards on the world.

> In the kingdom of the lotus of the heart
> Love chanting its pure hymeneal hymn
> Made life and body mirrors of sacred joy
> And all the emotions gave themselves to God.

Higher and Lower Nature

The movement of Nature is twofold, higher and lower, or, as we may choose to term it, divine and undivine. The distinction exists indeed for practical purposes only; for there is nothing that is not divine, and in a larger view it is as meaningless, verbally, as the distinction between natural and supernatural, for all things that are are natural. All things are in Nature and all things are in God. But, for practical purposes, there is a real distinction. The lower Nature, that which we know and are and must remain so long as the faith in us is not changed, acts through limitation and division, is of the nature of Ignorance and culminates in the life of the ego; but the higher Nature, that to which we aspire, acts by unification and transcendence of limitation, is of the nature of Knowledge and culminates in the life divine. The passage from the lower to the higher is the aim of Yoga; and this passage may effect itself by the rejection of the lower and escape into the higher, — the ordinary view-point, — or by the transformation of the lower and its elevation to the higher Nature. It is this, rather, that must be the aim of an integral Yoga.

It is a mistake to dwell too much on the lower nature and its obstacles, which is the negative side of the sadhana. They have to be seen and purified, but preoccupation with them as the one important thing is not helpful. The positive side of experience of the descent is the more important thing. If one waits for the lower nature to be purified entirely and for all time before calling down the positive experience, one might have to wait for ever. It is true that the more the lower nature is purified, the easier is the descent of the higher Nature, but it is also and more true that the more the higher Nature descends, the more the lower is purified.

All the grey inhibitions were torn off
And broken the intellect's hard and lustrous lid;
Truth unpartitioned found immense sky-room;
An empyrean vision saw and knew;
The bounded mind became a boundless light,
The finite self mated with Infinity.

Higher Consciousness

The sadhak (aspirant) becomes aware not only of a great, eventually an infinite peace, silence, wideness above us, above the head as it were and extending into all physical and supraphysical space, but also he can become aware of other things — a vast Force in which is all power, a vast Light in which is all knowledge, a vast Ananda in which is all bliss and rapture. At first they appear as something essential, indeterminate, absolute, simple, kevala: a Nirvana into any of these things seems possible. But we can come to see too that this Force contains all forces, this Light all lights, this Ananda all joy and bliss possible. And all this can descend into us. Any of them and all of them can come down, not peace alone; only the safest is to bring down first an absolute calm and peace, for that makes the descent of the rest more secure; otherwise it may be difficult for the external nature to contain or bear so much Force, Light, Knowledge or Ananda. All these things together make what we call the higher spiritual or Divine Consciousness. The psychic opening through the heart puts us primarily into connection with the individual Divine, the Divine in his inner relation with us; it is especially the source of love and bhakti. This upward opening puts us into direct relation with the whole Divine and can create in us the divine consciousness and a new birth or births of the spirit.

> His being lay down in bright immobile peace
> And bathed in wells of pure spiritual light;
> It wandered in wide fields of wisdom-self
> Lit by the rays of everlasting sun.

Higher Mental Opening

Man too has in himself, subliminal, unknown and unseen, concealed behind his waking consciousness and visible organism, this mental soul, mental nature, mental body and a mental plane, not materialised, in which the principle of Mind is at home and not as here at strife with a world which is alien to it, obstructive to its freedom and corruptive of its purity and clearness. All the higher faculties of man, his intellectual and psycho-mental being and powers, his higher emotional life awaken and increase in proportion as this mental plane in him presses upon him. (I include here in mind, not only the highest range of mind ordinarily known to man, but yet higher ranges to which he has either no current faculty of admission or else only a partial and mixed reception of some faint portion of their powers, — the illumined mind, the intuition and finally the creative Overmind or Maya which stands far above and is the source of our present existence). For he would enjoy powers and a vision and perceptions beyond the scope of this ordinary life and body; he would govern all by the clarities of pure knowledge; he would be united to other beings by a sympathy of love and happiness; his emotions would be lifted to the perfection of the psycho-mental plane, his sensations rescued from grossness, his intellect subtle, pure and flexible, delivered from the derivations of the impure pranic energy and the obstruction of matter. And he would develop too the reflection of a wisdom and bliss higher than any mental joy or knowledge; for he could receive more fully and without our incompetent mind's deforming and falsifying mixture the inspirations and intuitions that are the arrows of the supramental Light and from his perfected mental existence in the mould and power of that vaster splendour.

Then suddenly a luminous finger fell
On all things seen or touched or heard or felt
And showed his mind that nothing could be known;
That must be reached from which all knowledge comes.

Higher Mind

Our first decisive step out of our human intelligence, our normal mentality, is an ascent into a higher Mind, a mind no longer of mingled light and obscurity or half-light, but a large clarity of the Spirit. Its basic substance is a unitarian sense of being with a powerful multiple dynamisation capable of the formation of a multitude of aspects of knowledge, ways of action, forms and significances of becoming, of all of which there is a spontaneous inherent knowledge.

Higher Mind is one of the planes of the spiritual mind, the first and lowest of them.

The world of the Higher Mind is above those directly connected with the body-consciousness.

An opening into this Higher Mind is usually accompanied by a silence of the ordinary mental thought.

The power of the spiritual Higher Mind and its idea-force, modified and diminished as it must be by its entrance into our mentality, is not sufficient to sweep out all these obstacles and create the gnostic being, but it can make a first change, a modification that will capacitate a higher ascent and a more powerful descent and further prepare an integration of the being in a greater Force of consciousness and knowledge.

> A cosmic Thought spreads out its vastitudes;
> Its smallest parts are here philosophies
> Challenging with their detailed immensity,
> Each figuring an omniscient scheme of things.
> But higher still can climb the ascending light.

Hostile Forces

Men are being constantly invaded by the hostiles and there are great numbers of men who are partly or entirely under their influence. Some are possessed by them, others (a few) are incarnations of hostile beings. At the present moment they are very active all over the earth. Of course in the outside world there is no consciousness, such as is developed in yoga, by which they can either become aware of or consciously repel the attacks – the struggle in them between the psychic and the hostile force goes on mostly behind the veil or so far as it is on the surface is not understood by the mind.

The first attempt of the possessing entity is to separate the person from his psychic, and it is that that creates the struggle. All depends on the extent and persistence of the possession – how much of the being it occupies and whether it is constant or not.

The concentration in the heart is the way to get rid of them, but there must also be a detachment of the consciousness so that it can stand back from the attack and feel separate from it.

From the higher mind upwards, all is free from the action of the hostile forces. For they all belong to the spiritual consciousness though with varying degrees of light and power and completeness.

But the great obstinate world resists my word,
And the crookedness and evil in men's hearts
Is stronger than Reason, profounder than the Pit.
And the malignancy of hostile Powers
Puts craftily back the clock of destiny
And mightier seems than the eternal Will.

Human Nature

The human being forms in his superficial parts of being, mental, vital, physical, a habit of certain responses to these waves from outside. It is these responses that he takes as his own character (anger, desire, sex etc.) and thinks he cannot be otherwise. But that is not so; he can change. There is another consciousness deeper within him, his true inner being, which is his real self, but is covered over by the superficial nature. This the ordinary man does not know, but the yogi becomes aware of it as he progresses in his sadhana. As the consciousness of this inner being increases by sadhana, the surface nature and its responses are pushed out and can be got rid of altogether. But the ignorant universal Nature does not want to let go and throws the old movements on the sadhak and tries to get them inside again; owing to a habit the superficial nature gives the old responses. If one can get the firm knowledge that these things are from outside and not a real part of oneself, then it is easier for the sadhak to repel such returns, or if they lay hold, he can get rid of them sooner. That is why I say repeatedly that these things rise not in yourself, but from outside.

What we see of Nature and of human nature justifies this view of a birth of the individual soul from form to form until it reaches the human level of manifested consciousness which is its instrument for rising to yet higher levels. We see that Nature develops from stage to stage and in each stage takes up its past and transforms it into stuff of its new development. We see too that human nature is of the same make; all the earth-past is there in it. It has an element of matter taken up by life, an element of life taken up by mind, an element of mind which is being taken up by spirit: the animal is still present in its humanity; the very nature of the human being presupposes a material and a vital stage which prepared his emergence into mind and an animal past which moulded a first element of his complex humanity.

Was then the sun a dream because there is night?
Hidden in the mortal's heart the Eternal lives:
He lives secret in the chamber of thy soul,
A light shines there nor pain nor grief can cross.

Human Relations

If human relations as practised now by man are full of smallness and perversity and ignorance, yet are they disfigured shadows of something in the Divine and by turning to the Divine one finds that of which they are shadow and brings it down for manifestation in life.

All love is indeed in its nature self-existent because it springs from a secret oneness in being and a sense of that oneness or desire of oneness in the heart between souls that are yet able to conceive of themselves as different from each other and divided. Therefore all these other relations too can arrive at their self-existent motiveless joy of being for the sake of love alone. But still they start from and to the end they, to some extent, find a satisfaction of their play in other motives.

The danger of the vital is that of taking hold of love, Ananda, the sense of Beauty and using it for its own purposes, for vital human relations or interchange or else some kind of mere enjoyment of its own.

One glance could separate the true and false,
Or raise its rapid torch-fire in the dark
To check the claimants crowding through mind's gates
Covered by the forged signature of the gods,
Detect the magic bride in her disguise
Or scan the apparent face of thought and life.

Human Spirit's Destiny

The powers we are now satisfied to call gnosis, intuition or illumination are only fainter lights of which that (the Supermind) is the full and flaming source, and between the highest human intelligence and it there lie many levels of ascending consciousness, highest mental or overmental, which we would have to conquer before we arrived there or could bring down its greatness and glory here. Yet, however difficult, that ascent, that victory is the destiny of the human spirit and that luminous descent or bringing down of the divine Truth is the inevitable term of the troubled evolution of the earth-nature; that intended consummation is its raison d'être, our culminating state and the explanation of our terrestrial existence.

> All time-made difference they overcame;
> The world was fibered with their own heart-strings;
> Close-drawn to the heart that beats in every breast,
> They reached the one self in all through boundless love.

The true spiritual or psychic vision is this: "Whatever I may be, my soul is a child of the Divine and must reach the Divine sooner or later. I am imperfect, but seek after the perfection of the Divine in me and that not I but the Divine Grace will bring about; if I keep to that, the Divine Grace itself will do all." The "I" has to take its proper place here as a small portion and instrument of the Divine, something that is nothing without the Divine but with the Grace can be everything that the Divine wishes it to be.

Our object is not to remove all "limitations" on the expansion of the ego or to give a free field and make unlimited room for the fulfilment of the ideas of the human mind or the desires of the ego-centred life-force. None of us are here to "do as we like", or to create a world in which we shall at last be able to do as we like; we are here to do what the Divine wills and to create a world in which the Divine Will can manifest its truth no longer deformed by human ignorance or perverted and mistranslated by vital desire. The work which the sadhak of the supramental yoga has to do is not his own work for which he can lay down his own conditions, but the work of the Divine which he has to do according to the conditions laid down by the Divine. Our yoga is not for our own sake but for the sake of the Divine. It is not our own personal manifestation that we are to seek, the manifestation of the individual ego freed from all bounds and from all bonds, but the manifestation of the Divine. Of that manifestation our own spiritual liberation, perfection, fullness is to be a result and a part, but not in any egoistic sense or for any ego-centred or self-seeking purpose. This liberation, perfection, fullness too must not be pursued for our own sake, but for the sake of the Divine.

The soul must soar sovereign above the form
And climb to summits beyond mind's half-sleep;
Our hearts we must inform with heavenly strength,
Surprise the animal with the occult god.

The Seven Fold Ignorance

First - The Original ignorance

We are ignorant of the Absolute which is the source of all being and becoming; we take partial facts of being, temporal relations of the becoming for the whole truth of existence, that is the first, the original ignorance.

It is from the Ignorance that we proceed to the Knowledge; but this is not an intellectual knowledge which can be learned and completed in our present mould of consciousness; it must be an experience, a becoming, a change of consciousness, a change of being. This brings in the evolutionary character of the Becoming and the fact that our mental ignorance is only a stage in our evolution: a many-sided self-ignorance.

Our human ignorance moves towards the Truth
That Nescience may become omniscient:
Transmuted instincts shape to divine thoughts,
Thoughts house infallible immortal sight
And Nature climbs towards God's identity.

The Seven Fold Ignorance

Second - The Cosmic Ignorance

We are ignorant of the spaceless, timeless, immobile and immutable Self; we take the constant mobility and mutation of the cosmic becoming in Time and Space for the whole truth of existence, that is the second, the cosmic ignorance.

There none was weak, so falsehood could not live;
Ignorance was a thin shade protecting light,
Imagination the free-will of Truth,
Pleasure a candidate for heaven's fire.

The Seven Fold Ignorance

Third - The Egoistic Ignorance

We are ignorant of our universal self, the cosmic existence, the cosmic consciousness, our infinite unity with all being and becoming; we take our limited egoistic mentality, vitality, corporeality for our true self and regard everything other than that as not-self, that is the third, the egoistic ignorance.

> In the world of my knowledge and my ignorance
> Where God is unseen and only is heard a Name
> And knowledge is trapped in the boundaries of mind
> And life is hauled in the drag-net of desire
> And Matter hides the soul from its own sight,
> You are my Force at work to uplift earth's fate.

The Seven Fold Ignorance

Fourth – The Temporal Ignorance

We are ignorant of our eternal becoming in Time; we take this little life in a small span of Time, in a petty field of Space, for our beginning, our middle and our end, that is the fourth, the temporal ignorance.

When unity is won, when strife is lost
And all is known and all is clasped by Love
Who would turn back to ignorance and pain.

The Seven Fold Ignorance

Fifth - The Psychological Ignorance

Within this brief temporal becoming we are ignorant of our large and complex being, of that in us which is superconscient, intraconscient, circumconscient to our surface becoming; we take that surface becoming with its small selection of overtly mentalised experiences for our whole existence, that is the fifth, the psychological ignorance.

A body of the Superconscient's truth,
A native field of Supernature's mights:
It shall make earth's nescient ground truth's colony
Make even the Ignorance a transparent robe
Through which shall shine the brilliant limbs of Truth.

The Seven Fold Ignorance

Sixth - The Constitutional Ignorance

We are ignorant of the true constitution of our becoming; we take the mind or life or body or any two of these or all three for our true principle or the whole account of what we are, losing sight of that which constitutes them and determines by its occult presence and is meant to determine sovereignly by its emergence their operations, that is the sixth, the constitutional ignorance.

This world of bliss he saw and felt its call,
But found no way to enter into its joy;
Across the conscious gulf there was no bridge.
A darker air encircled still his soul

The Seven Fold Ignorance

Seventh - The Practical Ignorance

As a result of all these ignorances, we miss the true knowledge, government and enjoyment of our life in the world; we are ignorant in our thought, will, sensations, actions, return wrong or imperfect responses at every point to the questions of the world, wonder in maze of errors and desires, strivings and failures, pain and pleasure, sin and stumbling, follow a crooked road, grope blindly for a changing goal, - that is the seventh, the practical ignorance.

Pain is the signature of the Ignorance
Attesting the secret god denied by life:
Until life finds him pain can never end.
Calm is self's victory overcoming fate.
Bear; thou shalt find at last thy road to bliss.

Illumined Mind

The plane of the Illumined Mind is a level of consciousness much higher than the human intelligence. It is there that the Divine Light and Power come down to be transmitted to the human consciousness and from there they work and prepare the transformation of the human consciousness and even the physical nature.

The Illumined Mind does not work primarily by thought, but by vision; thought is here only a subordinate movement expressive of sight.

Here the clarity of the spiritual intelligence, its tranquil daylight, gives place or subordinates itself to an intense lustre, a splendour and illumination of the Spirit: a play of lightnings of spiritual truth and power breaks from above into the consciousness and adds to the calm and wide enlightenment and the vast descent of peace which characterise or accompany the action of the larger conceptual-spiritual principle, a fiery ardour of realisation and a rapturous ecstasy of knowledge.

There is also in this descent the arrival of a greater dynamic, a golden drive, a luminous "enthousiasmos" of inner force and power which replaces the comparatively slow and deliberate process of the Higher Mind by a swift, sometimes a vehement, almost a violent impetus of rapid transformation.

There are vasts of vision and eternal suns,
Oceans of an immortal luminousness,
Flame-hills assaulting heaven with peaks,
There dwellings all becomes a blaze of sight;
A burning head of vision leads the mind.

Illusion

When the Sadhaka has followed the discipline of withdrawal from the various identifications of the self with the ego, the mind, the life, the body, he has arrived at realisation by knowledge of a pure, still, self-aware existence, one, undivided, peaceful, inactive, undisturbed by the action of the world. The only relation that this Self seems to have with the world is that of disinterested Witness not at all involved in or affected or even touched by any of its activities. If this state of consciousness is pushed further one becomes aware of a self even more remote from world-existence; all that is in the world is in a sense in that Self and yet at the same time extraneous to its consciousness, non-existent in its existence, existing only in a sort of unreal mind, – a dream therefore, an illusion.

The integral Yoga of knowledge demands instead a divine return upon world-existence and its first step must be to realise the Self as the All, sarvam brahma.

Obeying the Eternal's deep command
They have built in the material front of things
This wide world-kindergarten of young souls
Where the infant spirit learns through mind and sense
To read the letters of the cosmic script
And study the body of the cosmic self
And search for the secret meaning of the whole.

Immortality of the Body

The change of the consciousness is the necessary thing and without it there can be no physical siddhi. But the fullness of the supramental change is not possible, if the body remains as it is, a slave of death, disease, decay, pain, unconsciousness and all the other results of the ignorance. If these are to remain the descent of the supramental is hardly necessary — for a change of consciousness which would bring mental-spiritual union with the Divine, the overmind is sufficient, even the Higher Mind is sufficient. The supramental descent is necessary for a dynamic action of the Truth in mind, vital and body. This would imply as a final result the disappearance of the unconsciousness of the body; it would no longer be subject to decay and disease. That would mean that it would not be subject to the ordinary processes by which death comes. If a change of body had to be made, it would have to be by the will of the inhabitant. This (not an obligation to live 3000 years, for that too would be a bondage) would be the essence of physical immortality. Still, if one wanted to live 1000 years or more, then supposing one had the complete siddhi, it should not be impossible.

As for immortality, it cannot come if there is attachment to the body, — for it is only by living in the immortal part of oneself which is unidentified with the body and bringing down its consciousness and force into the cells that it can come.

This knowledge was now made a cosmos' seed:
This seed was cased in the safety of the Light,
It needed not a sheath of Ignorance.
Then from the trance of that tremendous clasp
And from the throbbings of that single Heart
And from the naked Spirit's victory
A new and marvellous creation rose.

Impulsive Force

It is always necessary to keep the inner perception and will clear, conscious and in perfect balance and never to allow any force of impulsion, however it may present itself, to sweep without their discerning consent the vital or the body into action. Whatever appearance they may assume, such forces cannot be trusted; once the discriminating intelligence gives up its control, any kind of force can intervene and a path is opened for unbalanced vital impulses to be used to the detriment of the sadhana. A psychic or spiritual control replacing the mental would not act in this way, but whatever intensity or ardour it may give, would maintain a clear perception of things, a perfect discrimination, a harmony between the inward and the outward reality. It is only the vital that is swept away by these impulses; the vital must always be kept under the control of the intelligence, the psychic or when that becomes dynamic, the higher spiritual consciousness.

As the peace and contact grow, a double consciousness can develop — one engaged in the work, another behind, silent and observing or turned towards the Divine — in this consciousness the aspiration can be maintained even while the external consciousness is turned towards the work.

> Inconscience puts its seal on Nature's page
> Or else a mad disorder whirls the brain
> Posting along a ravaged nature's roads,
> A chaos of disordered impulses
> In which no light can come, no joy, no peace.
> This state now threatened, this she pushed from her.

Incapacity

A present incapacity, however heavy may seem its pressure, is only a trial of faith and a temporary difficulty and to yield to the sense of inability is for the seeker of the integral Yoga a non-sense, for his object is a development of a perfection that is there already, latent in his being, because man carries the seed of the divine life in himself, in his own spirit, the possibility of success is involved and implied in the effort and victory is assured because behind is the call and guidance of an omnipotent power.

All these defects you know are in you; to cast that out may take time, but if the will to be true to the inner self in all ways is strong and persistent and vigilant and always calls in the Mother's Force, it can be done sooner than now seems possible.

A difficult evolution from below
Called a masked intervention from above;
Else this great, blind inconscient universe
Could never have disclosed its hidden mind.

Inconscient

For below this conscient nature is the vast Inconscient out of which we come. The Inconscient is greater, deeper, more original, more potent to shape and govern what we are and do than our little derivative conscient nature. Inconscient to us, to our surface view, but not inconscient in itself or to itself, it is a sovereign guide, worker, determinant, creator. Not to know it is not to know our nether origins and the origin of the most part of what we are and do. And the Inconscient is not all.

The bed-rock of Inconscience is the fundamental basis of all resistance in the individual and in the world to the victory of the Spirit and the Divine Work that is leading toward that victory.

Inconscient is a status and power of involved consciousness in which being is plunged into another and opposite state of non-manifestation resembling non-existence so that out of it all in the material universe may be manifested.

Man in spite of its mental power is often impotent before the inconscient and subconscient which obscure its clarity and carry it away on the tide of instinct or impulse; inspite of its clarity it is fooled by vital and emotional suggestions into giving sanction to ignorance and error, to wrong thought and wrong action, or it is obliged to look on while the nature follows what it knows to be wrong, dangerous or evil.

Here everything is shut up from the first in the violently working inconscient sleep of material force; therefore the whole aim of any material becoming must be the waking of consciousness out of the inconscient; the whole consummation of a material becoming must be the removal of the veil of matter and the luminous revelation of the entirely self-conscious Being to its own imprisoned soul in the becoming. Since Man is such an imprisoned soul, this luminous liberation and coming to self-knowledge must be his highest object and the condition of his perfection.

God wrapped his head from sight in Matter's cowl,
His consciousness dived into inconscient depths,
All-knowledge seemed a huge dark Nescience;
Infinity wore a boundless zero's form.

His abysms of bliss became insensible deeps,
Eternity a blank spiritual Vast.

Indispensable Basis

The indispensable basis of our Yoga is sincerity, honesty, unselfishness, disinterested consecration to the work to be done, nobility of character and straight forwardness. They who do not practice these elementary virtues are not Sri Aurobindo's disciples.

If you desire this transformation, put yourself in the hands of the Mother and her Powers without cavil or resistance and let her do unhindered her work within you. Three things you must have, consciousness, plasticity, unreserved surrender. For you must be conscious in your mind and soul and heart and life and the very cells of your body, aware of the Mother and her Powers and their working; for although she can and does work in you even in your obscurity and your unconscious parts and moments, it is not the same thing as when you are in awakened and living communion with her.

Out of our thoughts we must leap up to sight,
Breathe her divine illimitable air,
Her simple vast supremacy confess,
Dare to surrender to her absolute.
Then the Unmanifest reflects his form
In the still mind as in a living glass;
The timeless Ray descends into our hearts
And we are rapt into eternity.

Individual

The individual is the meeting place of the play of the dual aspect of the Divine, Prakriti and Purusha or Soul and Nature. (Nature and Soul)

All life, spiritual, mental or material, is the play of the soul with the possibilities of its nature; for without this play there can be no self-expression and no relative self-experience.

For the nature of the divine existence is to possess always its unity, but to possess it also in an infinite experience, from many standpoints, on many planes, through many conscious powers or selves of itself, individualities — in our limited intellectual language — of the one conscious being. Each one of us is one of these individualities.

In the higher spiritual consciousness he becomes simultaneously one with both these aspects, and there he takes up and combines all the divine relations created by their interaction.

A Spirit who is no one and innumerable,
The one mystic infinite Person of his world
Multiplies his myriad personality,
On all his bodies seals his divinity's stamp
And sits in each immortal and unique.

Influencing Diversions

It is not safe while you are doing the yoga another influence, whatever it may be, which is not ours or part of the movement of this sadhana. If that takes place anything might happen and we would not be able to protect you against it because you would have stepped out of the circle of protection. A diversion of this kind which seems to be on the vital level might be a serious interference. No trust can be put on the beauty of the eyes or the face. There are many Beings of the inferior planes who have a captivating beauty and can enthral with it and they can give too an Ananda which is not the highest and may on the contrary by its lure take away from the path altogether. When you have reached the stage of clear discernment where the highest Light is turned on all things that come, then experiences of many kinds may be safely faced, but now a strict vigilance must be exercised and all diversions rejected. It is necessary to keep one's steps firmly on the straight road to the Highest; all else must wait for the proper time.

A fatal Influence upon creatures stole
Whose lethal touch pursued the immortal spirit,
On life was laid the haunting finger of Death
And overcast with error, grief and pain
The soul's native will for truth and joy and light.

Inner

While on our surface we are cut off from all around expect through an exterior mind and sense-contact which deliver but little of us to our world or our world to us, in these inner reaches the barrier between us and the rest of the existence is thin and easily broken; there we can feel at once — not merely infer from their results, but feel directly — the action of the secret world-forces, mind-forces, life-forces, subtle physical forces that constitute universal and individual existence; we shall even be able, if we will but train ourselves to it, to lay our hands on these world-forces that throw themselves on us or around us and more and more to control or at least strongly modify their action on us and others, their formations, their very movements. Yet again, above our human mind are still greater reaches superconscient to it and from there secretly descend influences, powers, touches which are the original determinants of things here and, if they were called down in their fullness, could altogether alter the whole make and economy of life in the material universe. It is all this latent experience and knowledge that the Divine Force working upon us by our opening to it in the integral Yoga, progressively reveals to us, uses and works out the consequences as means and steps towards a transformation of our whole being and nature. Our life is thenceforth no longer a little rolling wave on the surface, but interpenetrant if not coincident with the cosmic life. Our spirit, our self rises not only into an inner identity with some wide cosmic Self but into some contact with that which is beyond, though aware of and dominant over the action of the universe.

> In scenes forbidden to our pallid sense
> Amid miraculous scents and wonder-hues
> He met the forms that divinise the sight,
> To music that can immortalise the mind
> And make the heart wide as infinity.

Inner Experiences

The sadhak must understand that these experiences are not mere imaginations or dreams but actual happenings, for even when, as often occurs, they are formations only of a wrong or misleading or adverse kind, they have still their power as formations and must be understood before they can be rejected and abolished. Each inner experience is perfectly real in its own way, although the values of different experiences differ greatly, but it is real with the reality of the inner self and the inner planes. It is a mistake to think that we live physically only, with the outer mind and life. We are all the time living and acting on other planes of consciousness, meeting others there and acting upon them, and what we do and feel and think there, the forces we gather, the results we prepare have an incalculable importance and effect, unknown to us, upon our outer life. Not all of it comes through, and what comes through takes another form in the physical — though sometimes there is an exact correspondence; but this little is at the basis of our outward existence. All that we become and do and bear in the physical life is prepared behind the veil within us. It is therefore of immense importance for a yoga which aims at the transformation of life to grow conscious of what goes on within these domains, to be master there and be able to feel, know and deal with the secret forces that determine our destiny and our internal and external growth or decline.

> A passage for the Powers that move our days,
> Occult behind this grosser Nature's walls,
> A gossamer marriage-hall of Mind with Form
> Is hidden by a tapestry of dreams;
> Heaven's meanings steal through it as through a veil,
> Its inner sight sustains this outer scene.

Inner Mind

Though the inner mind-spaces have horizons, they stretch beyond those horizons — illimitably. The inner mind is something very wide projecting itself into the infinite and finally identifying itself with the infinity of universal Mind. When we break out of the narrow limits of the external physical mind we begin to see inwardly and to feel this wideness, in the end this universality and infinity of the mental self-space.

The inner mind has also a subtle sight, hearing, power of contact of its own which is not dependent on the physical organs. And it has, moreover, a power not only of direct communication of mind with object, — leading even at a high pitch of action to a sense of the contents of an object within or beyond the physical range,-but direct communication also of mind with mind. Mind is able too to alter, modify, inhibit the incidence, values, intensities of sense impacts. These powers of the mind we do not ordinarily use or develop; they remain subliminal and emerge sometimes in an irregular and fitful action, more readily in some minds than in others, or come to the surface in abnormal states of the being. They are the basis of clairvoyance, clairaudience, transference of thought and impulse, telepathy, most of the more ordinary kinds of occult powers.

> She looked out far and saw from inner mind
> This questionable world of outward things,
> Of false appearances and plausible shapes,
> This dubious cosmos stretched in the ignorant Void,
> The pangs of earth, the toil and speed of the stars
> And the difficult birth and dolorous end of life.

The Inner
Mind Vital Physical

There is an inner mind, an inner vital, an inner physical consciousness which can more easily than the outer receive the higher consciousness above and put itself into harmony with the psychic being; when that is done the outer nature is felt as only a fringe on the surface, not as oneself, and is more easily transformed altogether.

Only a little of the inner being escapes through the centres into the outer life, but that little is the best part of ourselves and responsible for our art, poetry, philosophy, ideals, religious aspirations, efforts at knowledge and perfection. But the inner centres are for the most part closed or sleep - to open them and make them awake and active is one aim of yoga. As they open the powers and possibilities of the inner being are also aroused in us; we awake first to a larger consciousness and then to a cosmic consciousness; we are no longer little separate personalities with limited lives but centres of a universal action and in direct contact with universal forces.

A mighty movement rocked the inner space
As if a world were shaken and found its soul:
Out of the Inconscient's soulless mindless Night
A flaming serpent rose released from sleep.

Inner Opening

The in going movement is indispensable. Its effect is to break or at least to open and pass the barrier between this outer instrumental consciousness and the inner being which it very partially strives to express, and to make possible in future a conscious awareness of all the endless riches of possibility and experience and new being and new life that lie untapped behind the veil of this small and very blind and limited material personality which men erroneously think to be the whole of themselves. It is the beginning and constant enlarging of this deeper and fuller and richer awareness that is accomplished between the inward plunge and the return from this inner world to the waking state.

The piercing of the veil between the outer consciousness and the inner being is one of the crucial movements in yoga. For yoga means union with the Divine, but it also means awaking first to your inner self and then to your higher self, – a movement inward and a movement upward. It is, in fact, only through the awakening and coming to the front of the inner being that you can get into union with the Divine.

> She forced her way through body to the soul.
> Across a perilous border line she passed
> Where life dips into the subconscient dusk
> Or struggles from Matter into chaos of mind.

Intense

This yoga can only be done to the end by those who are in total earnest about it and ready to abolish their little human ego and its demands in order to find themselves in the Divine. It cannot be done in a spirit of levity or laxity; the work is too high and difficult, the adverse powers in the lower Nature too ready to take advantage of the least sanction or the smallest opening, the aspiration and tapasya needed too constant and intense. It cannot be done if there is a petulant self-assertion of the ideas of the human mind or wilful indulgence of the demands and instincts and pretensions of the lowest part of the being, commonly justified under the name of human nature. It cannot be done if you insist on identifying these lowest things of the Ignorance with the divine Truth or even the lesser truth permissible on the way. It cannot be done if you cling to your past self and its old mental, vital and physical formations and habits; one has continually to leave behind his past selves and to see, act and live from an always higher and higher conscious level. It cannot be done if you insist on "freedom" for your human mind and vital ego. All the parts of the human being are entitled to express and satisfy themselves in their own way at their own risk and peril, if he so chooses, as long as he leads the ordinary life. But to enter into a path of yoga whose whole object is to substitute for these human things the law and power of a greater Truth and the whole heart of whose method is surrender to the Divine Shakti, and yet to go on claiming this so-called freedom, which is no more than a subjection to certain ignorant cosmic Forces, is to indulge in a blind contradiction and to claim the right to lead a double life.

Least of all can this yoga be done if those who profess to be its sadhaks continue always to make themselves centres, instruments or spokesmen of the forces of the Ignorance which oppose, deny and ridicule its very principle and object. On one side there is the supramental realisation, the overshadowing and descending power of the supramental Divine, the light and force of a far greater Truth than any yet realised on the earth, something therefore beyond what the little human mind and its logic regard as the only permanent realities, something whose nature and way and process of development here it cannot conceive or perceive by its own inadequate instruments or judge by its puerile standards; in spite of all opposition this is pressing down for manifestation in the physical

123

consciousness and the material life. On the other side is this lower vital nature with all its pretentious arrogance, ignorance, obscurity, dullness or incompetent turbulence, standing for its own prolongation, standing against the descent, refusing to believe in any real reality or real possibility of a supramental or superhuman consciousness and creation, or, still more absurd, demanding, if it exists at all, that it should conform to its own little standards, seizing greedily upon everything that seems to disprove it, denying the presence of the Divine, — for it knows that without that presence the work is impossible, — affirming loudly its own thoughts, judgments, desires, instincts, and, if these are contradicted, avenging itself by casting abroad doubt, denial, disparaging criticism, revolt and disorder. These are the two things now in presence between which every one will have to choose.

For this opposition, this sterile obstruction and blockade against the descent of the divine Truth cannot last for ever. Every one must come down finally on one side or the other, on the side of the Truth or against it. The supramental realisation cannot coexist with the persistence of the lower Ignorance; it is incompatible with continued satisfaction in a double nature.

> Once were my days like days of other men:
> To think and act was all, to enjoy and breathe;
> This was width and height of mortal hope:
> Yet there came glimpses of a deeper self
> That lives behind life and makes her act its scene.

Intermediate Zone

It is a borderland where all the worlds meet, mental, vital, subtle physical, pseudo-spiritual — but there is no order or firm foothold — a passage between the physical and the true spiritual realms.

A zone of transition between the ordinary consciousness in mind and the true yoga knowledge. One may cross without hurt through it, perceiving at once or at an early stage its real nature and refusing to be detained by its half-lights and tempting but imperfect and often mixed and misleading experiences; one may go astray in it, follow false voices and mendacious guidance, and that ends in a spiritual disaster; or one may take up one's abode in this intermediate zone, care to go no farther and build there some half-truth which one takes for the whole truth or become the instrument of the powers of these transitional planes, — that is what happens to many sadhaks and yogis. Overwhelmed by the first rush and sense of power of a supernormal condition, they get dazzled with a little light which seems to them a tremendous illumination or a touch of force which they mistake for the full Divine Force or at least a very great yoga Shakti; or they accept some intermediate Power (not always a Power of the Divine) as the Supreme and an intermediate consciousness as the supreme realisation.

Those galloping hooves in their enthusiast speed
Could bear to a dangerous intermediate zone
Where Death walks wearing a robe of deathless Life.
Or they enter the valley of the wandering Gleam
Whence, captives or victims of the specious Ray,
Souls trapped in that region never can escape.

Intermediate Zone

Its Experiences

All these experiences are of the same nature and what applies to one applies to another. Apart from some experiences of a personal character, the rest are either idea-truths, such as pour down into the consciousness from above when one gets into touch with certain planes of being, or strong formations from the larger mental and vital worlds which, when one is directly open to these worlds, rush in and want to use the sadhak for their fulfilment. These things, when they pour down or come in, present themselves with a great force, a vivid sense of inspiration or illumination, much sensation of light and joy, an impression of widening and power. The sadhak feels himself freed from the normal limits, projected into a wonderful new world of experience, filled and enlarged and exalted; what comes associates itself, besides, with his aspirations, ambitions, notions of spiritual fulfilment and yogic siddhi; it is represented even as itself that realisation and fulfilment. Very easily he is carried away by the splendour and the rush, and thinks that he has realised more than he has truly done, something final or at least something sovereignly true. At this stage the necessary knowledge and experience are usually lacking which would tell him that this is only a very uncertain and mixed beginning; he may not realise at once that he is still in the cosmic Ignorance, not in the cosmic Truth, much less in the Transcendental Truth, and that whatever formative or dynamic idea-truths may have come down into him are partial only and yet further diminished by their presentation to him by a still mixed consciousness. He may fail to realise also that if he rushes to apply what he is realising or receiving as if it were something definitive, he may either fall into confusion and error or else get shut up in some partial formation in which there may be an element of spiritual Truth but it is likely to be outweighted by more dubious mental and vital accretions that deform it altogether. It is only when he is able to draw back (whether at once or after a time) from his experiences, stand above them with the dispassionate witness consciousness, observe their real nature, limitations, composition, mixture that he can proceed on his way towards a real freedom and a higher, larger and truer siddhi. At each step this has to be done. For whatever comes in this way to the sadhak of this yoga, whether it be from overmind or Intuition or Illumined Mind or some exalted Life Plane or from all these together, it is not definitive and final; it is not the supreme Truth in which he can rest, but only a stage. And yet these stages have to be passed through, for the supramental or the Supreme Truth cannot be reached in one bound or even in many bounds; one has to pursue a calm patient steady progress through many intervening stages without getting bound or attached to their lesser Truth or Light or Power or Ananda.

Here in Life's nether realms all contraries meet;
Truth stares and does her work with bandaged eyes,
And Ignorance is Wisdom's patron here.

Intermediate Zone
False Mixtures

Very readily they come to think that they are in the full cosmic consciousness when it is only some front or small part of it or some larger Mind, Life-Power or subtle physical ranges with which they have entered into dynamic connection. Or they feel themselves to be in an entirely illumined consciousness, while in reality they are receiving imperfectly things from above through a partial illumination of some mental or vital plane; for what comes is diminished and often deformed in the course of transmission through these planes; the receiving mind and vital of the sadhak also often understands or transcribes ill what has been received or throws up to mix with it its own ideas, feelings, desires, which it yet takes to be not its own but part of the Truth it is receiving because they are mixed with it, imitate its form, are lit up by its illumination and get from this association and borrowed light an exaggerated value.

But I must pass leaving the ended search,
Truth's rounded outcome firm, immutable
And this harmonic building of world-fact,
This ordered knowledge of apparent things.
Here I can stay not, for I seek my soul.

Intermediate Zone

Its Dangers

There are worse dangers in this intermediate zone of experience. For the planes to which the sadhak has now opened his consciousness, — not as before getting glimpses of them and some influences, but directly, receiving their full impact, — send a host of ideas, impulses, suggestions, formations of all kinds, often the most opposite to each other, inconsistent or incompatible, but presented in such a way as to slur over their insufficiencies and differences, with great force, plausibility and wealth of argument or a convincing sense of certitude. Overpowered by this sense of certitude, vividness, appearance of profusion and richness, the mind of the sadhak enters into a great confusion which it takes for some larger organisation and order; or else it whirls about in incessant shiftings and changes which it takes for a rapid progress but which lead nowhere.

It is quite true that an inner purity and sincerity, in which one is motived only by the higher call, is one's best safeguard against the lures of the intermediate stage. It keeps one on the right track and guards from deviation, until the psychic being is fully awake and in front and, once that happens, there is no further danger.

A trenchant blade that shore the nets of doubt,
Its sword of discernment seemed almost divine.
Yet all that knowledge was a borrowed sun's;
The forms that came were not heaven's native births:
Its puissance dangerous and absolute
Could mingle poison with the wine of God.

Intermediate Zone
The Opposite Danger

Or there is the opposite danger that he may become the instrument of some apparently brilliant but ignorant formation; for these intermediate planes are full of little Gods or strong Daityas or smaller beings who want to create, to materialise something or to enforce a mental and vital formation in the earth life and are eager to use or influence or even possess the thought and will of the sadhak and make him their instrument for the purpose. This is quite apart from the well-known danger of actually hostile beings whose sole purpose is to create confusion, falsehood, corruption of the sadhana and disastrous unspiritual error. Anyone allowing himself to be taken hold of by one of these beings, who often take a divine Name, will lose his way in the yoga. On the other hand, it is quite possible that the sadhak may be met at his entrance into this zone by a Power of the Divine which helps and leads him till he is ready for greater things; but still that itself is no surety against the errors and stumblings of this zone; for nothing is easier than for the powers of these zones or hostile powers to imitate the guiding Voice or Image and deceive and mislead the sadhak or for himself to attribute the creations and formations of his own mind, vital or ego to the Divine.

> Its bottomless danger pits and swallowing gulfs,
> Its fear and joy and ecstasy and despair,
> Its occult wizardries, its simple lines
> And great communions and uplifting moves,
> Its faith in heaven, its intercourse with hell.

Intermediate Zone
The Region of Half Truths

For this intermediate zone is a region of half-truths — and that by itself would not matter, for there is no complete truth below the supermind; but the half-truth here is often so partial or else ambiguous in its application that it leaves a wide field for confusion, delusion and error. The sadhak thinks that he is no longer in the old small consciousness at all, because he feels in contact with something larger or more powerful, and yet the old consciousness is still there, not really abolished. He feels the control or influence of some Power, Being or Force greater than himself, aspires to be its instrument and thinks he has got rid of ego; but this delusion of egolessness often covers an exaggerated ego. Ideas seize upon him and drive his mind which are only partially true and by over-confident misapplication are turned into falsehoods; this vitiates the movements of the consciousness and opens the door to delusion.

> The Spirit's almighty freedom was not here:
> A schoolman mind had captured life's large space,
> But chose to live in bare paltry rooms
> Parked off from the top vast dangerous universe,
> Fearing to lose its soul in the infinite.

Intermediate Zone
Tempting Suggestions

Suggestions are made, sometimes of a romantic character, which flatter the importance of the sadhak or are agreeable to his wishes and he accepts them without examination or discriminating control. Even what is true, is so exalted or extended beyond its true pitch and limit and measure that it becomes the parent of error. This is a zone which many sadhaks have to cross, in which many wander for a long time and out of which a great many never emerge. Especially if their sadhana is mainly in the mental and vital, they have to meet here many difficulties and much danger; only those who follow scrupulously a strict guidance or have the psychic being prominent in their nature pass easily as if on a sure and clearly marked road across this intermediate region. A central sincerity, a fundamental humility also save from much danger and trouble. One can then pass quickly beyond into a clearer Light where if there is still much mixture, incertitude and struggle, yet the orientation is towards the cosmic Truth and not to a half-illumined prolongation of Maya and ignorance.

> These powers were not blunt with the dead weight of earth,
> They gave ambrosia's taste and poison's sting.
> There was an ardour in the gaze of Life
> They saw heaven blue in the grey air of Night:
> The impulses godward soared on passion's wings.

Intermediate Zone
And the Overmind

The overmind is indeed above and behind the whole action of the cosmic consciousness, but one can at first have only an indirect connection with it; things come down from it through intermediate ranges into a larger mind-plane, life-plane, subtle physical plane and come very much changed and diminished in the transmission, without anything like the full power and truth they have in the overmind itself on its native levels. Most of the movements come not from the overmind, but down from higher mind ranges. The ideas with which these experiences are penetrated and on which they seem to rest their claim to truth are not of the overmind, but of the higher Mind or sometimes of the illumined Mind; but they are mixed with suggestions from the lower mind and vital regions and badly diminished in their application or misapplied in many places.

A Witness sanctioning her will and works,
An Eye unseen in the unseeing vast;
There is an Influence from a Light above,
There are thoughts remote and sealed eternities:
A mystic motive drives the stars and suns.

Intermediate Zone
The Eagerness

The movement was made in a spirit of excessive hurry and eagerness, of exaggerated self-esteem and self-confidence, of a premature certitude, relying on no other guidance than that of one's own mind or of the "Divine" as conceived or experienced in a stage of very limited knowledge. But the sadhak's conception and experience of the Divine, even if it is fundamentally genuine, is never in such a stage complete and pure; it is mixed with all sorts of mental and vital ascriptions and all sorts of things are associated with this Divine guidance and believed to be part of it which come from quite other sources. Even supposing there is any direct guidance, — most often in these conditions the Divine acts mostly from behind the veil, — it is only occasional and the rest is done through a play of forces; error and stumbling and mixture of Ignorance take place freely and these things are allowed because the sadhak has to be tested by the world-forces, to learn by experience, to grow through imperfection towards perfection — if he is capable of it, if he is willing to learn, to open his eyes to his own mistakes and errors, to learn and profit by them so as to grow towards a purer Truth, Light and Knowledge.

> In our body's cells there sits a hidden Power
> That sees the unseen and plans eternity,
> Our smallest parts have room for deeper needs;
> There too the golden Messengers can come,
> A door is cut in the mud wall of self.

Intermediate Zone
The Self Assertions

The result of this state of mind is that one begins to affirm everything that comes in this mixed and dubious region as if it were all the Truth and the sheer Divine Will; the ideas or the suggestions that constantly repeat themselves are expressed with a self-assertive absoluteness as if they were Truth entire and undeniable. There is an impression that one has become impersonal and free from ego, while the whole tone of the mind, its utterance and spirit are full of vehement self-assertiveness justified by the affirmation that one is thinking and acting as an instrument and under the inspiration of the Divine. Ideas are put forward very aggressively that can be valid to the mind, but are not spiritually valid; yet they are stated as if they were spiritual absolutes. For instance, equality, which in that sense — for yogic Samata is a quite different thing — is a mere mental principle, the claim to a sacred independence, the refusal to accept anyone as Guru or the opposition made between the Divine and the human Divine etc., etc. All these ideas are positions that can be taken by the mind and the vital and turned into principles which they try to enforce on the religious or even the spiritual life, but they are not and cannot be spiritual in their nature.

> Agents, not masters, they serve Life's desires
> Toiling for ever in the snare of Time.
> Their bodies born out of some Nihil's womb
> Ensnare the spirit in the moment's dreams,
> Then perish vomiting the immortal soul
> Out of Matter's belly into the sink of Nought.

Intermediate Zone
The Suggestions

There also begin to come in suggestions from the vital planes, a pullulation of imaginations romantic, fanciful or ingenious, hidden interpretations, pseudo-intuitions, would-be initiations into things beyond, which excite or bemuse the mind and are often so turned as to flatter and magnify ego and self-importance, but are not founded on any well-ascertained spiritual or occult realities of a true order. This region is full of elements of this kind and, if allowed, they begin to crowd on the sadhak; but if he seriously means to reach the Highest, he must simply observe them and pass on. It is not that there is never any truth in such things, but for one that is true there are nine imitative falsehoods presented and only a trained occultist with the infallible tact born of long experience can guide himself without stumbling or being caught through the maze. It is possible for the whole attitude and action and utterance to be so surcharged with the errors of this intermediate zone that to go farther on this route would be to travel far away from the Divine and from the yoga.

Untouched they live by hope and doubt and fear.
Happy are men anchored on fixed belief
In this uncertain and ambiguous world,
Or who have planted in the heart's rich soil
One small grain of spiritual certitude.

Intermediate Zone
And this Yoga

Here the choice is still open whether to follow the very mixed guidance one gets in the midst of these experiences or to accept the true guidance. Each man who enters the realms of yogic experience is free to follow his own way; but this yoga is not a path for anyone to follow, but only for those who accept to seek the aim, pursue the way pointed out upon which a sure guidance is indispensable. It is idle for anyone to expect that he can follow this road far, — much less go to the end by his own inner strength and knowledge without the true aid or influence. Even the ordinary long-practised yogas are hard to follow without the aid of the Guru; in this which as it advances goes through untrodden countries and unknown entangled regions, it is quite impossible. As for the work to be done it also is not a work for any sadhak of any path; it is not, either, the work of the "Impersonal" Divine who, for that matter, is not an active Power but supports impartially all work in the universe. It is a training ground for those who have to pass through the difficult and complex way of this yoga and none other. All work here must be done in a spirit of acceptance, discipline and surrender, not with personal demands and conditions, but with a vigilant conscious submission to control and guidance. Work done in any other spirit results in an unspiritual disorder, confusion and disturbance of the atmosphere. In it too difficulties, errors, stumblings are frequent, because in this yoga people have to be led patiently and with some field for their own effort, by experience, out of the ignorance natural to Mind and Life to a wider spirit and a luminous knowledge. But the danger of an unguided wandering in the regions across the border is that the very basis of the yoga may be contradicted and the conditions under which alone the work can be done may be lost altogether. The transition through this intermediate zone — not obligatory, for many pass by a narrower but surer way — is a crucial passage; what comes out of it is likely to be a very wide or rich creation; but when one founders there, recovery is difficult, painful, assured only after a long struggle and endeavour.

Yet some uncaught, unslain can wearily pass

Carrying Truth's image in their sheltered heart,
Pluck Knowledge out of error's screening grip,
Break paths through the blind walls of little self,
Then travel on to reach a greater life.

Interruptions

You must remain vigilant always. For when the condition is good, the lower movements have a habit of subsiding and become quiescent, hiding as it were, — or they go out of the nature and remain at a distance. But if they see that the sadhak is losing vigilance, then they slowly begin to rise or draw near, most often unseen, and when he is quite off his guard, surge up suddenly or make a sudden irruption. This continues until the whole nature, mental, vital, physical down to the very subconscient is enlightened, conscious, full of the Divine. Till that happens, one must always remain watchful in a sleepless vigilance.

There is another thing which you must learn. If you are interrupted in sadhana. . . you must simply remain inwardly quiet and allow the interruption to pass. If you learn to do this, the inner state of experience will go on afterwards just as if nothing had happened. If you attach undue importance and get upset, on the contrary, you change the interruption into a disturbance and the inner state or experience ceases. Always keep the inner quiet and confidence in every circumstance; allow nothing to disturb it or to excite you. A steady inner calm and quiet will and psychic faith and bhakti are the one true foundation for your sadhana.

> Our life was born in pain and with a cry.
> Although earth-nature welcomes heaven's breath
> Inspiring Matter with the will to live,
> A thousand ills assail the mortal's hours
> And wear away the natural joy of life.

Intuition

What is thought-knowledge in the Higher Mind becomes illumination in the Illumined Mind and direct intimate vision in the Intuition. But the Intuition sees in flashes and combines through a constant play of light — through revelations, inspirations, intuitions, swift discriminations.

The Intuition is the first plane in which there is a real opening to the full possibility of realisation — it is through it that one goes farther — first to overmind and then to supermind.

One can get intuitions — communications from there (the Intuition plane) even while the ego exists — but to live in the wideness of the Intuition is not possible with the limitation of the ego.

In order to live in the Intuition plane one has to live in the cosmic consciousness because there the cosmic and individual run into each other as it were, and the mental separation between them is already broken down, so nobody can reach there who is still in the separative ego.

Intuition sees the truth of things by a direct inner contact, not like the ordinary mental intelligence by seeking and reaching out for indirect contacts through the senses etc. But the limitation of the Intuition as compared with the supermind is that it sees things by flashes, point by point, not as a whole.

In some minds often intuitions do come in, but immediately the ordinary thoughts surround it and eat it up alive, and then with some fragment of the murdered intuition shining through their non-intuitive stomachs they look up smiling at you and say, "I am an intuition, sir." But they are only intellect, intelligence or ordinary thought with part of a dismembered and therefore misleading intuition inside them. Now in a vacant mind, vacant but not inert, (that is important) intuitions have a chance of getting in alive and whole. But don't run away with the idea that all that comes into an empty mind will be intuitive. Anything, any blessed kind of idea can come in. One has to be vigilant and examine the credentials of the visitor. In other words, the mental being must be there, silent but vigilant, impartial but discriminating.

Thought there has revelation's sun-bright eyes;
The Word, a mighty and inspiring Voice,
Enters Truth's inmost cabin of privacy
And tears away the veil from God and life.

Journey

This cannot be a smooth and even process; alterations there are of day and night, illumination and darkness, calm and construction or battle and upheaval, the presence of the growing Divine Consciousness and its absence, heights of hope and abysses of despair, the clasp of the Beloved and the anguish of its absence, the overwhelming invasion, the compelling deceit, the fierce opposition, the disabling mockery of hostile Powers or the help and comfort and communion of the gods and the Divine Messengers.

We must always go beyond, always renounce the lesser for the greater, the finite for the Infinite; we must be prepared to proceed from illumination to illumination, from experience to experience, from soul-state to soul-state so as to reach the utmost transcendence of the Divine and its utmost universality.

> The superconscient's screen was ripped by thought,
> Idea rotated symphonies of sight,
> Sight was a flame-throw from identity;
> Life was a marvellous journey of the spirit,
> Feeling a wave from the universal Bliss.
> In the kingdom of the Spirit's power and light,
> As if one who arrived out of infinity's womb
> He came new-born, infant and limitless
> And grew in the wisdom of the timeless Child;

Knowledge

It is only when we have seen both our Self and our outer nature as a whole, in the depths as well as on the surface, then we can acquire a true basis for knowledge.

Mental knowledge is of little use except sometimes as an introduction pointing towards the real knowledge which comes from a direct consciousness of things.

A surface knowledge of the physical universe is an imperfect guide; for the thinking animal it may be enough, but not for a race of mental beings in labour of spiritual evolution.

The one thing always is to let the Peace and Power work and not allow the mind to seek after things and get disturbed. All the values of the mind are constructions of ignorance — it is only when your psychic being comes forward that you have the true knowledge — for your psychic being knows.

The mind in its higher parts is aware of being one with the Divine, in all ways, in all things - having that supreme knowledge, it is not disturbed by its own ignorance and impotence in its lower instrumental parts; it looks on all that with a smile and remains happy and luminous with the light of the supreme knowledge.

The consciousness of union with the Divine is for the spiritual seeker the supreme knowledge.

An inspired Knowledge sat enthroned within
Whose seconds illumined more than reason's years.

Liberated Soul

The rules which the intellect of men lays down cannot apply to the liberated soul, — by the external criteria and tests which their mental associations and prejudgments prescribe, such a one cannot be judged; he is outside the narrow jurisdiction of these fallible tribunals. It is immaterial whether he wears the garb of the ascetic or lives the full life of the householder; whether he spends his days in what men call holy works or in the many-sided activities of the world. whether he devotes himself to the direct leading of men to the Light like Buddha, Christ or Shankara or governs kingdoms like Janaka or stands before men like Sri Krishna as a politician or a leader of armies; what he eats or drinks; what are his habits or his pursuits; whether he fails or succeeds; whether his work be one of construction or destruction; whether his life and deeds are approved by his contemporaries or he is condemned as a misleader of men and a fomenter of religious, moral or social heresies. He is not governed by the judgements of men or the laws laid down by the ignorant; he obeys an inner voice and is moved by an unseen Power. His real life is within and this is its description that he lives, moves and acts in God, in the Divine, in the Infinite.

> Across the cosmic field through narrow lanes
> Asking a scanty dole from the Fortune's hands
> And garbed in beggar's robes there walks the One.
> Even in the theatre of these small lives
> Behind the act a secret sweetness breathes,
> An urge of miniature divinity.

Life

Life is everywhere, secret or manifest, organised or elemental, involved or evolved, but universal, all-pervading, imperishable; only its forms and organisings differ.

Life then reveals itself as essentially the same everywhere from the atom to man, the atom containing the subconscious stuff and movement of being which are released into consciousness in the animal, with plant life as a midway stage in the evolution.

Life is really a universal operation of Conscious-Force acting subconsciously on and in Matter; it is the operation that creates, maintains, destroys and re-creates forms or bodies and attempts by play of nerve-force, that is to say, by currents of interchange of stimulating energy to awake conscious sensation in those bodies.

There is an Intuition in Matter which holds the action of the material world from the electron to the sun and planets and their contents. There is an Intuition in Life which similarly supports and guides the play and development of Life in Matter till it is ready for the mental evolution of which man is the vehicle. In man also the creation follows the same upward process, — the Intuition within develops according to the stage he has reached in his progress.

There is no end of seeking and of birth,
There is no end of dying and return;
The life that wins its aim asks greater aims,
The life that fails and dies must live again;
Till it has found itself it cannot cease.

Life Nature

The vital's cherished desires, emotions, feelings, impulses, grooves of sensation, forceful mechanism of action and reaction.

This is to be replaced by a luminous, desireless, free and yet automatically self-determining force, the force of a centralised universal and impersonal knowledge, power, delight of which the life must become an instrument and an epiphany, but of which it has at present no inkling and no sense of its greater joy and strength for fulfilment.

It has been said as long ago as the Upanishads (hard is the path to tread, sharp like a razor's edge); it was said later by Christ 'hard is the way and narrow the gate by which one enters into the kingdom of heaven' and also 'many are called, few chosen' — because of these difficulties. But it has also always been known that those who are sincere and faithful in heart and remain so and those who rely on the Divine will arrive in spite of all difficulties, stumbles or falls.

The cry of the psychic is always, "Let the Truth prevail, let Thy will be done and not mine". But the clamour of the vital is the very opposite: it calls to the Divine, "Let my will be Thine; obey my insistences, satisfy my desires, then only will I seek and accept Thee, for then only will I consent to see the Divine in Thee". It is hardly necessary to say which is the way to the Truth or which the right solution of any struggle in the nature.

The lower nature is ignorant and undivine, not in itself hostile but shut to the Light and Truth. The hostile forces are anti-divine, not merely undivine; they make use of the lower nature, pervert it, fill it with distorted movements and by that means influence man and even try to enter and possess or at least entirely control him.

Cast from thee sense that veils thy spirit's sight:
In the enormous emptiness of thy mind
Thou shalt see the Eternal's body in the world.

Light

Light is the power that enlightens whatever it falls upon — the result may be vision, memory, knowledge, right will, right impulse, etc.

When you see Light, that is a vision; when you feel Light entering into you, that is an experience; when Light settles in you and brings illumination and knowledge, that is a realisation. The Light descending recedes if there is an attachment to obscurity or to any form of the Ignorance.

A descent brings naturally a deep inward condition and a silence of the mind, and it may bring much more — peace, a sense of liberation, happiness, Ananda. It is very often attended as in this experience by a light or luminosity. It was felt enveloping the upper part of the body down to the cardiac centre, because it is these centres, the head and heart centres that are first invaded and occupied by whatever descends from above, Consciousness, Force, Light or Ananda. Usually, there is at first a pressure from above on the head, then one feels something entering the higher part of the head and then the whole head is occupied, as you feel now with the "fourmillement" at the time of concentration. Once the head with its mental centres is open and occupied, the Force descends rapidly to the heart centre, unless there is some obstacle or a resistance in the higher vital parts. From there it sends its stream into the whole body and begins to occupy the vital and physical centres — from the navel to the Muladhara. The coming of this experience, occupation of the body, by the Force from above, is a great step forward in the sadhana.

All Light is not the light of the spirit, much less the light of the supermind. The mind, vital and physical have their own lights which can be very exhilarating and aspiring.

More and more souls shall enter into light,
Minds lit, inspired, the occult summoner hear
And lives blaze with a sudden inner flame
And heart grow enamoured of divine delight
And humans wills tune to the divine will.

Love

Love is a passion and it seeks for two things, eternity and intensity, and in the relation of the Lover and Beloved the seeking for eternity and for intensity is instinctive and self-born. Love is a seeking for mutual possession, and it is here that the demand for mutual possession becomes absolute. Passing beyond desire of possession which means a difference, it is a seeking for oneness, and it is here that the idea of oneness, of two souls merging into each other and becoming one finds the acme of its longing and the utterness of its satisfaction. Love, too, is a yearning for beauty, and it is here that the yearning is eternally satisfied in the vision and touch and the joy of the All-Beautiful. Love is a child and a seeker of Delight, and it is here that it finds the highest possible ecstasy both of the heart-consciousness and of every fibre of the being. Moreover, this relation is that which as between human being and human being demands the most and, even while reaching the greatest intensities, is still the least satisfied, because only in the Divine can it find its real and its utter satisfaction. Therefore it is here most that the turning of human emotion Godwards finds its full meaning and discovers all the truth of which love is the human symbol, all its essential instincts divinised, raised, satisfied in the bliss from which our life was born and towards which by oneness it returns in the Ananda of the divine existence where love is absolute, eternal and unalloyed.

> Thy spirit's strength shall make thee one with God,
> Thy agony shall change to ecstasy,
> Indifference deepen into infinity's calm
> And joy laugh nude on the peaks of the Absolute.

Love and Knowledge

Love fulfilled does not exclude knowledge, but itself brings knowledge; and the completer the knowledge, the richer the possibility of love. "By Bhakti," says the Lord in the Gita, "shall a man know Me in all my extent and greatness and as I am in the principles of my being, and when he has known Me in the principles of my being, then he enters into Me." Love without knowledge is a passionate and intense, but blind, crude, often dangerous thing, a great power, but also a stumbling-block; love, limited in knowledge, condemns itself in its fervour and often by its very fervour to narrowness; but love leading to perfect knowledge brings the finite and absolute union. Such love is not inconsistent with, but rather throws itself with joy into divine works; for it loves God and is one with him in all his being, and therefore in all beings, and to work for the world is then to feel and fulfil multitudinously one's love for God.

Love is the power and passion of the divine self-delight and without love we may get the rapt peace of its infinity, the absorbed silence of the Ananda, but not its absolute depth of richness and fullness. Love leads us from the suffering of division into the bliss of perfect union, but without losing that joy of the act of union which is the soul's greatest discovery and for which the life of the cosmos is a long preparation. Therefore to approach God by love is to prepare oneself for the greatest possible spiritual fulfilment.

> In all who have risen to greater Life
> A voice of unborn things whispers to the ear,
> To their eyes visited by some high sunlight
> Aspiration shows the image of a crown:
> To work out a seed that she has thrown within,
> To achieve her power in them her creatures live.

Lower Vital

The lower vital is occupied with small desires and feelings, such as make the greater part of daily life, e.g. food desire, sexual desire, small likings, dislikings, vanity, quarrels, love of praise, anger at blame, little wishes of all kinds — and a numberless host of other things.

Most people live in the vital. That means that they live in their desires, sensations, emotional feelings, vital imaginations and see and experience and judge everything from that point of view. It is the vital that moves them, the mind being at its service, not its master. In yoga also many people do sadhana from that plane and their experience is full of vital visions, formations, experiences of all kinds, but there is no mental clarity or order, neither do they rise above the mind. It is only the minority of men who live in the mind or in the psychic or try to live in the spiritual plane.

It was inevitable that in the course of the sadhana these inferior parts of the nature should be brought forward in order that like the rest of the being they may make the crucial choice and either accept or refuse transformation. My whole work depends upon this movement; it is the decisive ordeal of this yoga. For the physical consciousness and the material life cannot change if this does not change. Nothing that may have been done before, no inner illumination, experience, power or Ananda is of any eventual value, if this is not done. If the little external personality is to persist in retaining its obscure and limited, its petty and ignoble, its selfish and false and stupid human consciousness, this amounts to a flat negation of the work and the sadhana. I have no intention of giving my sanction to a new edition of the old fiasco, a partial and transient spiritual opening within with no true and radical change in the law of the external nature. If, then, any sadhak refuses in practice to admit this change or if he refuses even to admit the necessity for any change of his lower vital being and his habitual external personality, I am entitled to conclude that, whatever his professions, he has not accepted either myself or my yoga.

The difficulty in the lower vital being is that it is still wedded to its old self and in revolt against the Light; it has not only not surrendered either to a greater Truth or to myself and the Mother, but it has up to now no such will and hardly any idea even of what true surrender is. When the lower vital assumes this attitude it takes its stand upon a constant affirmation of the old personality and the past forms of the lower nature. Every time they are discouraged, it supports and brings them back and asserts its right to freedom, — the freedom to affirm and follow its own crude and egoistic ideas, desires, fancies, impulses or convenience whenever it chooses. It claims secretly or in so many words the right to follow its nature, — its human unregenerate nature, the right to be itself, — its natural original unchanged self with all the falsehood, ignorance and incoherence proper to this part of the being. And it claims or, if it does not claim in theory, it asserts in practice the right to express all this impure and inferior stuff in speech and act and behaviour. It defends, glosses over, paints in specious colours and tries to prolong indefinitely the past habitual ways of thinking, speaking and feeling and to eternise what is distorted and misformed in the character.

Absorbed they lived in the passion of the scene,
But knew not who they were and or why they lived:
Life had for them no aim save Nature's joy
And the stimulus and delight of outer things.

Mantra

OM is the mantra, the expressive sound-symbol of the Brahman Consciousness in its four domains from the Turiya to the external or material plane. The function of a mantra is to create vibrations in the inner consciousness that will prepare it for the realisation of what the mantra symbolises and is supposed indeed to carry within itself. The mantra OM should therefore lead towards the opening of the consciousness to the sight and feeling of the One Consciousness in all material things, in the inner being and in the supraphysical worlds, in the causal plane above now superconscient to us and, finally, the supreme liberated transcendence above all cosmic existence.

One must say, "Since I want only the Divine, my success is sure, I have only to walk forward in all confidence and His own Hand will be there secretly leading me to Him by His own way and at His own time." That is what you must keep as your constant mantra.

In this yoga there is no fixed mantra, no stress is laid on mantras, although sadhaks can use one if they find it helpful or so long as they find it helpful. The stress is rather on an aspiration in the consciousness and a concentration of the mind, heart, will, all the being. If a mantra is found helpful for that, one uses it. OM if rightly used (not mechanically) might very well help the opening upwards and outwards (cosmic consciousness) as well as the descent.

As a rule the only mantra used in this sadhana is that of the Mother or of my name and the Mother's. The concentration in the heart and the concentration in the head can both be used — each has its own result. The first opens up the psychic being and brings bhakti, love and union with the Mother, her presence within the heart and the action of her Force in the nature. The other opens the mind to self-realisation, to the consciousness of what is above mind, to the ascent of the consciousness out of the body and the descent of the higher consciousness into the body.

The name of the Divine is usually called in for protection, for adoration, for increase of bhakti, for the opening up of the inner consciousness, for the realisation of the Divine in that aspect. As far as it is necessary to work in the subconscious for that, the Name must be effective there.

Namajapa has a great power in it.

A hand from some Greatness opened her heart's locked doors
And showed the work for which her strength was born.
As when the mantra sinks in Yoga's ear,
Its message enters stirring the blind brain
And keeps in the dim ignorant cells its sound;
The hearer understands a form of words
And, musing on the index thought it holds,
He strives to read it with the labouring mind,
But finds bright hints, not the embodied truth:

Material Physical

This is the material consciousness; it is mostly subconscient, but the part of it that is conscious is mechanical, inertly moved by habits or by the forces of the lower nature. Always repeating the same unintelligent and unenlightened movements, it is attached to the routine and established rule of what already exists, unwilling to change, unwilling to receive the Light or obey the higher Force. Or, if it is willing, then it is unable. Or, if it is able, then it turns the action given to it by the Light or the Force into a new mechanical routine and so takes out of it all soul and life. It is obscure, stupid, indolent, full of ignorance and inertia, darkness and slowness of tamas.

The physical consciousness in everybody is like that. It is inert, conservative, does not want to move, to change — it clings to its habits (what people call their character) or its habits (habitual movements) cling to it and repeat themselves like a clock working in a persistent mechanical way. When you have cleared your vital somewhat, things go down and stick there. You see, if you have become self-conscious, you put pressure, perhaps, but the physical responds very slowly, hardly at first it seems to move at all.

If there is faith, quietude, openness in the rest of the being, the material is bound to open also. Tamas, inertia, ignorance, stupidity, littleness, obstruction to the true movement are universal characteristics of the material consciousness, so long as it is not enlightened, regenerated and transformed from above...

The physical consciousness is constitutionally ignorant — it may be made to understand, but it goes on forgetting and feeling as if it had never known — till the Force and Light finally get hold of it and then it forgets no more.

Infernal elements, demon powers are there.
Man's lower nature hides these awful guests.

Materialisation

In fact, there are different planes of substance, gross, subtle and more subtle going back to what is called causal (Karana) substance. What is more gross can be reduced to the subtle state and the subtle brought into the gross state; that accounts for dematerialisation and rematerialisation. These are occult processes and are vulgarly regarded as magic. Ordinarily the magician knows nothing of the why and wherefore of what he is doing, he has simply learned the formula or process or else controls elemental beings of the subtler states (planes or worlds) who do the thing for him. The Tibetans indulge widely in occult processes; if you see the books of Madame David Neel who has lived in Tibet you will get an idea of their expertness in these things. But also the Tibetan Lamas know something of the laws of occult (mental and vital) energy and how it can be made to act on physical things. That is something which goes beyond mere magic. The direct power of mind-force or life-force upon Matter can be extended to an almost illimitable degree. It must be remembered that Energy is fundamentally one in all the planes, only taking more and more dense forms, so there is nothing a priori impossible in mind-energy or life-energy acting directly on material energy and substance; if they do, they can make a material object do things or rather can do things with a material object which would be to that object in its ordinary poise or "law" unhabitual and therefore apparently impossible.

This bodily appearance is not all;
The form deceives, the person is a mask;
Hid deep in man celestial powers can dwell.
His fragile ship conveys through the sea of years
An incognito of the Imperishable

Materialism and its Value

Through many centuries a great army of shining witnesses, saints and teachers, names sacred to Indian memory and dominant in Indian imagination, have borne always the same witness and swelled always the same lofty and distant appeal, - renunciation the sole path of knowledge, acceptation of physical life the act of the ignorant, cessation from birth the right use of human birth, the call of the Spirit, the recoil from Matter.

We seek indeed a larger and completer affirmation. We perceive that in the Indian ascetic ideal the great Vedantic formula, "One without a second", has not been read sufficiently in the light of that other formula equally imperative, "All this is the Brahman". The passionate aspiration of man upward to the Divine has not been sufficiently related to the descending movement of the Divine leaning downward to embrace eternally its manifestation. Its meaning in Matter has not been so well understood as Its truth in the Spirit. The Reality which the Sannyasin seeks has been grasped in its full height, but not, as by the ancient Vedantins, in its full extent and comprehensiveness. But in our completer affirmation we must not minimise the part of the pure spiritual impulse. As we have seen how greatly Materialism has served the ends of the Divine, so we must acknowledge the still greater service rendered by Asceticism to Life. We shall preserve the truths of material Science and its real utilities in the final harmony, even if many or even if all of its existing forms have to be broken or left aside.

> There poured a wide and intimate and blissful Dawn,
> Healed were all things that Time's torn heart has made
> And sorrow could live no more in Nature's breast:
> Division ceased to be, for God was there.
> The soul lit the conscious body with its ray,
> Matter and Spirit mingled and were one.

Materialistic Approach

Materialism can hardly be spiritual in its basis, because its basic method is just the opposite of the spiritual way of doing things. The spiritual works from within outward, the way of materialism is to work from out inwards. It makes the inner the result of the outer, fundamentally a phenomenon of Matter and it works upon that view of things. It seeks to "perfect" humanity by outward means and one of its efforts is to construct a perfect social machine which will train and oblige men to be what they ought to be. The loss of the ego in the Divine is the spiritual ideal; here it is replaced by the immolation of the individual to the military and industrial State. Where is there any spirituality in all that? Spirituality can only come by opening of the mind, vital and physical to the inmost soul, to the higher Self, to the Divine, and their subordination to the spiritual forces and instrumentation as channels of the inner Light, the higher Knowledge and Power. Other things, mental, aesthetic, vital, are often misnamed 'spirituality', but they lack the essential character without which the word loses its true significance.

A giant Ignorance surrounds his lore.
Assigned to meet the cosmic mystery
In the dumb figure of a material world,
His passport of entry false and his personage,
He is compelled to be what he is not;
He obeys the Inconscience he has come to rule
And sinks in Matter to fulfill his soul.

Matter

It is seen that the creative Energy in Matter is a movement of the power of the Spirit. Matter itself cannot be the original and ultimate reality. At the same time the view that divorces Matter and Spirit and puts them as opposites is unacceptable; Matter is a form of Spirit, a habitation of Spirit, and here in Matter itself there can be a realisation of Spirit.

Matter or body itself is a limiting form of substance of spirit in which life and mind and spirit are involved, self-hidden, self-forgetful by absorption in their own externalising action, but bound to emerge from it by a self-compelling evolution. But matter too is capable of refining to subtler forms of substance in which it becomes more apparently a formal density of life, of mind, of spirit. Man himself has, besides this gross material body, an encasing vital sheath, a mental body, a body of bliss and gnosis. But all matter, all body contains within it the secret powers of these higher principles; matter is a formation of life that has no real existence apart from the informing universal spirit which gives it its energy and substance.

In finite things the conscious Infinite dwells:
Involved it sleeps in Matter's helpless trance,
It rules the world from its sleeping senseless Void;
Dreaming it throws out mind and heart and soul.

Meditation

These are the ordinary normal experiences of the sadhana when there is an opening from above — the contact with the peace of the Brahman, Self or Divine and the contact with the higher Power, the Power of the Mother.

Behind the heart is the psychic centre. If one concentrates in the head, as many do, it is a mental-spiritual meditation one seeks for; if in the heart it is a psychic meditation; these are the usual places where one concentrates. But what rises up first or opens first may not be the mental or the psychic, but the emotional or the vital; that depends on the nature — for whatever is easiest to open in it, is likely to open first. If it is in the vital, then the meditation tends to project the consciousness into the vital plane and its experiences. But from that we can get to the psychic by drawing more and more inwards, not getting absorbed into the vital experiences but separating oneself and looking at them with detachment as if one were deep inside and observing things outside oneself. Similarly one can get the mental experiences by concentrating in the thought and by it bringing a corresponding experience, e.g. the thought of all being the Brahman, or one can draw back from the thought also and observe one's own thoughts as outside things until one enters into silence and the pure spiritual experience.

The stillness in the meditation is a very good sign. It comes usually in that pervading way when there has been sufficient purification to make it possible. On the other side, it is itself the beginning of the laying of the foundation of the higher spiritual consciousness.

Love, bhakti, surrender, the psychic opening are the only short cuts to the Divine...

But now her spirit's flame of conscient force
Retiring from a sweetness without fruit
Called back her thoughts from speech to sit within
In a deep room in meditation's house.
For only there could dwell the soul's firm truth:

Mental

Man is in his characteristic power of nature a mental being, but in the first steps of his emergence he is more of the mentalised animal, preoccupied like the animal with his bodily existence; he employs his mind for the uses, interests, desires of the life and the body, as their servant and minister, not yet as their sovereign and master.

Mental nature thinks, sees, wills, feels, senses with division as a starting-point and has only a constructed understanding of unity; even when it experiences oneness, it has to act from the oneness on a basis of limitation and difference.

The intellect of the thinker regards the phenomenal world from the standpoint of the reason; reason is there the judge and the authority and no suprarational authority can prevail against it: but behind the phenomenal world is a transcendent Reality which the intuition alone can see; there reason, — at least a finite dividing limited reason, — cannot prevail against the intuitive experience, it cannot even relate the two, it cannot therefore solve the mystery of the universe.

Our gain in becoming more perfect mental being is that we get to the possibility of a subtler, higher and wider existence, consciousness, force, happiness and delight of being.

The too great activity of the intellectual mind and its attachments to its own pride of ideas, its prejudices, its fixed notions and its ignorant reason may shut the doors to the inner light and prevent the full tide of bhakti from flooding everything; it may also cling to a surface mental activity and refuse to go inside and allow the psychic vision and the feelings of the inner heart to become its guides, though it is by this vision and this feeling that bhakti grows and conquers.

A demi-god animal, came thinking man.
He wallows in mud, yet heavenward soars in thought;
He plays and ponders, laughs and weeps and dreams,
Satisfies his little longings like the beast.

Mental Knowledge

A thousand questions can be asked about anything whatsoever, but to answer would require a volume, and even then the mind would understand nothing. It is only by a growth in the consciousness itself that you can get some direct perception of these things. But for that the mind must be quiet and a direct feeling and intuition take its place.

It is not enough to devote ourselves by the reading of Scriptures or by the stress of philosophical reasoning to an intellectual understanding of the Divine; for at the end of our long mental labour we might know all that has been said of the Eternal, possess all that can be thought about the Infinite and yet we might not know him at all.

You may have all the mental knowledge in the world and yet be impotent to face vital difficulties. Courage, faith, sincerity towards the Light, rejection of opposite suggestions and adverse voices are there the true help. Then only can knowledge itself be at all effective.

As so he grew into his larger self,
Humanity framed his movements less and less,
A greater being saw a greater world.
A fearless will for knowledge dared to erase
The lines of safety reason draws that bar
Mind's soar, soul's dive into the Infinite.

Mental Physical

The nature of the mental physical to go on repeating without use the movement that has happened. It is what we call the mechanical mind — it is strong in childhood because the thinking mind is not developed and has besides a narrow range of interests. Afterwards it becomes an undercurrent in the mental activities.

Everything has a physical part — even the mind has a physical part; there is a mental physical, a mind of the body and the material. So the emotional being has a physical part. It has no location separate from the rest of the emotional. One can only distinguish that when the consciousness becomes sufficiently subtle to do so.

It [the material] is the most physical grade of the physical — there is the mental physical, the vital physical, the material physical.

The mind in the physical or mental physical is limited by the physical view and experience of things, it mentalises the experiences brought by the contacts of outward life and things, and does not go beyond that (though it can do that much very cleverly),

All developed mental men, those who get beyond the average, have in one way or other or at least at certain times and for certain purposes to separate the two parts of the mind, the active part which is a factory of thoughts and the quiet masterful part which is at once a Witness and a Will, observing them, judging, rejecting, eliminating, accepting, ordering corrections and changes, the Master in the House of Mind, capable of self-empire, sāmrājya.

The yogi goes still farther; he is not only a master there, but even while in mind in a way, he gets out of it as it were, and stands above or quite back from it and free. For him the image of the factory of thoughts is no longer quite valid; for he sees that thoughts come from outside, from the universal Mind or universal Nature, sometimes formed and distinct, sometimes unformed and then they are given shape somewhere in us.

Advancing tardily from a limping start,
Crutching hypothesis upon argument,
Throning its theories as certitudes,
It reasons from the half-known to the unknown.

Mental Plane

Beyond the vital plane is a mental plane, a world of mental existence in which neither life, nor matter, but mind is the first determinant. Mind there is not determined by material conditions or by the life-force, but itself determines and uses them for its own satisfaction. There mind, that is to say, the psychical and the intellectual being, is free in a certain sense, free at least to satisfy and fulfil itself in a way hardly conceivable to our body-bound and life-bound mentality; for the Purusha there is the pure mental being and the relations with Prakriti are determined by that purer mentality, Nature there is mental rather than vital and physical.

This world of mental existence also is constantly acting upon us and our world, has its powers and its beings, is related to us through our mental body. There we find the psychical and mental heavens to which the Purusha can ascend when it drops this physical body and can there sojourn till the impulse to terrestrial existence again draws it downward. Here too are many planes, the lowest converging upon and melting into the worlds below, the highest at the heights of the mind-power into the worlds of a more spiritual existence.

A great all-ruling consciousness is there
And Mind unwitting serves a higher Power;
It is a channel, not the source of all.
The cosmos is no accident in Time;
There is a meaning in each play of Chance,
There is a freedom in each face of Fate.

Mental Vital

There are four parts of the vital being (mental vital, emotional vital, central vital and lower vital) — first, the mental vital which gives a mental expression by thought, speech or otherwise to the emotions, desires, passions, sensations and other movements of the vital being.

It is not enough then to have a great vital energy acting in you; it must be put in contact with the higher consciousness, it must be surrendered to the true control, it must be placed under the government of the Divine. That is why there is sometimes felt a contempt for the action of the vital force or a condemnation of it, because it has an insufficient light and control and is wedded to an ignorant undivine movement. That also is why there is the necessity of opening to inspiration and power from a higher source. The vital energy by itself leads nowhere, runs in chequered, often painful and ruinous circles, takes even to the precipice, because it has no right guidance; it must be connected with the dynamic power of the higher consciousness and with the Divine Force acting through it for a great and luminous purpose.

Its thoughts were kneaded by the shocks of sense;
It captured not the spirit in the form,
It entered not the heart of what it saw;
It looked not for the power behind the act,
It studied not the hidden motive in things
Nor strove to find the meaning of it all.

Mind

Mind in the ordinary use of the word covers indiscriminately the whole consciousness, for man is a mental being and mentalises everything; but in the language of this yoga the words "mind" and "mental" are used to connote specially the part of the nature which has to do with cognition and intelligence, with ideas, with mental or thought perceptions, the reactions of thought to things, with the truly mental movements and formations, mental vision and will, etc., that are part of his intelligence.

Mind indeed can never be a perfect instrument of the Spirit; a supreme self-expression is not possible in its movements because to separate, divide, limit is its very character.

All Mind can do is to piece together the fragments or deduce a unity; truth of Mind is only a half-truth or a portion of a puzzle. Mental knowledge is always relative, partial and inconclusive, and its outgoing action and creation come out still more confused in its steps or precise only in narrow limits and by imperfect piecings together.

It clamours to be impressed at every turn by miraculous power and easy success and dazzling splendour; otherwise it cannot believe that here is the Divine.

If you follow your mind, it will not recognise the Mother even when she is manifested before you. Follow your soul and not your mind, your soul that answers to the Truth, not your mind that leaps at appearances.

Mind is the author, spectator, actor, stage:
Mind only is and what it thinks is seen.
If Mind is all, renounce the hope of bliss;
If Mind is all, renounce the hope of Truth.
For Mind can never touch the body of Truth
And Mind can never see the soul of God.

Mind, Life and Body

Always the greater part of the motive and action of these powers clings to the old law, the deceiving tablets, the cherished inferior movements of Nature and they meet with reluctance, alarm or revolt or obstructing inertia the voices and the forces that call and impel us to exceed and transform ourselves into a greater being and a wider Nature. In their major part the response is either a resistance or a qualified or temporising acquiescence; for even if they follow the call, they yet tend — when not consciously, then by automatic habit — to bring into the spiritual action their own natural disabilities and errors.

A Yoga of integral perfection regards man as a divine spiritual being involved in mind, life and body; it aims therefore at a liberation and a perfection of his divine nature. It seeks to make an inner living in the perfectly developed spiritual being his constant intrinsic living and the spiritualised action of mind, life and body only its outward human expression.

> She felt the leaden inevitable hand
> Invade the secrecy of her guarded soul
> And smite with sudden pain its still content
> And the empire of her hard-won quietude.
> Awhile she fell to the level of the human mind,
> A field of mortal grief and Nature's law
> She shared, she bore the common lot of men
> And felt what common hearts endure in Time.

Mind, Life and Matter

The three powers and planes of being, of which we are even at present aware, form a lower hemisphere of the manifestation, a hemisphere of Mind, Life and Matter. These are in themselves powers of the superior principles; but wherever they manifest in a separation from their spiritual sources, they undergo as a result a phenomenal lapse into a divided in place of the true undivided existence: this lapse, this separation creates a state of limited knowledge exclusively concentrated on its own limited world-order and oblivious of all that is behind it and of the underlying unity, a state therefore of cosmic and individual Ignorance.

In the descent into the material plane of which our natural life is a product, the lapse culminates in a total Inconscience out of which an involved Being and Consciousness have to emerge by a gradual evolution. This inevitable evolution first develops, as it is bound to develop, Matter and a material universe; in Matter, Life appears and living physical beings; in Life, Mind manifests and embodied thinking and living beings; in Mind, ever increasing its powers and activities in forms of Matter, the Supermind or Truth-Consciousness must appear, inevitably, by the very force of what is contained in the Inconscience and the necessity in Nature to bring it into manifestation.

> Earth wheeled abandoned in the hollow gulfs
> Forgetful of her spirit and her fate.
> The impassive skies were neutral, empty, still.
> Then something in the inscrutable darkness stirred;
> A nameless movement, an unthought idea
> Insistent, dissatisfied, without an aim,
> Something that wished but knew not how to be,
> Teased the Inconscient to wake Ignorance.

Mind - Nature

The mind's moulds, its ideas, mental formations, opinions, all its habits of intellectual observation and judgement — that it may be replaced first by an intuitive and then by an overmind or supramental functioning which inaugurates the action of a direct Truth-Consciousness, Truth-sight, Truth-discernment.

At first what is necessary is that the pure touch of the spiritual force must intervene in mental nature: that awakening pressure must stamp itself upon mind and heart and life and give them their upward orientation; a subtle light or a great transmuting power must purify, refine and uplift their motions and suffuse them with a higher consciousness that does not belong to their own normal capacity and character. This can be done from within by an invisible action through the psychic entity and the psychic personality; a consciously felt descent from above is not indispensable.

Cast thought from thee, that nimble ape of Light:
In his tremendous hush stilling thy brain
His vast Truth wake within and know and see.

Money

Money is the visible sign of a universal force, and this force in its manifestation on earth works on the vital and physical planes and is indispensable to the fullness of the outer life. In its origin and its true action it belongs to the Divine. But like other powers of the Divine it is delegated here and in the Ignorance of the lower Nature can be usurped for the uses of the ego or held by Asuric influences and perverted to their purpose. This is indeed one of the three forces — power, wealth, sex — that have the strongest attraction for the human ego and the Asura and are most generally misheld and misused by those who retain them...

You must neither turn with an ascetic shrinking from the money power, the means it gives and the objects it brings, nor cherish a rajasic attachment to them or a spirit of enslaving self-indulgence in their gratifications. Regard wealth simply as a power to be won back for the Mother and placed at her service.

All wealth belongs to the Divine and those who hold it are trustees, not possessors. It is with them today, tomorrow it may be elsewhere. All depends on the way they discharge their trust while it is with them, in what spirit, with what consciousness in their use of it, to what purpose.

In your personal use of money look on all you have or get or bring as the Mother's. Make no demand but accept what you receive from her and use it for the purposes for which it is given to you. Be entirely selfless, entirely scrupulous, exact, careful in detail, a good trustee; always consider that it is her possessions and not your own that you are handling. On the other hand, what you receive for her, lay religiously before her; turn nothing to your own or anybody else's purpose.

The future's road is hid from mortal sight:
He moves towards a veiled and secret face.
To light one step in front is all his hope
And only for a little strength he asks
To meet the riddle of his shrouded fate.

Money and its Possessors

The seekers or keepers of wealth are more often possessed rather than its possessors; few escape entirely a certain distorting influence stamped on it by its long seizure and perversion by the Asura. For this reason most spiritual disciplines insist on a complete self-control, detachment and renunciation of all bondage to wealth and of all personal and egoistic desire for its possession. Some even put a ban on money and riches and proclaim poverty and bareness of life as the only spiritual condition. But this is an error; it leaves the power in the hands of the hostile forces. To conquer it for the Divine to whom it belongs and use it divinely for the divine life is the supramental way for the Sadhaka. ...

The ideal Sadhaka in this kind is one who if required to live poorly can so live and no sense of want will effect him or interfere with the full inner play of the divine consciousness, and if he is required to live richly, can so live and never for a moment fall into desire or attachment to his wealth or to the things that he uses or servitude to self-indulgence or a weak bondage to the habits that the possession of riches creates. The divine Will is all for him and the divine Ananda.

In the supramental creation the money-force has to be restored to the Divine Power and used for a true and beautiful and harmonious equipment and ordering of a new and divinised vital and physical existence in whatever way the Divine Mother herself decides in her creative vision. But first it must be conquered back for her and those will be strongest for the conquest who are in this part of their nature strong and large and free from ego and surrendered without any claim or withholding or hesitation, pure and powerful channels for the Supreme Puissance.

All that thou hast, shall be for others' bliss,
All that thou art, shall to my hands belong,
I will pour delight from thee as from a jar,
I will whirl thee as my chariot through the ways,
I will use thee as my sword and as my lyre,
I will play on thee my minstrelsies of thought.

The Mother

The one whom we adore as the Mother is the divine Conscious Force that dominates all existence, one and yet so many-sided that to follow her movement is impossible even for the quickest mind and for the freest and most vast intelligence. The Mother is the consciousness and force of the Supreme and far above all she creates. But something of her ways can be seen and felt through her embodiments and the more seizable because more defined and limited temperament and action of the goddess forms in whom she consents to be manifest to her creatures.

Determining all that shall be in this universe and in the terrestrial evolution by what she sees and feels and pours from her, she stands there above the Gods and all her Powers and Personalities are put out in front of her for the action and she sends down emanations of them into these lower worlds to intervene, to govern, to battle and conquer, to lead and turn their cycles to direct the total and the individual lines of their forces. These Emanations are the many divine forms and personalities in which men have worshipped her under different names throughout the ages.

The power that mediates between the sanction and the call is the presence and power of the Divine Mother. The Mother's power and not any human endeavour and tapasya can alone rend the lid and tear the covering and shape the vessel and bring down into this world of obscurity and falsehood and death and suffering Truth and Light and Life divine and immortal's Ananda.

> Above the stretch and blaze of cosmic Sight,
> Above the silence of the wordless Thought,
> Formless creator of immortal forms,
> Nameless, investitured with the name divine,
> Transcending Time's hours, transcending Timelessness,
> The Mighty Mother sits in lucent calm
> And holds the eternal Child upon her knees,
> Attending the day when he shall speak to Fate.

The Mother's Personalities

At the summit of the manifestation of which we are a part there are worlds of infinite existence, consciousness, force and bliss over which the Mother stands as unveiled Power. She sends down emanations into these lower worlds to intervene, to govern, to battle and conquer, to lead and turn the cycles. These Emanations are the many divine forms and personalities in which men worshipped her throughout the ages.

Four great Aspects of the Mother, four of her leading Powers and Personalities have stood in front in her guidance of the Universe and in her dealing with the terrestrial play. To the four we give four great names, Maheswari, Mahakali, Mahalakshmi, Mahasaraswati. When her Personalities are all gathered in her and manifested and their separate working has been turned into a harmonious unity and they rise in her to their supramental godheads, then is the Mother revealed as the supramental mahashakti and brings pouring down her luminous transcendences from their ineffable ether. Then can human nature change into dynamic divine nature because all the elemental lines of the supramental Truth-consciousness and Truth-force are strung together and the harp of life is fitted for the rhythms of the Eternal. All knowledge, all strengths, all triumph and victory, all skill and works are in her hands and they are full of the treasures of the Spirit and of all perfections and siddhis.

> In its deep lotus home her being sat
> As if on concentration's marble seat,
> Calling the mighty Mother of the worlds
> To make this earthly tenement her house.
> As in a flash from supernal light,
> A living image of the original Power,
> A face, a form came down into her heart
> And made of it its temple and pure abode.

Mahakali

Embodies her power of splendid strength and irresistible passion, her warrior mood, her overwhelming will, her impetuous swiftness and world-shaking force.

She is Mahakali, goddess of the supreme strength, and with her are all mights and spiritual force and severest austerity of Tapas and swiftness to the battle and the victory and the laughter, the attahãsya, that makes light of defeat and death and the powers of the ignorance...

There is in her an overwhelming intensity, a mighty passion of force to achieve, a divine violence rushing to shatter every limit and obstacle. All her divinity leaps out in a splendour of tempestuous action; she is there for swiftness, for the immediately effective process, the rapid and direct stroke, the frontal assault that carries everything before it. Terrible is her face to the Asura, dangerous and ruthless her mood against the haters of the Divine; for she is the Warrior of the Worlds who never shrinks from the battle. Intolerant of imperfection, she deals roughly with all in man that is unwilling and she is severe to all that is obstinately ignorant and obscure; her wrath is immediate and dire against treachery and falsehood and malignity, ill-will is smitten at once by her scourge. Indifference, negligence and sloth in the divine work she cannot bear and she smites awake at once with sharp pain, if need be, the untimely slumberer and the loiterer. The impulses that are swift and straight and frank, the movements that are unreserved and absolute, the aspiration that mounts in flame are the motion of Mahakali. Her spirit is tameless, her vision and will are high and far-reaching like the flight of an eagle, her feet are rapid on the upward way and her hands are outstretched to strike and to succour. For she too is the Mother and her love is as intense as her wrath and she has a deep and passionate kindness. When she is allowed to intervene in her strength, then in one moment are broken like things without consistence the obstacles that immobilise or the enemies that assail the seeker. If her anger is dreadful to the hostile and the vehemence of her pressure painful to the weak and timid, she is loved and worshipped by the great, the strong and the noble; for they feel that her blows beat what is rebellious in their material into strength and perfect truth, hammer straight what is wry and perverse and expel what is impure or defective. But for her what is done in a day might have taken centuries; without her Ananda might be wide and grave or soft and sweet and beautiful but would lose the flaming joy of its most absolute intensities. To knowledge she gives a conquering might, brings to beauty and harmony a high and mounting movement and imparts to the slow and difficult labour after perfection an impetus that multiplies the power and shortens the long way. Nothing can satisfy her that falls short of the supreme ecstasies, the highest heights, the noblest aims, the largest vistas. Therefore with her is the victorious force of the Divine and it is by grace of her fire and passion and speed if the great achievement can be done now rather than hereafter.

Wearing the mighty Mother's form and face.
Armed, bearer of the weapon and the sign
Whose occult might no magic can imitate,
Manifold yet one she sat, a guardian force:
A savior gesture stretched her lifted arm,
And symbol of some native cosmic strength,
A sacred beast lay prone below her feet,
A silent flame-eyed mass of living force.

Mahalakshmi

Mahalakshmi is vivid and sweet and wonderful with her deep secret of beauty and harmony and fine rhythm, her intricate and subtle opulence, her compelling attraction and captivating grace.

She is Mahalakshmi, the goddess of the supreme love and delight, and her gifts are the spirit's grace and the charm and the beauty of the Ananda and protection and every divine and human blessing.

Wisdom and Force are not the only manifestations of the supreme Mother; there is a subtler mystery of her nature and without it Wisdom and Force would be incomplete things and without it perfection would not be perfect. Above them is the miracle of eternal beauty, an unseizable secret of divine harmonies, the compelling magic of an irresistible universal charm and attraction that draws and holds things and forces and beings together and obliges them to meet and unite that a hidden Ananda may play from behind the veil and make of them its rhythms and its figures. This is the power of Mahalakshmi and there is no aspect of the Divine Shakti more attractive to the heart of embodied beings. Maheswari can appear too calm and great and distant for the littleness of earthly nature to approach or contain her, Mahakali too swift and formidable for its weakness to bear; but all turn with joy and longing to Mahalakshmi. For she throws the spell of the intoxicating sweetness of the Divine: to be close to her is a profound happiness and to feel her within the heart is to make existence a rapture and a marvel; grace and charm and tenderness flow out from her like light from the sun and wherever she fixes her wonderful gaze or lets fall the loveliness of her smile, the soul is seized and made captive and plunged into the depths of an unfathomable bliss. Magnetic is the touch of her hands and their occult and delicate influence refines mind and life and body and where she presses her feet course miraculous streams of an entrancing Ananda.

And yet it is not easy to meet the demand of this enchanting Power or to keep her presence. Harmony and beauty of the mind and soul, harmony and beauty of the thoughts and feelings, harmony and beauty in every outward act and movement, harmony and beauty of the life and surroundings, this is the demand of Mahalakshmi. Where there is affinity to the rhythms of the secret world-bliss and response to the call of the All- Beautiful and concord and unity and the glad flow of many lives turned towards the Divine, in that atmosphere she consents to abide. But all that is ugly and mean and base, all that is poor and sordid and squalid, all that is brutal and coarse repels her advent. Where love and beauty are not or are reluctant to be born, she does not come; where they are mixed and disfigured with baser things, she turns soon to depart or cares little to pour her riches. If she finds herself in men's hearts surrounded with selfishness and hatred and jealousy and malignance and envy and strife, if treachery and greed and ingratitude are mixed in the sacred chalice, if grossness of passion and unrefined desire degrade devotion, in such hearts the gracious and beautiful Goddess will not linger. A divine disgust seizes upon her and she withdraws, for she is not one who insists or strives; or, veiling her face, she waits for this bitter and poisonous devil's stuff to be rejected and disappear before she will found anew her happy influence. Ascetic bareness and harshness are not pleasing to her nor the suppression of the heart's deeper emotions and the rigid repression of the soul's and the life's parts of beauty. For it is through love and beauty that she lays on men the yoke of the Divine. Life is turned in her supreme creations into a rich work of celestial art and all existence into a poem of sacred delight; the world's riches are brought together and concerted for a supreme order and even the simplest and commonest things are made wonderful by her intuition of unity and the breath of her spirit. Admitted to the heart she lifts wisdom to pinnacles of wonder and reveals to it the mystic secrets of the ecstasy that surpasses all knowledge, meets devotion with the passionate attraction of the Divine, teaches to strength and force the rhythm that keeps the might of their acts harmonious and in measure and casts on perfection the charm that makes it endure for ever.

All here shall be one day her sweetness's home,
All contraries prepare her harmony;
Towards her our knowledge climbs, our passion gropes,
In her miraculous rapture we shall dwell,
Her clasp will turn to ecstasy our pain.
Our self shall be one self with all through her.

Mahasaraswati

Mahasaraswati is equipped with her close and profound capacity of intimate knowledge and careful flawless work and quiet and exact perfection in all things. For She is the goddess of divine skill and of the works of the Spirit, and hers is the Yoga that is skill in works, and the utilities of divine knowledge and the self-application of the spirit to life and the happiness of its harmonies.

Mahasaraswati is the Mother's Power of Work and her spirit of perfection and order. The youngest of the Four, she is the most skilful in executive faculty and the nearest to physical Nature. Maheshwari lays down the large lines of the world-forces, Mahakali drives their energy and impetus, Mahalakshmi discovers their rhythms and measures, but Mahasaraswati presides over their detail of organization and execution, relation of parts and effective combination of forces and unfailing exactitude of result and fulfillment. The science and craft and technique of things are Mahasaraswati's province. Always she holds in her nature and can give to those whom she has chosen the intimate and precise knowledge, the subtlety and patience, the accuracy of intuitive mind and conscious hand and discerning eye of the perfect worker. This Power is the strong, the tireless, the careful and efficient builder, organiser, administrator, technician, artisan and classifier of the worlds. When she takes up the transformation and new-building of the nature, her action is laborious and minute and often seems to our impatience slow and interminable, but it is persistent, integral and flawless. For the will in her works is scrupulous, unsleeping, indefatigable; leaning over us she notes and touches every little detail, finds out every minute defect, gap, twist or incompleteness, considers and weighs accurately all that has been done and all that remains still to be done hereafter. Nothing is too small or apparently trivial for her attention; nothing however impalpable or disguised or latent can escape her. Moulding and remoulding she labours each part till it has attained its true form, is put in its exact place in the whole and fulfils its precise purpose. In her constant and diligent arrangement and rearrangement of things her eye is on all needs at once and the way to meet them and her intuition knows what is to be chosen and what rejected and successfully determines the right instrument, the right time, the right condition and the right process. Carelessness and negligence and indolence she abhors; all scamped and hasty and shuffling work, all clumsiness and à peu près and misfire, all false adaptation and misuse of instruments and faculties and leaving of things undone or half done is offensive and foreign to her temper. When her work is finished, nothing has been forgotten, no part has been misplaced or omitted or left in a faulty condition; all is solid, accurate, complete, admirable. Nothing short of a perfect perfection satisfies her and she is ready to face an eternity of toil if that is needed for the fullness of her creation. Therefore of all the Mother's powers she is the most long-suffering with man and his thousand imperfections. Kind, smiling, close and helpful, not easily turned away or discouraged, insistent even after repeated failure, her hand sustains our every step on condition that we are single in our will and straightforward and sincere; for a double mind she will not tolerate and her revealing irony is merciless to drama and histrionics and self-deceit and pretence. A mother to our wants, a friend in our difficulties, a persistent and tranquil counselor and mentor, chasing away with her radiant smile the clouds of gloom and fretfulness and depression, reminding always of the ever-present help, pointing to the eternal sunshine, she is firm, quiet and persevering in the deep and continuous urge that drives us towards the integrality of the higher nature. All the work of the other Powers leans on her for its completeness; for she assures the material foundation, elaborates the stuff of detail and erects and rivets the armour of the structure.

In her confirmed because transformed in her,
Our life shall find in its fulfilled response
Above, the boundless hushed beatitudes,
Below, the wonder of the embrace divine.

Maheswari

Of calm wideness and comprehending wisdom and tranquil benignity and inexhaustible compassion and sovereign and surpassing majesty and all-ruling greatness.

She is Maheshwari, goddess of the supreme knowledge, and brings to us her vision for all kinds and widenesses of truth, her rectitude of the spiritual will, the calm and passion of her supramental largeness, her felicity of illumination...

Imperial Maheshwari is seated in the wideness above the thinking mind and will and sublimates and greatens them into wisdom and largeness or floods with a splendour beyond them. For she is the mighty and wise One who opens us to the supramental infinities and the cosmic vastness, to the grandeur of the supreme Light, to a treasure-house of miraculous knowledge, to the measureless movement of the Mother's eternal forces. Tranquil is she and wonderful, great and calm for ever. Nothing can move her because all wisdom is in her; nothing is hidden from her that she chooses to know; she comprehends all things and all beings and their nature and what moves them and the law of the world and its times and how all was and is and must be. A strength is in her that meets everything and masters and none can prevail in the end against her vast and intangible wisdom and high tranquil power. Equal, patient, unalterable in her will she deals with men according to their nature and with things and happenings according to their Force and the truth that is in them. Partiality she has none, but she follows the decrees of the Supreme and some she raises up and some she casts down or puts away from her into the darkness. To the wise she gives a greater and more luminous wisdom; those that have vision she admits to her counsels; on the hostile she imposes the consequence of their hostility; the ignorant and foolish she leads according to their blindness. In each man she answers and handles the different elements of his nature according to their need and their urge and the return they call for, puts on them the required pressure or leaves them to their cherished liberty to prosper in the ways of the Ignorance or to perish. For she is above all, bound by nothing, attached to nothing in the universe. Yet has she more than any other the heart of the universal Mother. For her compassion is endless and inexhaustible; all are to her eyes her children and portions of the

One, even the Asura and Rakshasa and Pisacha and those that are revolted and hostile. Even her rejections are only a postponement, even her punishments are a grace. But her compassion does not blind her wisdom or turn her action from the course decreed; for the Truth of things is her one concern, knowledge her centre of power and to build our soul and our nature into the divine Truth her mission and her labour.

All Nature dumbly calls to her alone
To heal with her feet the aching throb of life
And break the seals on the dim soul of man
And kindle her fire in the closed heart of things.

Nature's Grip

The spiritual seeker grows aware of in himself and finds all around him and has to struggle and combat incessantly to be rid of their grip and dislodge the long-entrenched mastery they have exercised over his own being as over the environing human existence. The difficulty is great; for their hold is so strong, so apparently invincible that it justifies the disdainful dictum which compares human nature to a dog's tail, — for, straighten it never so much by force of ethics, religion, reason or any other redemptive effort, it returns in the end always to the crooked curl of Nature. And so great is the vim, the clutch of that more agitated Life-Will, so immense the peril of its passions and errors, so subtly insistent or persistently invasive, so obstinate up to the very gates of Heaven the fury of its attack or the tedious obstruction of its obstacles that even the saint and the Yogin cannot be sure of their liberated purity or their trained self-mastery against its intrigue or its violence. All labour to straighten out this native crookedness strikes the struggling will as a futility...

A remedy yet there should be and is, a way of redress and a chance of transformation for this troubled vital nature; but for that the cause of deviation must be found and remedied at the heart of Life itself and in its very principle, since Life too is a power of the Divine and not a creation of some malignant Chance or dark Titanic impulse, however obscure or perverted may be its actual appearance. Not to be immersed, enmeshed and bound by Nature, not to hate and destroy her, is the first thing we must learn if we would be complete Yogins and proceed towards our divine perfection.

> This is the ephemeral creature's daily life,
> As long as the human animal is lord
> And a dense nether nature screens the soul,
> As long as intellect's outward-gazing sight
> Serves earthy interest and creature joys,
> An incurable littleness pursues his days.

New Consciousness

A spiritual consciousness is emerging and it is through this spiritual consciousness that one can meet the Divine. Religions, full of vital and mental, mixed, troubled and ignorant stuff, can only get glimpses of the Divine; positivist reason with its questioning based upon things as they are and refusing to believe in anything that may or will be cannot get any vision at all. The spiritual is a new consciousness that has to evolve and has been evolving. It is quite natural that at first and for a long time only a few should get the full light, while a greater number but still only a few compared with the mass of humanity, should get it partially. But what has been gained by the few can at a stage of the evolution be completed and more generalised and that is the attempt which we are making. But if this greater consciousness of light, peace and joy is to be gained, it cannot be by questioning and scepticism which can only fall back on what is and say: "It is impossible, what has not been in the past cannot be in the future, what is so imperfectly realised as yet cannot be better realised in the future." A faith, a will, or at least a persistent demand and aspiration are needed – a feeling that with this and this alone I can be satisfied and a push towards it that will not cease till it is done. That is why a spirit of scepticism and denial stands in the way, because they stand against the creation of the conditions under which spiritual experience can unroll itself.

Since God has made earth, earth must make in her God;
What hides within her breast she must reveal.
I claim thee for the world that thou hast made.
If man lives bound by his humanity,
If he is tied for ever to his pain,
Let a greater being then arise from man,
The Superhuman with the Eternal mate
And the Immortal shine through earthly forms.

New Creation

The supramental creation, since it is to be a creation upon earth, must be not only an inner change but a physical and external manifestation also. And it is precisely for this part of the work, the most difficult of all, that surrender is most needful, for this reason, that it is the actual descent of the supramental Divine into Matter and the working of the Divine Presence and Power there that can alone make the physical and external change possible. Even the most powerful self-assertion of human will and endeavour is impotent to bring it about; as for egoistic insistence and vital revolt, they are, so long as they last, insuperable obstacles to the descent. Only a calm, pure and surrendered physical consciousness, full of the psychic aspiration, can be its field; this alone can make an effective opening of the material being to the Light and Power and the supramental change a thing actual and practicable. It is for this that we are here in the body.

This Light comes not by struggle or by thought;
In the mind's silence the Transcendent acts
And the hushed heart hears the unuttered Word.
A vast surrender was his only strength.
A Power that lives upon the heights must act,
Bring into life's closed room the Immortal's air
And fill the finite with the Infinite.

New Species

Ordinarily, as a constant factor or basis, there is the reproduction of that which was already evolved; for new characteristic to be propagated in the species they must have been accepted, received, sanctioned in the vital and mental world. Then only can they be automatically self-reproduced from the material seed. When the mind-world and the life-world are ready, they are poured out freely on fit recipients.

It is the pressure of the Life-world which enables life to evolve and develop here in the forms we already know; it is that increasing pressure which drives it to aspire in us to a greater revelation of itself and will one day deliver the mortal from his subjection to the narrow limitations of his present incompetent and restricting physicality. It is the pressure of the Mind-world which evolves and develops mind here and helps us to find a leverage for our mental self-uplifting and expansion, so that we may hope to enlarge continually our self of intelligence and even to break the prison-walls of our matter-bound physical mentality. It is the pressure of the supramental and spiritual worlds which is preparing to develop here the manifest power of the Spirit and by it open our being on the physical plane into the freedom and infinity of the superconscient Divine; that contact, that pressure can alone liberate from the apparent Inconscience, which was our starting-point, the all-conscient Godhead concealed in us.

There dwell earth nature's shining origins:
The perfect plans on which she moulds her works,
The distant outcomes of her travailing force
Repose in a framework of established fate.

Nirvana

Nirvana is nothing but the peace and freedom of the Spirit which can exist in itself, be there world or no world, world-order or world-disorder.

I myself had my experience of Nirvana and silence in the Brahman, etc. long before there was any knowledge of the overhead spiritual planes...

If the redemption of the soul from the physical vesture be the object, then there is no need of supramentalisation. Spiritual Mukti and Nirvana are sufficient. If the object is to rise to supraphysical planes, then also there is no need of supramentalisation. One can enter into some heaven above by devotion to the Lord of that heaven. But that is no progression. The other worlds are typal worlds, each fixed in its own kind and type and law. Evolution takes place on the earth and therefore the earth is the proper field for progression. The beings of the other worlds do not progress from one world to another. They remain fixed to their own type.

The psychic and the spiritual opening with their experiences and consequences can lead away from life or to a Nirvana; but they are here being considered solely as steps in a transformation of the nature.

In him Nirvana lives and speaks and acts
Impossibly creating a universe.
An eternal zero is his formless self,
His spirit the void impersonal absolute.

Nirvana

A Personal Experience

Now to reach Nirvana was the first radical result of my own yoga. It threw me suddenly into a condition above and without thought, unstained by any mental or vital movement; there was no ego, no real world — only when one looked through the immobile senses, something perceived or bore upon its sheer silence a world of empty forms, materialised shadows without true substance. There was no One or many even, only just absolutely That, featureless, relationless, sheer, indescribable, unthinkable, absolute, yet supremely real and solely real. This was no mental realisation nor something glimpsed somewhere above, — no abstraction, — it was positive, the only positive reality, — although not a spatial physical world, pervading, occupying or rather flooding and drowning this semblance of a physical world, leaving no room or space for any reality but itself, allowing nothing else to seem at all actual, positive or substantial. I cannot say there was anything exhilarating or rapturous in the experience, as it then came to me, — (the ineffable Ananda I had years afterwards), — but what it brought was an inexpressible Peace, a stupendous silence, an infinity of release and freedom. I lived in that Nirvana day and night before it began to admit other things into itself or modify itself at all, and the inner heart of experience, a constant memory of it and its power to return remained until in the end it began to disappear into a greater Superconsciousness from above. But meanwhile realisation added itself to realisation and fused itself with this original experience. At an early stage the aspect of an illusionary world gave place to one in which illusion (Footnote: In fact it is not an illusion in the sense of an imposition of something baseless and unreal on the consciousness, but a misinterpretation by the conscious mind and sense and a falsifying misuse of manifested existence.) is only a small surface phenomenon with an immense Divine Reality behind it and a supreme Divine Reality above it and an intense Divine Reality in the heart of everything that had seemed at first only a cinematic shape or shadow. And this was no reimprisonment in the senses, no diminution or fall from supreme experience, it came rather as a constant heightening and widening of the Truth; it was the spirit that saw objects, not the senses, and the Peace, the Silence, the freedom in Infinity remained always, with the world or all worlds only as a continuous incident in the timeless eternity of the Divine.

Now, that is the whole trouble in my approach to Mayavada. Nirvana in my liberated consciousness turned out to be the beginning of my realisation, a first step towards the complete thing, not the sole true attainment possible or even a culminating finale. It came unasked, unsought for, though quite welcome. I had no least idea about it before, no aspiration towards it, in fact my aspiration was towards just the opposite, spiritual power to help the world and to do my work in it, yet it came — without even a "May I come in" or a "By your leave". It just happened and settled in as if for all eternity or as if it had been really there always. And then it slowly grew into something not less but greater than its first self.

In a sublimer and more daring soar
To the wide summit of the triple stairs
Bare steps climbed up like glowing rocks of gold
Burning their way to a pure absolute sky.

Offering

It is possible so to turn life into an act of adoration to the Supreme by the spirit in one's works; for, says the Gita, "He who gives to me with a heart of adoration a leaf, a flower, a fruit or a cup of water, I take and enjoy that offering of his devotion," and it is not only any dedicated external gift that can be so offered with love and devotion, but all our thoughts, all our feelings and sensations, all our outward activities and their forms and objects can be such gifts to the Eternal. It is true that the special act or form of action has its importance, even a great importance, but it is the spirit in the act that is the essential factor; the spirit of which it is the symbol or materialised expression gives it its whole value and justifying significance.

If you desire this transformation, put yourself in the hands of the Mother and her Powers without cavil or resistance and let her do unhindered her work within you. Three things you must have, consciousness, plasticity, unreserved surrender. For you must be conscious in your mind and soul and heart and life and the very cells of your body, aware of the Mother and her Powers and their working; for although she can and does work in you even in your obscurity and your unconscious parts and moments, it is not the same thing as when you are in awakened and living communion with her.

> The mastery free nature's have was his
> And their assent to joy and spacious calm;
> One with the single Spirit inhabiting all,
> He laid experience at the Godhead's feet;
> His mind was open to her infinite mind,
> His acts were rhythmic with her primal force;
> He had subdued his mortal thought to hers.

Ordinary Consciousness

The ordinary consciousness is that in which one knows things only or mainly by the intellect, the external mind and the senses and knows forces etc. only by their outward manifestations and results and the rest by inferences from these data. There may be some play of mental intuition, deeper psychic seeing or impulsions, spiritual intimations, etc. — but in the ordinary consciousness these are incidental only and do not modify its fundamental character.

Most people live in their ordinary outer ignorant personality which does not easily open to the Divine; but there is an inner being within them of which they do not know, which can easily open to the Truth and the Light. But there is a wall which divides them from it, a wall of obscurity and unconsciousness. When it breaks down, then there is the release; the feeling of calm, Ananda, joy...

A consciousness that knows not its own truth,
A vagrant hunter of misleading dawns,
Between the being's dark and luminous ends
Moves here in a half-light that seems the whole:

Other Yogas and this Integral Yoga

Our synthesis takes man as a spirit in mind much more than a spirit in body and assumes in him the capacity to begin on that level, to spiritualise his being by the power of the soul in mind opening itself directly to a higher spiritual force and being and to perfect by that higher force so possessed and brought into action the whole of his nature. For that reason our initial stress has fallen upon the utilisation of the powers of soul in mind and the turning of the triple key of knowledge, works and love in the locks of the spirit; the Hathayogic methods can be dispensed with, – though there is no objection to their partial use, – the Rajayogic will only enter in as an informal element. To arrive by the shortest way at the largest development of spiritual power and being and divinise by it a liberated nature in the whole range of human living is our inspiring motive.

The old yoga demanded a complete renunciation extending to giving up the worldly life itself. This yoga aims instead at a new and transformed life. But it insists as inexorably on a complete throwing away of desire and attachment in the mind, life and body. Its aim is to refound life in the truth of the spirit and for that purpose to transfer the roots of all we are and do from the mind, life and body to a greater consciousness above the mind. That means that in the new life all the connections must be founded on a spiritual intimacy and a truth other than any which supports our present connections.

This yoga demands a total dedication of the life to the aspiration for the discovery and embodiment of the Divine Truth and to nothing else whatever. All clinging to mental preferences must fall away from you, all insistence on vital aims and interests and attachments must be put away, all egoistic clinging to family, friends, country must disappear if you want to succeed in this yoga.

A new creation from the old shall rise,
A Knowledge inarticulate find speech,
Beauty suppressed burst into paradise bloom,
Pleasure and pain dive into absolute bliss.

Our Relationship with God

He is the friend, the adviser, helper, saviour in trouble and distress, the defender from enemies, the hero who fights our battles for us or under whose shield we fight, the charioteer, the pilot of our ways. And here we come at once to a closer intimacy; he is the comrade and eternal companion, the playmate of the game of living.

Afterwards we do not obey, but move to his will as the string replies to the finger of the musician. To be the instrument is this higher stage of self-surrender and submission. But this is the living and loving instrument and it ends in the whole nature of our being becoming the slave of God, rejoicing in his possession and its own blissful subjection to the divine grasp and mastery.

> If human will could be made one with God's,
> If human thought could echo the thoughts of God,
> Man might be all-knowing and omnipotent;
> But now he walks in Nature's doubtful ray.
> Yet can the mind of man receive God' light,
> The force of man can be driven by God's force,
> Then is he a miracle doing miracles.
> For only so can he be Nature's King.

Our World

We regard the world not as an invention of the devil or a self-delusion of the soul, but as the manifestation of the Divine, although as yet a partial because a progressive and evolutionary manifestation. Therefore for us renunciation of life cannot be the goal of life nor rejection of the world the object for which the world was created. We seek to realise our unity with God, but for us that realisation involves a complete and absolute recognition of our unity with man and we cannot cut the two asunder. To use Christian language, the Son of God is also the Son of Man and both elements are necessary to the complete Christhood.

If the world is ruled by the flesh and the devil, all the more reason that the children of Immortality should be here to conquer it for God and the Spirit. If life is an insanity, then there are so many million souls to whom there must be brought the light of divine reason.

> Earth made a stepping-stone to conquer heaven,
> The soul saw beyond heaven's limiting boundaries,
> Met a great light from the Unknowable
> And dreamed of a transcendent action's sphere.

Ourselves

This little mind, vital and body which we call ourselves is only a surface movement and not our "self" at all. It is an external bit of personality put forward for one brief life, for the play of the Ignorance. It is equipped with an ignorant mind stumbling about in search of fragments of truth, an ignorant vital rushing about in search of fragments of pleasure, an obscure and mostly subconscious physical receiving the impacts of things and suffering rather than possessing a resultant pain or pleasure. All that is accepted until the mind gets disgusted and starts looking about for the real Truth of itself and things, the vital gets disgusted and begins wondering whether there is not such a thing as real bliss and the physical gets tired and wants liberation from itself and its pains and pleasures. Then it is possible for the little ignorant bit of personality to get back to its real Self and with it to these greater things — or else to extinction of itself, Nirvana.

That which we call ourselves is only a trembling ray on the surface; behind is all the vast subconscient, the vast superconscient.

Our observable consciousness, that which we call ourselves, is only the little visible part of our being. It is a small field below which are depths and farther depths and widths and ever wider widths which support and supply it but to which it has no visible access. All that is our self, our being; what we see at the top is only our ego and its visible nature.

Even the movements of this little surface nature cannot be understood nor its true law discovered until we know all that is below or behind and supplies it — and know too all that is around it and above.

If we learn to live within, we infallibly awaken to the presence within us which is our more real self, a presence profounder, calm, joyous and puissant of which the world is not a master — a presence which, if it is not the Lord Himself, is the radiation of the Lord within. And if we can go back into ourselves and identify ourselves, not with our superficial experience, but with that radiant penumbra of the Divine, we can live in that attitude towards the contacts of the world and, standing back in our consciousness from the pleasures and pains of the body, vital being and mind, possess them as experiences whose nature being superficial does not touch or impose itself on our core and our being. The truth of ourselves lies within and not on the surface.

In our depths we ourselves are that One, since in the reality of our being we are the indivisible All-Consciousness and therefore the inalienable All-Bliss, the disposition of our sensational experience in the three vibrations of pain, pleasure and indifference can only be a superficial arrangement created by that limited part of ourselves which is uppermost in our waking consciousness. Behind there must be something in us, — much vaster, profounder, truer than the superficial consciousness, — which takes delight impartially in all experiences; it is that delight which secretly supports the superficial mental being and enables it to persevere through all labours, sufferings and ordeals in the agitated movement of the Becoming.

> The All-containing was contained in form,
> Oneness was carved into units measureable,
> The limitless built into a cosmic sum:
> Unending Space was beaten into a curve,
> Indivisible Time into small minutes cut,
> The infinitesmal massed to keep secure
> The mystery of the Formless cast into form.

Ourselves and Others

The Lord is there in all equally in all beings, we have to make no essential distinctions between ourselves and others, the wise and the ignorant, friend and enemy, man and animal, the saint and the sinner. We must hate none, despise none, be repelled by none; for in all we have to see the One disguised or manifested at his pleasure. He is a little revealed in one or more revealed in another or concealed and wholly distorted in others according to his will and his knowledge of what is best for that which he intends to become in form in them and to do in works in their nature. All is our self, one self that has taken many shapes.

Aware of the universal Self in all
She turned to living hearts and human forms;
Her soul's reflections, complements, counterparts,
The close outlying portions of her being
Divided from her by walls of body and mind
Yet to her spirit bound by ties divine.

Outer Man

The outer physical man is only an instrumental personality and by himself he cannot arrive at this union with the Divine, — he can only get occasional touches, religious feelings, imperfect intimations. And even these come not from the outer consciousness but from what is within us.

Most men are, like animals, driven by the forces of Nature: whatever desires come, they fulfill them, whatever emotions come they allow them to play, whatever physical wants they have, they try to satisfy...

When people do sadhana, there is a higher Nature that works within, the psychic and spiritual, and they have to put their nature under the influence of the psychic being and the higher spiritual self or of the Divine. Not only the vital and the body but the mind also has to learn the Divine Truth and obey the divine rule. But because of the lower nature and its continued hold on them, they are unable at first and for a long time to prevent their nature from following the old ways — even when they know or are told from within what to do or what not to do. It is only by persistent sadhana, by getting into the higher spiritual consciousness and spiritual nature that this difficulty can be overcome; but even for the strongest and best sadhaks it takes a long time.

The yogi arrives at a sort of division in his being in which the inner Purusha, fixed and calm, looks at the perturbations of the outer man as one looks at the passions of an unreasonable child; that once fixed, he can proceed afterwards to control the outer man also; but a complete control of the outer man needs a long and arduous tapasya.

One rejects from oneself the identification with the mind, vital, body, saying continually "I am not the mind", "I am not the vital", "I am not the body", seeing these things as separate from one's real self — and after a time one feels all the mental, vital, physical processes and the very sense of mind, vital, body becoming externalised, an outer action, while within and detached from them there grows the sense of a separate self-existent being which opens into the realisation of the cosmic and transcendent spirit. There is also the method-a very powerful method — of the Sankhyas, the separation of the Purusha and the Prakriti. One enforces on the mind the position of the Witness — all action of mind, vital, physical becomes an outer play which is not myself or mine, but belongs to Nature and has been enforced on an outer me. I am the witness Purusha; I am silent, detached, not bound by any of these things.

> I strove to find its hints through Beauty and Art,
> But Form cannot unveil the indwelling Power;
> Only it throws its symbols at our hearts.
> It evoked a mood of self, invoked a sign
> Of all the brooding glory hidden in sense:
> I lived in the ray but faced not the Sun.

Overmind

The Overmind sees calmly, steadily, in great masses and large extensions of space and time and relation, globally; it creates and acts in the same way — it is the world of the great Gods, the divine Creators. Only, each creates in his own way, he sees all but sees all from his viewpoint. There is not the absolute supramental harmony and certitude. These, inadequately expressed, are some of the differences. I speak, of course, of these planes in themselves — when acting in the human consciousness they are necessarily much diminished in their working by having to depend on the human instrumentation of mind, vital and physical. Only when these are quieted, they get a fuller force and reveal more their character.

Overmind and Supermind are also involved and occult in earth-Nature, but they have no formations on the accessible levels of our subliminal inner consciousness; there is as yet no overmind being or organised overmind nature, no supramental being or organised supermind nature acting either on our surface or in our normal subliminal parts: for these greater powers of consciousness are superconscient to the level of our ignorance. In order that the involved principles of Overmind and Supermind should emerge from their veiled secrecy, the being and powers of the Superconscience must descend into us and uplift us and formulate themselves in our being and powers; this descent is a sine qua non of the transition and transformation.

> The cosmic empire of the Overmind,
> Time's buffer state bordering Eternity,
> Too vast for the experience of man's soul:
> All here gathers beneath one golden sky:
> The powers that build the cosmos station take
> In its house of infinite possibility;
> Each god from there builds his own nature's world.

Parts of the Being

We are composed of many parts each of which contributes something to the total movement of our consciousness, our thought, will, sensation, feeling, action...

What the parts of the body correspond to are planes — subtle physical, higher, middle and lower vital, mental. Each plane is in communication with various worlds that belong to it.

In the yoga one becomes aware of the different parts and their proper action, and puts each in its place and to its proper action under the control of the Higher Consciousness or else under the control of the Divine Power. Afterwards all gets charged with the spiritual consciousness and there is an automatic right perception and right action of the different parts because they are controlled entirely from above and do not falsify or resist or confuse its dictates. What the parts of the body correspond to are planes. Every part of us has as it were its own complex individuality and natural formation independent of the rest and these parts of the consciousness are like fields into which forces from the same planes of consciousness in the universal Nature are constantly entering or passing.

> He knows not his own greatness nor his aim;
> He has forgotten why he has come and whence;
> His spirit and his members are at war.

Peace

The first calm that comes is of the nature of peace, the absence of all unquiet, grief and disturbance. As the equality becomes more intense, it takes a fuller substance of positive happiness and spiritual ease.

This complete self-surrender must be the chief mainstay of the Sadhaka because it is the only way, apart from complete quiescence and indifference to all action, — and that has to be avoided, — by which the absolute calm and peace can come.

The calm established in the whole being must remain the same whatever happens, in health and disease, in pleasure and in pain, in good fortune and misfortune, our own or that of those we love, in success and failure, honour and insult, praise and blame, justice done to us or injustice, everything that ordinarily affects the mind. This is the joy of the spirit in itself, dependent on nothing external for its absolute existence.

> O radiant fountain of the world's delight
> World-free and unattainable above,
> O Bliss who ever dwellst deep hid within
> While men seek thee outside and never find,
> Mystery and Muse with hieratic tongue,
> Incarnate the white passion of thy force,
> Mission to earth some living form of thee.

Perception

To know the world, so to perceive and experience it, it is not enough to have an intellectual idea or imagination that so it is; a certain divine vision, divine sense, divine ecstasy is needed, an experience of union of ourselves with the objects of our consciousness. In that experience not only the Beyond but all here, not only the totality, the All in its mass, but each thing in the All becomes to us our self, God, the Absolute and Infinite, Sachchidananda. This is the secret of complete delight in God's world, complete satisfaction of the mind and heart and will, complete liberation of the consciousness. It is the supreme experience at which art and poetry and all the various efforts of subjective and objective knowledge and all desire and effort to possess and enjoy objects are trying more or less obscurely to arrive; their attempt to seize the forms and properties and qualities of things is only a first movement which cannot give the deepest satisfaction unless by seizing them perfectly and absolutely they get the sense of the infinite reality of which these are the outer symbols.

A pure perception lent its lucent joy:
Its intimate vision waited not to think;
It enveloped all Nature in a single glance,
It looked into the very self of things;
Deceived no more by form he saw the soul.

Perfection

When you are completely identified with the Divine Mother and feel yourself to be no longer another and separate being, instrument, servant or worker, but truly a child and eternal portion of her consciousness and force. Always she will be in you and you in her; it will be your constant, simple and natural experience that all your thought and seeing and action, your very breathing or moving come from her and are hers. You will know and see and feel that you are a person and power formed by her out of herself, put out from her for the play and yet always safe in her, being of her being, consciousness of her consciousness, force of her force, Ananda of her Ananda. When this condition is entire and her supramental energies can freely move you, then you will be perfect in divine works, knowledge, will, action will become sure, simple, luminous, spontaneous, flawless, an outflow from the Supreme, a divine movement of the Eternal.

If our souls could see and love and clasp God's Truth,
Its infinite radiance would seize our hearts,
Our being in God's image be remade
And earthly life become the life divine.

Personal Greatness

A man becomes a leader of men or eminent in a large or lesser circle and feels himself full of a power that he knows to be beyond his own ego-Force; he may be aware of a Fate acting through him or a Will mysterious and unfathomable or a Light within of great brilliance. There are extraordinary results of his thoughts, his actions or his creative genius. He effects some tremendous destruction that clears the path for humanity or some great construction that becomes its momentary resting-place. He is a scourge or he is a bringer of light and healing, a creator of beauty or a messenger of knowledge. Or, if his work and its effects are on a lesser scale and have a limited field, still they are attended by the strong sense that he is an instrument and chosen for his mission or his labour. Men who have this destiny and these powers come easily to believe and declare themselves to be mere instruments in the hands of God or of Fate: but even in the declaration we can see that there can intrude or take refugee an intenser and more exaggerated egoism than ordinary men have the courage to assert or the strength to house within them. And often if men of this kind speak of God, it is to erect an image of him which is really nothing but a huge shadow of themselves or their own nature, a sustaining Deific Essence of their own type of will and thought and quality and force. This magnified image of their ego is the Master whom they serve. This happens only too often in Yoga to strong but crude vital natures or minds too easily exalted when they allow ambition, pride or the desire of greatness to enter into their spiritual seeking and vitiate its purity of motive; a magnified ego stands between them and their true being and grasps for its own personal purpose the strength from a greater unseen Power, divine or undivine, acting through them of which they become vaguely or intensely aware.

A much worse thing may befall those who break something of the human bonds but have not purity and have not the knowledge, for they may become instruments, but not of the Divine; too often, using his name, they serve unconsciously his masks and black Contraries, the Powers of Darkness.

Then he could see the hidden heart of Night:
The labour of its stark unconsciousness
Revealed the endless terrible Inane.

203

A spiritless blank Infinity was there;
A Nature that denied the eternal Truth
In the vain braggart freedom of its thought
Hoped to abolish God and reign alone.

Personality

The soul comes into birth for experience, for growth, for evolution till it can bring the Divine into Matter. It is the central being that incarnates, not the outer personality — the personality is simply a mould that it creates for its figures of experience in that one life. In another birth it will create for itself a different personality, different capacities, a different life and career. Supposing Virgil is born again, he may take up poetry in one or two other lives, but he will certainly not write an epic but rather perhaps slight but elegant and beautiful lyrics such as he wanted to write, but did not succeed, in Rome. In another birth he is likely to be no poet at all, but a philosopher and a yogin seeking to attain and to express the highest truth — for that too was an unrealised trend of his consciousness in that life...

As the evolving being develops still more and becomes more rich and complex, it accumulates its personalities, as it were. Sometimes they stand behind the active elements, throwing in some colour, some trait, some capacity here and there, — or they stand in front and there is a multiple personality. Though it all remains in a kind of seed memory, it does not ordinarily emerge.

The psychic when it departs from the body, shedding even the mental and vital on its way to its resting place, carries with it the heart of its experiences, — not the physical events, not the vital movements, not the mental buildings, not the capacities or characters, but something essential that it gathered from them, what might be called the divine element for the sake of which the rest existed. That is the permanent addition, it is that that helps in the growth towards the Divine. That is why there is usually no memory of the outward events and circumstances of past lives — for this memory there must be a strong development towards unbroken continuance of the mind, the vital, even the subtle physical; for though it all remains in a kind of seed memory, it does not ordinarily emerge.

> Only the Self that builds this figure of self
> Can raise the fixed interminable line
> That joins these changing names, these numberless lives,
> These new oblivious personalities.

Physical Being

The physical being of man has always been felt by the seekers of perfection to be a great impediment and it has been the habit to turn from it with contempt, denial or aversion and a desire to suppress altogether or as far as may be the body and the physical life. But this cannot be the right method for the integral Yoga. The body is given us as one instrument necessary to the totality of our works and it is to be used, not neglected, hurt, suppressed or abolished. If it is imperfect, recalcitrant, obstinate, so are also the other members, the vital being, heart and mind and reason. It has like them to be changed and perfected and to undergo a transformation. As we must get ourselves a new life, new heart, new mind, so we have in a certain sense to build for ourselves a new body.

The first thing the will has to do with the body is to impose on it progressively a new habit of all its being, consciousness, force and outward and inward action. It must be taught an entire passivity in the hands first of the higher instruments, but eventually in the hands of the spirit and its controlling and informing Shakti. It must be accustomed not to impose its own limits on the nobler members, but to shape its action and its response to their demands, to develop, one might say, a higher notation, a higher scale of responses.

> To cast the spirit into physical form,
> To lend speech and thought to the Ineffable;
> She is pushed to reveal the ever Unmanifest.
> I saw them cross the twilight of an age,
> The sun-eyed children of a marvellous dawn,
> The great creators with wide brows of calm,
> The massive barrier-breakers of the world
> And wrestlers with destiny in her lists of will,
> And labourers in the quarries of the gods,
> The messengers of the Incommunicable,
> The architects of immortality.

Physical Energy

It is the universal Prana, as the ancients knew, which in various forms sustains or drives material energy in all physical things from the electron, and atom and gas up through the metal, plant, animal, physical man. To get this pranic Shakti to act more freely and forcibly in the body is knowingly or unknowingly the attempt of all who strive for a greater perfection of or in the body. The ordinary man tries to command it mechanically by physical exercises and other corporal means, the Hathayogin more greatly and flexibly, but still mechanically by Asana and Pranayama; but for our purpose it can be commanded by more subtle, essential and pliable means; first, by a will in the mind widely opening itself to and potently calling in the universal pranic Shakti on which we draw and fixing its stronger presence and more powerful working in the body; secondly, by the will in the mind opening itself rather to the spirit and its power and calling in higher pranic energy from above, a supramental pranic force; thirdly, the last step, by the highest supramental will of the spirit entering and taking up directly the task of the perfection of the body...

Most men are not conscious of this pranic force in the body or cannot distinguish it from the more physical form of energy which it informs and uses for its vehicle. But as the consciousness becomes more subtle by practice of Yoga, we can come to be aware of the sea of pranic Shakti around us, feel it with the mental consciousness, concretely with a mental sense, see its courses and movements, and direct and act upon it immediately by the will. But until we thus become aware of it, we have to possess a working or at least an experimental faith in its presence and in the power of the will to develop a greater command and use of this Prana force.

A mighty Presence still defends thy frame.
Perhaps the heavens guard thee for some great soul,
Thy fate, thy work are kept somewhere afar,
Thy spirit came not down a star alone.

Physical Limitation

It is evident that however much we may analyse the physical and sensible, we cannot by that means arrive at the Knowledge of the Self or of ourselves or of that which we call God. The telescope, the microscope, the scalpel, the retort and alembic cannot go beyond the physical, although they may arrive at subtler and subtler truths about the physical. If then we confine ourselves to what the senses and their physical aids reveal to us and refuse from the beginning to admit any other reality or any other means of knowledge, we are obliged to conclude nothing is real except the physical and that there is no Self in us or in the universe, no God within and without, no ourselves even except this aggregate of brain, nerves and body. But this we are only obliged to conclude because we have assumed it firmly from the beginning and therefore cannot but circle round to our original assumption.

If, then, there is a Self, a Reality not oblivious to the senses, it must be by other means than those of physical Science that it is to be sought and known. The intellect is not that means.

> The Illimitable they measured with number's rods
> And traced the last formula of limited things,
> In transparent systems bodied termless truths,
> The Timeless made accountable to Time
> And valued the incommensurable Supreme.
> To park and hedge the ungrasped infinitudes
> They erected absolute walls of thought and speech
> And made a vacuum to hold the One.

Physical Mind

This part of the mind is the instrument of understanding and ordered action on physical things.

It is obscure and ignorant and fumbling guided only by an external knowledge.

It is agile and active and competent only in its own limits. When it has to deal with supraphysical things it becomes incompetent, often imbecile and yet positive and arrogant and dogmatic in its ignorance.

A principle of dark and dull inertia is at its base; all are tied down by the body and its needs and desires to a trivial mind, petty desires and emotions, an insignificant repetition of small worthless functionings, needs, cares, occupations, pains, pleasures that lead to nothing beyond themselves and bear the stamp of an ignorance that knows not its own why and whither. This physical mind of inertia believes in no divinity other than its small earth-gods; it aspires perhaps to a greater comfort, order, pleasure, but asks for no uplifting and no spiritual deliverance.

We arrive at the conception and at the knowledge of a divine existence by exceeding the evidence of the senses and piercing beyond the walls of the physical mind. So long as we confine ourselves to sense-evidence and the physical consciousness, we can conceive nothing and know nothing except the material world and its phenomena.

It has to become conscious of the Divine and to act in accordance with an inner light, will and knowledge putting itself into contact and an understanding unity with the physical world.

In this bound thinking's narrow leadership
Tied to the soil, inspired by common things,
Attached to a confined familiar world,
Amid the multitude of her motived plots,
Her changing actors and her million masks,
Life was a play monotonously the same.

Planes

Sat, Chit, Ananda, Supermind, Mind, Life, Matter are the seven planes described in the Veda — but in this yoga one sees many levels of consciousness...

Each plane is a world or a conglomeration or series of worlds, each organized in its own way.

Each plane, in spite of its connection with others above and below it, is yet a world in itself, with its own movements, forces, beings, types, forms existing as if for its and their own sake, under its own laws, for its own manifestation without apparent regard for the other members of the great series.

Mind has its own realms and life has its own realms just as matter has. In the mental realms life and substance are entirely subordinated to Mind and obey its dictates. Here on earth there is the evolution with matter as the starting-point, life as the medium, mind emerging from it. There are many grades, realms, combination in the cosmos — there are even many universes. Ours is only one of many.

A hidden Bliss is at the root of things.
A mute Delight regards Time's countless works:
To house God's joy in things Space gave wide room,
To house God's joy in self our souls were born.

Planes and their Influence

If we regard the gradation of worlds or planes as a whole, we see them as a great connected complex movement; the higher precipitate their influences on the lower, the lower react to the higher and develop or manifest in themselves within their own formula something that corresponds to the superior power and its action. The material world has evolved life in obedience to a pressure from the vital plane, mind in obedience to a pressure from the mental plane. It is now trying to evolve supermind in obedience to a pressure from the supramental plane.

There is a vital plane (self-existent) above the material universe which we see; there is a mental plane (self-existent) above the vital and material. These three together, — mental, vital, physical, — are called the triple universe of the lower hemisphere. They have been established in the earth-consciousness by evolution — but they exist in themselves before the evolution, above the earth-consciousness and the material plane to which the earth belongs.

We are all the time living and acting on other planes of consciousness, meeting others there and acting upon them, and what we do and feel and think there, the forces we gather, the results we prepare have an incalculable importance and effect, unknown to us, upon our outer life.

A mightier task remained than all he had done.
To that he turned from which all being comes,
A sign attending from the Secrecy
Which knows the Truth ungrasped behind our thoughts
And guards the world with its all-seeing gaze.

Planes and Sub-Planes

A plane is not fixed in one hardly variable formula as physical life seems to be, but is capable of many variations of its poise, admits many sub-planes ranging from those which touch material existence and, as it were, melt into that, to those which touch at the height of the life-power the planes of pure mental and psychic existence and melt into them. For in Nature in the infinite scale of being there are no wide gulfs, no abrupt chasms to be overleaped, but a melting of one thing into another, a subtle continuity; out of that her power of distinctive experience creates the orderings, the definite ranges, the distinct gradations by which the soul variously knows and possesses its possibilities of world-existence.

The sole creation; the creation or manifestation is very vast and contains many planes and worlds that existed before the evolution, all different in character and with different kinds of beings. The fact of being prior to the evolution does not make them undifferentiated. The world of the Asuras is prior to the evolution, so are the worlds of the mental, vital or subtle physical Devas — but these beings are all different from each other. The great Gods belong to the overmind plane; in the supermind they are unified as aspects of the Divine, in the overmind they appear as separate personalities. Any godhead can descend by emanation to the physical plane and associate himself with the evolution of a human being with whose line of manifestation he is in affinity. But these are things which cannot be very easily understood by the mind, because the mind has too rigid an idea of personality — the difficulty only disappears when one enters into a more flexible consciousness above where one is nearer to the experience of One in all and All in one.

> As one who sets his sail towards mysteried shores
> Driven through huge oceans by the breath of God,
> The fathomless below, the unknown around,
> His soul abandoned the blind star-field, Space.
> Afar from all that makes the measured world,
> Plunging to hidden eternities it withdrew
> Back from mind's foaming surface to the Vasts
> Voiceless within us in omniscient sleep.

Possession by the True Self

When you are completely identified with the Divine Mother and feel yourself to be no longer another and separate being, instrument, servant or worker, but truly a child and eternal portion of her consciousness and force. When this condition is entire and her supramental energies can freely move you, then you will be perfect in divine works, knowledge, will, action will become sure, simple, luminous, spontaneous, flawless, an outflow from the Supreme, a divine movement of the Eternal.

If our souls could see and love and clasp God's Truth,
Its infinite radiance would seize our hearts,
Our being in God's image be remade
And earthly life become the life divine.

Prayer

Its power and sense is to put the will, aspiration and faith of man into touch with the divine Will as that of a conscious Being with whom we can enter into conscious and living relations.

Prayer helps to prepare this relation for us at first on the lower plane even while it is there consistent with much that is mere egoism and self-delusion; but afterwards we can draw towards the spiritual truth which is behind it. It is not then the giving of the thing asked for that matters, but the relation itself, the contact of man's life with God, the conscious interchange. In spiritual matters and in the seeking of spiritual gains, this conscious relation is a great power; it is a much greater power than our own entirely self-reliant struggle and effort and it brings a fuller spiritual growth and experience...

It is true that the universal will executes always its aim and cannot be deflected by egoistic propitiation and entreaty, but neither is that order or the execution of the universal will altogether effected by mechanical Law, but by powers and forces of which for human life at least, human will, aspiration and faith are not among the least important.

Prayers should be full of confidence without sorrow or lamenting.

Aspiration, call, prayer are forms of one and the same thing and are all effective; you can take the form that comes to you or is easiest to you.

As for the prayers, the fact of praying and the attitude it brings, especially unselfish prayer for others, itself opens you to the higher Power, even if there is no corresponding result in the person prayed for.

A prayer, a master act, a king idea
Can link man's strength to a transcendent Force.
Then miracle is made the common rule,
One mighty deed can change the course of things;
A lonely thought becomes omnipotent.

Preparation

At first there may have to be a prolonged, often tedious and painful period of preparation and purification of all our being till it is ready and fit for an opening to a greater Truth and Light or to the Divine Influence and Presence. Even when centrally fitted, prepared, open already, it will still be long before all our movements of mind, life and body, all the multiple and conflicting members and elements of our personality consent or, consenting, are able to bear the difficult and exacting process of the transformation. And hardest of all, even if all in us is willing, is the struggle we shall have to carry through against the universal forces attached to the present unstable creation when we seek to make the final supramental conversion and reversal of consciousness by which the Divine Truth must be established in us in its plenitude and not merely what they would more readily permit, an illumined Ignorance.

It is for this that a surrender and submission to That which is beyond us enabling the full and free working of its Power is indispensable. As that self-giving progresses, the work of the sacrifice becomes easier and more powerful and the prevention of the opposing Forces loses much of its strength, impulsion and substance. Two inner changes help most to convert what now seems difficult or impracticable into a thing possible and even sure. There takes place a coming to the front of some secret inmost soul within which was veiled by the restless activity of the mind, by the turbulence of our vital impulses and by the obscurity of the physical consciousness, the three powers which in their confused combination we now call our self. There will come about as a result a less impeded growth of a Divine Presence at the centre with its liberating Light and effective Force and an irradiation of it into all the conscious and subconscious ranges of our nature. These are the two signs, one marking our completed conversion and consecration to the great Quest, the other the final acceptance by the Divine of our sacrifice.

A static Oneness and dynamic Power
Descend in him, the integral Godhead's seals;
His soul and body take that splendid stamp.
A long dim preparation is man's life,
A circle of toil and hope and war and peace

Tracked out by Life on Matter's obscure ground
In his climb to a peak no feet have ever trod,
He seeks through a penumbra shot with flame
A veiled reality half-known, ever missed,
A search for something or someone never found,
Cult of an ideal never made real here,
An endless spiral of ascent and fall
Until at last is reached the giant point
Through which his Glory shines for whom we were made
And we break into the infinity of God.

Psychic Being

Aspiration, constant and sincere, and the will to turn to the Divine alone are the best means to bring forward the psychic.

The psychic being is a spiritual personality put forward by the soul in its evolution; its growth marks the stage which the spiritual evolution of the individual has reached and its immediate possibilities for the future.

The psychic is the divine element in the individual being and its characteristic power is to turn everything towards the Divine, to bring a fire of purification, aspiration, devotion, true light of discernment, feeling, will, an action which transforms by degrees the whole nature. Quietude, peace and silence in the heart and therefore in the vital part of the being are necessary to reach the psychic, to plunge in it, for the perturbations of the vital nature, desire, emotion turned ego-wards or world-wards are the main part of the screen that hides the soul from the nature. It is better, therefore, to be free from the mental constructions when you take the plunge and to have only the sense of aspiration, of devotion, of self-giving to the Divine.

The soul, the psychic being is in direct touch with the divine Truth, but it is hidden in man by the mind, the vital being and the physical nature. One may practise yoga and get illuminations in the mind and the reason; one may conquer power and luxuriate in all kinds of experiences in the vital; one may establish even surprising physical Siddhis; but if the true soul-power behind does not manifest, if the psychic nature does not come into the front, nothing genuine has been done. In this yoga the psychic being is that which opens the rest of the nature to the true supramental light and finally to the supreme Ananda.

But once the hidden doors are flung apart
Then the veiled king steps out in Nature's front;
A Light comes down into the ignorance,
Its heavy painful knot loosens its grasp:
The mind becomes a mastered instrument
And life a hue and figure of the soul.

Psychic Light

There is no absolute certitude of the guidance, the surrender is not sure, so long as we are besieged by mind formations and life impulses and instigations of ego which may easily betray us into the hands of a false experience. This danger can only be countered by the opening of a now nine-tenths concealed inmost soul or psychic being that is already there but not commonly active within us. That is the inner light we must liberate; for the light of this inmost soul is our one sure illumination so long as we walk still amidst the siege of the Ignorance and the Truth consciousness has not taken up the entire control of our God-ward endeavour.

As if reversing a deformation's spell,
Released from the black magic of the Night,
Renouncing servitude to the dark Abyss,
It shall learn at last who lived within unseen
And seized with marvel in the adoring heart
To the enthroned Child-Godhead kneel aware,
Trembling with beauty and delight and love.

Purification

A great and long revolution and churning of the Ocean of Life with strong emergences of its nectar and its poison is enforced till all is ready and the increasing Descent finds a being, a nature prepared and conditioned for its complete rule and its all-encompassing presence. But if the equality and the psychic light and will are already there, then this process, though it cannot be dispensed with, can still be much lightened and facilitated: it will be rid of its worst dangers; an inner calm, happiness, confidence will support the steps through all the difficulties and trials of the transformation and the growing Force profiting by the full assent of the nature will rapidly diminish and eliminate the power of the opposing forces. A sure guidance and protection will be present throughout, sometimes standing in front, sometimes working behind the veil, and the power of the end will be already there in the beginning and in the long middle stages of the great endeavour. For at all times the seeker will be aware of the Divine Guide and Protector or the working of the supreme Mother-Force; he will know that all is done for the best, the progress assured, the victory inevitable. In either case the process is the same and unavoidable, a taking up of the whole nature, of the whole life, of the internal and of the external, to reveal and handle and transform its forces and their movements under the pressure of a diviner Life from above, until all here has been possessed by greater spiritual powers and made an instrumentation of a spiritual action and a divine purpose.

In this process and at an early stage of it it becomes evident that what we know of ourselves, our present conscious existence, is only a representative formation, a superficial activity, a changing external result of a vast mass of concealed existence.

In forms not too remote from human grasp
Some passion of the inviolate purity
Broke through, a ray of the original Bliss.
Heaven's joys might have been earth's if earth were pure.

219

Purpose

The yoga we practice is not for ourselves alone, but for the Divine; its aim is to work out the will of the Divine in the world, to effect a spiritual transformation and to bring down a divine nature and a divine life into the mental, vital and physical nature and life of humanity. Its object is not personal Mukti, although Mukti is a necessary condition of the yoga, but the liberation and transformation of the human being. It is not personal Ananda, but the bringing down of the divine Ananda, the God's kingdom of heaven upon the earth. Of liberation we have no personal need; for the soul is eternally free and bondage is an illusion.

It is to have this joy of union as the ultimate crown of all the varied experiences of spiritual relation between the individual soul and God that the One became many in the universe.

Let not the impatient Titan drive thy heart,
Ask not the imperfect fruit, the partial prize.
Only one boon, to greaten thy spirit, demand;
Only one joy, to raise thy kind, desire.

Recognising Nature

Truly, we do not think, will or act but thought occurs in us, will occurs in us, impulse and act occurs in us; our ego-sense gathers around itself, refers to itself all this flow of natural activities. It is a cosmic force, it is Nature that forms the thought, imposes the will, imparts the impulse. Our body, mind and the ego are a wave of that sea of force in action and do not govern it, but by it are governed and directed. The Sadhaka in his progress towards truth and self-knowledge must come to a point where the soul opens its eyes of vision and recognises this truth of ego and this truth of works. He gives up the idea of a mental, vital, physical "I" that acts or governs action; he recognises that Prakriti, Force of Cosmic nature following her fixed modes, is in him and in all things and creatures the one and only worker.

> The master of existence lurks in us
> And plays at hide and seek with his own Force;
> In nature's instrument loiters secret God.

Rejection

Rejection is the throwing out of all that is not the true Truth of the Divine.

Detect first what is false or obscure in you and persistently reject it, then alone can you rightly call for the Divine Power to transform you.

Two rules alone there are that will diminish the difficulty and obviate the danger. One must reject all that comes from the ego, from vital desire, from the mere mind and its presumptuous reasoning incompetence, all that ministers to these agents of the Ignorance. One must learn to hear and follow the voice of the inmost soul, the direction of the Guru, the command of the Master, the working of the Divine Mother. Whoever clings to the desires and weaknesses of the flesh, the cravings and passions of the vital in its turbulent ignorance, the dictates of his personal mind unsilenced and unillumined by a greater knowledge, cannot find the true inner law and is heaping obstacles in the way of the divine fulfilment. Whoever is able to detect and renounce these obscuring agencies and to discern and follow the true Guide within and without will discover the spiritual law and reach the goal of Yoga.

Do not imagine that truth and falsehood, light and darkness, surrender and selfishness can be allowed to dwell together in the house consecrated to the Divine. The transformation must be integral, and integral therefore the rejection of all that withstands it.

> All that denies must be torn out and slain
> And crushed the many longings for whose sake
> We lose the One for whom our lives were made.

Relationship

The whole principle of this yoga is to give oneself entirely to the Divine alone and to nobody and nothing else, and to bring down into ourselves by union with the Divine Mother-Power all the transcendent light, force, wideness, peace, purity, truth — consciousness and Ananda of the supramental Divine. In this yoga, therefore, there can be no place for vital relations or interchanges with others; any such relation or interchange immediately ties down the soul to the lower consciousness and its lower nature, prevents the true and full union with the Divine and hampers both the ascent to the supramental Truth-consciousness and the descent of the supramental Ishwari Shakti. Still worse would it be if this interchange took the form of a sexual relation or a sexual enjoyment, even if kept free from any outward act; therefore these things are absolutely forbidden in the sadhana. It goes without saying that any physical act of the kind is not allowed; but also any subtler form is ruled out. It is only after becoming one with the supramental Divine that we can find our true spiritual relations with others in the Divine; in that higher unity this kind of gross lower vital movement can have no place.

No error can be more perilous than to accept the immixture of the sexual desire and some kind of subtle satisfaction of it and look on this as a part of the sadhana. It would be the most effective way to head straight towards spiritual downfall and throw into the atmosphere forces that would block the supramental descent, bringing instead the descent of adverse vital powers to disseminate disturbance and disaster. This deviation must be absolutely thrown away, should it try to occur and expunged from the consciousness, if the Truth is to be brought down and the work is to be done.

It is flesh that calls to flesh to serve its lust;
It is thy mind that seeks an answering mind
And dreams awhile that it has found its mate.

Religion and Yoga

In ordinary religion this adoration wears the form of external worship and that again develops a most external form of ceremonial worship. This element is ordinarily necessary because the mass of men live in their physical minds, cannot realise anything except by the force of a physical symbol and cannot feel that they are living anything except by the force of a physical action.

It is evident that even real religion, — and Yoga is something more than religion, — only begins when this quite outward worship corresponds to something really felt within the mind, some genuine submission, awe or spiritual aspiration, to which it becomes an aid, an outward expression and also a sort of periodical or constant reminder helping to draw back the mind to it from the preoccupations of ordinary life. But so long as it is only an idea of the Godhead to which one renders reverence or homage, we have not yet got to the beginning of Yoga. The aim of Yoga being union, its beginning must always be a seeking after the Divine, a longing after some kind of touch, closeness or possession. When this comes on us, the adoration becomes always primarily an inner worship; we begin to make ourselves a temple of the Divine, our thoughts and feelings a constant prayer of aspiration and seeking, our whole life an external service and worship. It is as this change, this new soul-tendency grows, that the religion of the devotee becomes a Yoga, a growing contact and union. It does not follow that the outward worship will necessarily be dispensed with, but it will increasingly become only a physical expression or outflowing of the inner devotion and adoration, the wave of the soul throwing itself out in speech and symbolic act.

The Divine Truth is greater than any religion or creed or scripture or idea or philosophy — so you must not tie yourself to any of these things.

For Truth is wider, greater than her forms.
A thousand icons they have made of her
And find her in the idols they adore;
But she remains herself and Infinite.

Repel

The Sadhaka must be on the watch as the witnessing and willing Purusha behind or, better, as soon as he can manage it, above the mind, and repel even the least indices or incidence of trouble, anxiety, grief, revolt, disturbance in his mind. If these things come, he must at once detect their source, the defect which they indicate, the fault of egoistic claim, vital desire, emotion or idea from which they start and this he must discourage by his will, his spiritualised intelligence, his soul unity with the Master of his being. On no account must he admit any excuse for them, however natural, righteous in seeming or plausible, or any inner or outer justification.

> Always the dark Adventurers seem to win;
> Nature they fill with evil's institutes,
> Turn into defeats the victories of Truth,
> Proclaim as falsehoods the eternal laws,
> And load the dice of Doom with wizard lies;
> The world's shrines they have occupied, usurped its thrones.

Revolution

There must be an ascension of the whole being, an ascension of spirit chained here and trammelled by its instruments and its environment to sheer Spirit free above, an ascension of soul towards some blissful Super-soul, an ascension of mind towards some luminous Supermind, an ascension of life towards some vast Super-life, an ascension of our very physicality to join its origin in some pure and plastic spirit-substance. And this cannot be a single swift upsoaring but, like the ascent of the sacrifice described in the Veda, a climbing from peak to peak in which from each summit one looks up to the much more that has still to be done. At the same time there must be a descent too to affirm below what we have gained above: on each height we conquer we have to turn to bring down its power and its illumination into the lower mortal movement; the discovery of the Light for ever radiant on high must correspond with the release of the same Light secret below in every part down to the deepest caves of subconscient Nature.

> Here the mind's wisdom stopped; it felt complete;
> For nothing more was left to think or know;
> In a spiritual zero it sat throned
> And took its vast silence for the Ineffable.

Right Functionings

The will to enjoy is proper to the vital being but not the choice or reaching after the enjoyment which must be determined and acquired by higher functionings; therefore the vital being must be trained to accept whatever gain or enjoyment comes to it in the right functioning of the life in obedience to the working of the divine Will and to rid itself of craving and attachment. Similarly the heart must be freed from subjection to the cravings of the life-principle and the senses and thus rid itself of the false emotions of fear, wrath, hatred, lust, etc. which constitute the chief impurity of the heart. The will to love is proper to the heart, but here also the choice and reaching after love have to be foregone or tranquillised and the heart taught to love with depth and intensity indeed, but with a calm depth and a settled and equal, not a troubled and disordered intensity. The tranquillisation and mastery of these members is a first condition for the immunity of the understanding from error, ignorance and perversion.

Leave not thy goal to follow a beautiful face.
Only when thou hast climbed above thy mind
And liv'st in the calm vastness of the One
Can love be eternal in the eternal bliss
And Love divine replace the human tie.

Sachchidananda

Sachchidananda is the One with a triple aspect. In the Supreme the three are not three but one — existence is consciousness, consciousness is bliss, and they are thus inseparable, not only inseparable but so much each other that they are not distinct at all. In the superior planes of manifestation they become triune — although inseparable, one can be made more prominent and base or lead the others. In the lower planes below they become separable in appearance, though not in their secret reality, and one can exist phenomenally without the others so that we become aware of what seems to us an inconscient or a painful existence or a consciousness without Ananda. Indeed, without this separation of them in experience pain and ignorance and falsehood and death and what we call inconscience could not have manifested themselves — there could not have been this evolution of a limited and suffering consciousness out of the universal nescience of Matter.

As it is evident from the description of Chinese Tao and the Buddhist Shunya that that is a Nothingness in which all is, so with the negation of consciousness here.

It is the supramental Power that transforms mind, life and body — not the Sachchidananda consciousness which supports impartially everything. But it is by having experience of the Sachchidananda, pure existence-consciousness-bliss, that the ascent to the supramental and the descent of the supramental become (at a much later stage) possible. For first one must get free from the ordinary limitation by the mental, vital and physical formations, and the experience of the Sachchidananda peace, calm, purity and wideness gives this liberation.

All our existence depends on that Existence, it is that which is evolving in us; we are a being of that Existence, a state of consciousness of that Consciousness, an energy of that conscious Energy, a will-to-delight of being, delight of consciousness, delight of energy born of that Delight: this is the root principle of our existence. But our surface formulation of these things is not that, it is a mistranslation into the terms of the Ignorance.

A reflected static realisation of Sachchidananda is possible on any of the cosmic planes, but the full entering into it, the entire union with the Supreme Divine dynamic as well as static, comes with the transcendence.

> The One by whom all live, who lives by none,
> An immeasurable luminous secrecy
> Guarded by the veils of the Unmanifest,
> Above the changing cosmic interlude
> Abode supreme, immutably the same,
> A silent Cause occult, impenetrable,
> Infinite, eternal, unthinkable, alone.

Sacrifice

If we can break down the veil of the intellectual, emotional, sensational mind which our ordinary existence has built between us and the Divine, we can then take up through the Truth-mind all our mental, vital and physical experience and offer it up to the spiritual — this was the secret or mystic sense of the old Vedic "sacrifice" — to be converted into the terms of the infinite truth of Sachchidananda, and we can receive the powers and illuminations of the infinite Existence in forms of a divine knowledge, will and delight to be imposed on our mentality, vitality, physical existence till the lower is transformed into the perfect vessel of the higher.

And the fruit also of the sacrifice of works varies according to the work, according to the intention in the work and according to the spirit that is behind the intention. But all other sacrifices are partial, egoistic, mixed, temporal, incomplete, — even those offered to the highest Powers and Principles keep this character: the result too is partial, limited, temporal, mixed in its reactions, effective only for a minor or intermediate purpose. The one entirely acceptable sacrifice is a last and highest and uttermost self-giving, — it is that surrender made face to face, with devotion and knowledge, freely and without any reserve to One who is at once our immanent Self, the environing constituent All, the Supreme Reality beyond this or any manifestation and, secretly, all these together, concealed everywhere, the immanent Transcendence. For to the soul that wholly gives itself to him, God also gives himself altogether. Only the one who offers his whole nature, finds the Self. Only the one who can give everything, enjoys the Divine All everywhere. Only a supreme self-abandonment attains to the Supreme. Only the sublimation by sacrifice of all that we are, can enable us to embody the Highest and live here in the immanent consciousness of the transcendent Spirit.

> He can recreate himself and all around
> And fashion new the world in which he lives:
> He, ignorant, is the Knower beyond Time,
> He is the Self above Nature, above Fate.

Sadhana

Sadhana means the purification of the nature, the consecration of the being, the opening of the psychic and the inner mind and vital, the contact and presence of the Divine, the realisation of the Divne in all things, surrender, devotion, the widening of the consciousness into the cosmic Consciousness, the Self one in all, the psychic and spiritual transformation of the nature. If these things are neglected and only poetry and mental development and social contact occupy all the time, then that is not sadhana.

In our yoga we begin with the idea, the will, the aspiration of the complete surrender; but at the same time we have to reject the lower nature, deliver our consciousness from it, deliver the self involved in the lower nature by the self rising to freedom in the higher nature. If we do not do this double movement, we are in danger of making a tamasic and therefore unreal surrender, making no effort, no tapas and therefore no progress; or else we may make a rajasic surrender not to the Divine but to some self-made false idea or image of the Divine which masks our rajasic ego or something still worse.

A perfect confidence in the Divine Mother and a vigilance to repel all wrong suggestions and influences is the main law of this yoga.

A quieted mind (not necessarily motionless or silent, though it is good if one can have that at will) and a persistent aspiration in the heart are the two main keys of the yoga.

The object of the sadhana can only be to live in the divine consciousness and to manifest it in life.

Ascend from Nature to divinity's heights;
Face the high gods, crowned with felicity,
Then meet a greater God, thy self beyond Time.
This word was seed of all the thing to be.
A hand from some Greatness opened her heart's locked doors
And showed the work for which her strength was born.

Samadhi

This concentration proceeds by the Idea, using thought, form and name as keys which yield up to the concentrating mind the Truth that lies concealed behind all thought, form and name. By concentration upon the Idea the mental existence which at present we are breaks open the barrier of our mentality and arrives at the state of consciousness, the state of being, the state of power of conscious-being and bliss of conscious-being to which the Idea corresponds and of which it is the symbol, movement and rhythm. Concentration by the Idea is, then, only a means, a key to open us to the superconscient planes of our existence; a certain self-gathered state of our whole existence lifted into that superconscient truth, unity and infinity of self-aware, self-blissful existence is the aim and culmination; and that is the meaning we shall give to the term Samadhi.

> Eternity drew close disguised as Love
> And laid its hand upon the body of Time.
> A little gift comes from the Immensitudes,
> But measureless to life its gain of joy;
> All the untold Beyond is mirrored there.

Samadhi and its Development

In Yoga various devices are used to seal up the doors of the physical sense, some of them physical devices; but the one all-sufficient means is a force of concentration by which the mind is drawn inward to depths where the call of physical things can no longer easily attain to it. A second necessity is to get rid of the intervention of physical sleep. The ordinary habit of the mind when it goes in away from contact with physical things is to fall into the torpor of sleep or its dreams, and therefore when called in for the purposes of Samadhi, it gives or tends to give, at the first chance, by sheer force of habit, not the response demanded, but its usual response of physical slumber. This habit of the mind has to be got rid of; the mind has to learn to be awake in the dream state, in possession of itself, not with the outgoing, but with an ingathered wakefulness in which, though immersed in itself, it exercises all its powers.

Still like a statue on its pedestal,
Lone in the silence and to vastness bared,
Against midnight's dumb abysses piled in front
A columned shaft of fire and light she rose.

Samadhi from Inner to Outer

By an absorbed inner joy and emotion, as in a sealed and secluded chamber of the soul, prepare itself for the delight of union with the divine Beloved, the Master of all bliss, rapture and Ananda.

As it becomes the master of its Samadhi, it is able to pass without any gulf of oblivion from the inner to the outer waking. Secondly, when this has been once done, what is attained in the inner state, becomes easier to acquire by the waking consciousness and to turn into the normal experience, powers, mental status of the waking life.

The subtle mind which is normally eclipsed by the insistence of the physical being, becomes powerful even in the waking state, until even there the enlarging man is able to live in his several subtle bodies as well as in his physical body, to be aware of them and in them, to use their senses, faculties, powers, to dwell in possession of supraphysical truth, consciousness and experience.

A heavenlier function with a finer mode
Lit with its grace man's outward earthliness;
No more slept drugged by Matter's dominance.

Sat Chit Ananda

If you speak of the upper hemisphere as the supernal, there are three, Sat plane, Chit plane and Ananda plane. The supermind could be added as a fourth, as it draws upon the other three and belongs to the upper hemisphere.

The upper hemisphere contains the Divine existence-consciousness-bliss, with the supermind as its means of self-formulation.

The worlds where all beings live and move in ineffable completeness and unalterable oneness, because the Mother carries them safe in her arms forever. There will and knowledge and sensation and all the rest of our faculties, powers, modes of experience are not merely harmonious, concomitant, unified, but are one being of consciousness and power of consciousness.

If supermind were to start here from the beginning as the direct creative Power, a world of the kind we see now would be impossible; it would have been full of the divine Light from the beginning, there would be no involution in the inconscience of Matter, consequently no gradual striving evolution of consciousness in Matter. A line is therefore drawn between the higher half of the universe of consciousness, parārdha, and the lower half, aparārdha. The higher half is constituted of Sat, Chit, Ananda, Mahas (the supramental) — the lower half of mind, life, Matter. This line is the intermediary overmind which, though luminous itself, keeps from us the full indivisible supramental Light, depends on it indeed, but in receiving it, divides, distributes, breaks it up into separated aspects, powers, multiplicities of all kinds, each of which it is possible by a further diminution of consciousness, such as we reach in Mind, to regard as the sole or the chief Truth and all the rest as subordinate or contradictory to it.

There is a consciousness mind cannot touch,
Its speech cannot utter nor its thought reveal.
It has no home on earth, no centre in man,
Yet is the source of all things thought and done,
The fount of the creation and its works.

Satisfaction

In the possession of the divine Beloved all the life of the soul is satisfied and all the relations by which it finds and in which it expresses itself, are wholly fulfilled. He is sought within in the heart and therefore apart from all by an inward-gathered concentration of the being in the soul itself; but he is also seen and loved everywhere where he manifests his being. All the beauty and joy of existence is seen as his joy and beauty; he is embraced by the spirit in all beings; the ecstasy of love enjoyed pours itself out in a universal love; all existence becomes a radiation of its delight and even in its very appearances is transformed into something other than its outward appearance. The world itself is experienced as a play of the divine Delight, a Lila, and that in which the world loses itself is the heaven of beatitude of the eternal.

It is not by insistence on petty demands and satisfactions in the external field pleasing to the vital nature and its pride or desire that you can get the true relation with the Divine in this province.

My mind is a torch lit from the eternal sun,
My life a breath drawn by the immortal Guest,
My mortal body is the Eternal's house.

236

Science of Appearances

The knowledge which the senses and intellectual reasoning from the data of the senses can bring us, is not true knowledge; it is a science of appearances. And even appearances cannot be properly known unless we know first the Reality of which they are images.

Yogic knowledge seeks to enter into a secret consciousness beyond mind which is only occultly here, concealed at the basis of all existence. For it is that consciousness alone that truly knows and only by its possession can we possess God and rightly know the world and its real nature and secret forces.

All this world visible or sensible to us and all too in it that is not visible is merely the phenomenal expression of something beyond the mind and the senses. This Reality is their self and there is one self of all; when that is seized, all other things can then be known in their truth and no longer as now only in their appearance.

All things are the Divine because the Divine is there, but hidden not manifest; when the mind goes out to things, it is not with the sense of the Divine in them, but for the appearances only which conceal the Divine. It is necessary therefore for you as a sadhak to turn entirely to the Mother in whom the Divine is manifest and not run after the appearances, the desire of which or the interest in which prevents you from meeting the Divine. Once the being is consecrated, then it can see the Divine everywhere — and then it can include all things in the one consciousness without a separate interest or desire.

> Small lights kindled by touches of groping thought,
> Incapable of the soul's direct inlook
> She sees by spasms and solders by knowledge-scrap,
> Makes Truth the slave-girl of her indigence,
> Expelling Nature's mystic unity
> Cuts into quantum and mass the moving All;
> She takes for measuring-rod her ignorance.

Self

It is necessary to understand clearly the difference between the evolving soul (psychic being) and the pure Atman, self or spirit. The pure self is unborn, does not pass through death or birth, is independent of birth or body, mind or life or this manifested Nature. It is not bound by these things, not limited, not affected, even though it assumes and supports them.

Atman, our true self, is Brahman, it is pure indivisible Being, self-luminous, self concentrated in consciousness, self-concentrated in force, self-delighted. Its existence is light and bliss. It is timeless, spaceless and free.

The method of the traditional way of knowledge, eliminating all these things arrives at the conception and realisation of a pure conscious existence, self-aware, self-blissful, unconditioned by mind and life and body, and to its ultimate positive experience that is Atman, the Self, the original and essential nature of our existence.

You must remain always aware of the self and the obscure nature must not be felt as the self but as an instrument which has to be put into tune with the self.

The first realisation of the Self or Brahman is often a realisation of something that separates itself from all form, name, action, movement, exists in itself only, regarding the cosmos as only a mass of cinematographic shapes unsubstantial and empty of reality. That was my own first complete realisation of the Nirvana in the Self. That does not mean a wall between Self and Brahman, but a scission between the essential self-existence and the manifested world.

It looks for the source of Light with vision's lamp;
It works to find the doer of all works,
The unfelt Self within who is the guide,
The unknown Self above who is the goal.
All is not here a blinded Nature's task:
A Word, a Wisdom watches us from on high.

Self-Will

Self-will in thought and action has, we have already seen, to be quite renounced if we would be perfect in the way of divine works; it has equally to be renounced if we are to be perfect in divine knowledge. This Self-will means an egoism in the mind which attaches itself to its preferences, its habits, its past or present formations of thought and view and will because it regards them as itself or its own, weaves around them the delicate threads of "I-ness" and "my-ness" and lives in them like a spider in its web. It hates to be disturbed as a spider hates attack on its web, and feels foreign and unhappy if transplanted to fresh viewpoints and formations as a spider feels foreign in another web than its own. This attachment must be entirely excised from the mind. Not only must we give up the ordinary attitude to the world and life to which the unawakened mind clings as its natural element; but we must not remain bound in any mental construction of our own or in any intellectual thought-system or arrangement of religious dogmas or logical conclusions; we must not only cut asunder the snare of the mind and the senses, but flee also beyond the snare of the thinker, the snare of the theologian and the church-builder, the meshes of the Word and the bondage of the Idea. All these are within us waiting to wall in the spirit with forms; but we must always go beyond, always renounce the lesser for the greater, the finite for the Infinite; we must be prepared to proceed from illumination to illumination, from experience to experience, from soul-state to soul-state so as to reach the utmost transcendence of the Divine and its utmost universality. Nor must we attach ourselves even to the truths we hold most securely, for they are but forms and expressions of the Ineffable who refuses to limit himself to any form or expression; always we must keep ourselves open to the higher Word from above that does not confine itself to its own sense and the light of the Thought that carries in it its own opposites.

In the ordinary Nature we live in the Ignorance and do not know the Divine. The forces of the ordinary Nature are undivine forces because they weave a veil of ego and desire and unconsciousness which conceals the Divine from us. To get into the higher and deeper consciousness which knows and lives luminously in the Divine, we have to get rid of the forces of the lower nature and open to the action of the Divine Shakti which will transform our consciousness into that of Divine Nature.

Only for good the secret Will can work.
Our destiny is written in double terms:
Through Nature's contraries we draw near God;
Out of darkness we still grow to light.

Sense Mind

The sense mind which merely consists of the recording of perceptions of all kinds without distinction whether they be right or wrong, true or mere illusory phenomena, penetrating or superficial.

Manas, the sense mind, depends in our ordinary consciousness on the physical organs of receptive sense for knowledge and on the organs of the body for action directed towards the objects of sense. The superficial and outward action of the senses is physical and nervous in its character, and they may easily be thought to be merely results of nerve-action.

Man's initial mentality is not at all a thing of reason and will; it is an animal, physical or sense mentality which constitutes its whole experience from the impressions made on it by the external world and by its own embodied consciousness which responds to the outward stimulus of this kind of experience.

A half-enlightened physical or sense mentality is the ordinary type of the mind of man.

This sense mind, this intelligence, this reason, however inadequate, are the instruments in which he has learned to put his trust and he has erected by their means certain foundations which he is not over-willing to disturb and has traced limits outside of which he feels all to be confusion, uncertainty and a perilous adventure.

Manas, sense-mind, is the activity, emerging from the basic consciousness, which makes up the whole essentiality of what we call sense. Sight, hearing, taste, smell, touch are really properties of the mind, not of the body.

The plane we inhabit is the plane of Matter; the present predominant principle in our nature is the mental intelligence with the sense-mind, which depends upon Matter, as its support and pedestal. As a consequence, the preoccupation of the mental intelligence and its powers with the material existence as it is shown to it through the senses, and with life as it has been formulated in a compromise between life and matter, is a special stamp of the constitutional Ignorance.

They worked for the body's wants, they craved no more,
Content to breathe, to feel, to sense, to act,
Identified with the spirit's outer shell.

Service to Humanity

If light, peace, deliverance, a better state of existence are to come, they must descend into the soul from something wider than the individual but also from something higher than the collective ego. Altruism, philanthropy, the service of mankind are in themselves mental or moral ideals, not laws of the spiritual life. It is the transcendent Source which we must seek and serve.

The greatest service to humanity, the surest foundation for its true progress, happiness and perfection is to prepare or find the way by which the individual and the collective man can transcend the ego and live in its true self, no longer bound to ignorance, incapacity, disharmony and sorrow.

There are many things in the ordinary man of which he is not conscious, because the vital hides them from the mind and gratifies them without the mind realising what is the force that is moving the action — thus things that are done under the plea of altruism, philanthropy, service, etc. are largely moved by ego which hides itself behind these justifications; in yoga the secret motive has to be pulled out from behind the veil, exposed and got rid of. Secondly, some things are suppressed in the ordinary life and remain lying in the nature, suppressed but not eliminated; they may rise up any day or they may express themselves in various nervous forms or other disorders of the mind or vital or body without it being evident what is their real cause. This has been recently discovered by European psychologists and much emphasised, even exaggerated in a new science called psycho-analysis. Here again, in sadhana one has to become conscious of these suppressed impulses and eliminate them — this may be called rising up, but that does not mean that they have to be raised up into action but only raised up before the consciousness so as to be cleared out of the being.

> Happiest who stand on faith as on a rock.
> But I must pass leaving the ended search,
> Truth's rounded outcome firm, immutable
> And this harmonic building of world-fact,
> This ordered knowledge of apparent things.
> Here I can stay not, for I seek my soul.

Shakti

The power of the Infinite and the Eternal.

Shakti, Will, Power is the driver of the worlds and, whether it be Knowledge-Force or Love-Force or Life-Force or Action-Force or Body-Force, is always spiritual in its origin and divine in its native character. It is the use of it made in the Ignorance by brute, man or Titan that has to be cast aside and replaced by its greater natural — even if to us supernormal — action led by an inner consciousness which is in tune with the Infinite and the Eternal. The integral Yoga cannot reject the works of Life and be satisfied with an inward experience only; it has to go inward in order to change the outward, making the Life-Force a part and a working of a Yoga-Energy which is in touch with the Divine and divine in its guidance.

Aware of the Divine as the Master of our being and action, we can learn to become channels of his Shakti, the Divine Puissance, and act according to her dictates or her rule of light and power within us. Our action will not then be mastered by our vital impulse or governed by a mental standard, for she acts according to the permanent yet plastic truth of things, — not that which the mind constructs, but the higher, deeper and subtler truth of each movement and circumstance as it is known to the supreme knowledge and demanded by the supreme will in the universe. The liberation of the will follows upon the liberation in knowledge and is its dynamic consequence; it is knowledge that purifies, it is truth that liberates: evil is the fruit of a spiritual ignorance and it will disappear only by the growth of a spiritual consciousness and the light of spiritual knowledge.

If behind your devotion and surrender you make a cover for your desires, egoistic demands and vital insistences, if you put these things in place of the true aspiration or mix them with it and try to impose them on the Divine Shakti, then it is idle to invoke the divine Grace to transform you.

The Absolute, the Perfect, the Alone;
Has entered with his silence into space:
He has fashioned these countless persons of one self;
He lives in all, who lived in his vast alone;
Space is himself and Time is only he.

Sheaths

Man, for instance, has, besides his gross physical body, subtler sheaths or bodies by which he lives behind the veil in direct connection with supraphysical planes of consciousness and can be influenced by their powers, movements and beings. What takes place in life has always behind it pre-existent movements and forms in the occult vital planes; what takes place in mind presupposes pre-existent movements and forms in the occult mental planes. That is an aspect of things which becomes more and more evident, insistent and important, the more we progress in a dynamic yoga.

We use, normally, only our corporeal senses and live almost wholly in the body and the physical vitality and the physical mind, and it is not directly through these that the life-world enters into relations with us. That is done through other sheaths of our being, — so they are termed in the Upanishads, — other bodies, as they are called in a later terminology, the mental sheath or subtle body in which our true mental being lives and the life sheath or vital body which is more closely connected with the physical or food-sheath and forms with it the gross body of our complex existence. These possess powers, senses, capacities which are always secretly acting in us, are connected with and impinge upon our physical organs and the plexuses of our physical life and mentality. By self-development we can become aware of them, possess our life in them, get through them into conscious relation with the life-world and other worlds and use them also for a more subtle experience and more intimate knowledge of the truths, facts and happenings of even the material world itself. We can by this self-development live more or less fully on planes of our existence other than the material which is now all in all to us.

What has been said of the life-world applies with the necessary differences to still higher planes of the cosmic existence.

But all this must not be taken in too rigid and mechanical a sense. It is an immense plastic movement full of the play of possibilities and must be seized by a flexible and subtle tact or sense in the seeing consciousness. It cannot be reduced to a too rigorous logical or mathematical formula. Two or three points must be pressed in order that this plasticity may not be lost to our view.

If we regard the vital or the subtle physical plane, we see great ranges of it, (most of it), existing in themselves, without any relation with the material world and with no movement to affect or influence it, still less to precipitate a corresponding manifestation in the physical formula. At most we can say that the existence of anything in the vital, subtle physical or any other plane creates a possibility for a corresponding movement of manifestation in the physical world. But something more is needed to turn that static or latent possibility into a dynamic potentiality or an actual urge towards a material creation. That something may be a call from the material plane, e.g., some force or someone on the physical existence entering into touch with a supraphysical power or world or part of it and moved to bring it down into the earth-life. Or it may be an impulse in the vital or other plane itself, e.g., a vital being moved to extend his action towards the earth and establish there a kingdom for himself or the play of the forces for which he stands in his own domain. Or it may be a pressure from above; let us say, some supramental or mental power precipitating its formation from above and developing forms and movements on the vital level as a means of transit to its self-creation in the material world. Or it may be all these things acting together, in which case there is the greatest possibility of an effective creation.

Next, as a consequence, it follows that only a limited part of the action of the vital or other higher plane is concerned with the earth-existence. But even this creates a mass of possibilities which is far greater than the earth can at one time manifest or contain in its own less plastic formulas. All these possibilities do not realise themselves; some fail altogether and leave at the most an idea that comes to nothing; some try seriously and are repelled and defeated and, even if in action for a time, come to nothing. Others effectuate a half manifestation, and this is the most usual result, the more so as these vital or other supraphysical forces come into conflict and have not only to overcome the resistance of the physical consciousness and of matter, but their own internecine resistance to each other. A certain number succeed in precipitating their results in a more complete and successful creation, so that if you compare this creation with its original in the higher plane, there is something like a close resemblance or even an apparently exact reproduction or translation from the supraphysical to the physical formula. And yet even there the exactness is only apparent; the very fact of translation into another substance and another rhythm of manifestation makes a difference. It is something new that has manifested and it is that that makes the creation worth while. What for instance would be the utility of a supramental creation on earth if it were just the same thing as a supramental creation on the supramental plane? It is that, in principle, but yet something else, a triumphant new self-discovery of the Divine in conditions that are not elsewhere.

Our souls can visit in great lonely hours
Still regions of imperishable Light,
All-seeing eagle-peaks of silent Power
And moon-flame oceans of swift fathomless Bliss
And calm immensities of spirit Space.

Silence

The individual ego must cease to strive, the mind fall silent, the desire-will learn not to initiate. Our personality must join its source and all thought and initiation come from above.

To get the capacity of this silence and peace is a most important step in the sadhana. My whole Yoga is founded upon and it is through it that there come afterwards all the inexhaustible riches of a greater Knowledge, Will and Joy. The cup has often to be emptied before it can be new-filled; the yogin ought not to be afraid of emptiness or silence. It is the spirit that feels a release in the silence empty of all mental or other activities, for in that silence it becomes self-aware.

A silent mind is a result of yoga; the ordinary mind is never silent. The thinkers and philosophers do not have the silent mind. It is the active mind they have, only of course they concentrate so the common incoherent mentalising stops. There are always two things that can rise up and assail the silence, — vital suggestions, the physical mind's mechanical recurrences. Calm rejection for both is the cure.

The psychic is the soul that develops in the evolution — the spirit is the Self that is not affected by the evolution, it is above it — only it is covered or concealed by the activity of mind, vital and the body. The removal of this covering is the release of the spirit — and it is removed when there is a full and wide spiritual silence.

The Silence bears the Eternal's great dumb seal,
His light inspires the eternal Word;
He is the Immobile's deep and deathless hush.

Silencing the Mind

It was my great debt to Lele that he showed me this. "Sit in meditation," he said, "but do not think, look only at your mind; you will see thoughts coming into it; before they can enter throw these away from your mind till your mind is capable of entire silence." I had never heard before of thoughts coming visibly into the mind from outside, but I did not think either of questioning the truth or the possibility, I simply sat down and did it. In a moment my mind became silent as a windless air on a high mountain summit and then I saw one thought and then another coming in a concrete way from outside; I flung them away before they could enter and take hold of the brain and in three days I was free. From that moment, in principle, the mental being in me became a free Intelligence, a universal Mind, not limited to the narrow circle of personal thought as a labourer in a thought factory, but a receiver of knowledge from all the hundred realms of being and free to choose what it willed in this vast sight-empire and thought-empire.

> His centre was no more in earthly mind,
> A power of seeing silence filled his limps:
> Caught by a voiceless white epiphany
> Into a vision that surpasses forms,
> Into a living that surpasses life,
> He neared the still consciousness sustaining all.

Sincerity

A will for purity, a readiness for obedience to the Truth, for surrender to the Highest, a readiness to lose or to subject to a divine yoke the limiting and self-affirming ego.

Sincere is simply an adjective meaning that the will must be a true will. If you simply think "I aspire" and do things inconsistent with the aspiration, or follow your desires or open yourself to contrary influences, then it is not a sincere will.

Be true to your true self always — that is the real sincerity. Persist and conquer.

If there is too much egoism in the nature of the seeker or a strong passion or an excessive ambition, vanity or other dominating weakness, or an obscurity of the mind or a vacillating will or a weakness of the life-force or an unsteadiness in it or want of balance, he is likely to be seized on through these deficiencies and to be frustrated or to deviate, misled from the true way of the inner life and seeking into false paths, or to be left wandering about in an intermediate chaos of experiences and fail to find his way out into the true realisation. These perils were well-known to a past spiritual experience and have been met by imposing the necessity of initiation, of discipline, of methods of purification and testing by ordeal, of an entire submission to the directions of the path-finder or path-leader, one who has realised the Truth and himself possesses and is able to communicate the light, the experience, a guide who is strong to take by the hand and carry over difficult passages as well as to instruct and point out the way. But even so the dangers will be there and can only be surmounted if there is or there grows up a complete sincerity.

There is one indispensable condition, sincerity.
Let Fate do with me what she will or can;
I am stronger than death and greater than my fate;
My love shall outlast the world, doom falls from me
Helpless against my immortality.
Fate's law may change, but not my spirit's will.

Soul

The soul is a spark of the Divine in the heart of the living creatures of Nature. It is not seated above the manifested being; it enters into the manifestation of the self, consents to be a part of its natural phenomenal becoming, supports its evolution in the world of material Nature. It carries with it at first an undifferentiated power of the divine consciousness containing all possibilities which have not yet taken form but to which it is the function of evolution to give form. This spark of Divinity is there in all terrestrial living beings from the earth's highest to its lowest creatures.

It belongs to the transcendent and because of it we can open to the higher Nature beyond.

It is necessary to understand clearly the difference between the evolving soul (psychic being) and the pure Atman, self or spirit. The pure self is unborn, does not pass through death or birth, is independent of birth or body, mind or life or this manifested Nature. It is not bound by these things, not limited, not affected, even though it assumes and supports them. The soul, on the contrary, is something that comes down into birth and passes through death — although it does not itself die, for it is immortal — from one state to another, from the earth plane to other planes and back again to the earth-existence. It goes on with this progression from life to life through an evolution which leads it up to the human state and evolves through it all a being of itself which we call the psychic being that supports the evolution and develops a physical, a vital, a mental human consciousness as its instruments of world-experience and of a disguised, imperfect, but growing self-expression. All this it does from behind a veil showing something of its divine self only in so far as the imperfection of the instrumental being will allow it. But a time comes when it is able to prepare to come out from behind the veil, to take command and turn all the instrumental nature towards a divine fulfilment. This is the beginning of the true spiritual life. The soul is able now to make itself ready for a higher evolution of manifested consciousness than the mental human — it can pass from the mental to the spiritual and through degrees of the spiritual to the supramental state. Till then there is no reason why it should cease from birth, it cannot in fact do so. If having reached the spiritual state, it wills to pass out of the terrestrial manifestation, it may indeed do so — but there is also possible a higher manifestation, in the Knowledge and not in the Ignorance.

The soul, the psychic being is in direct touch with the divine Truth, but is hidden in man by the mind, the vital being and the physical nature.

The mind thinks and the vital craves, but the soul feels and knows the Divine.

The soul or psyche is immutable only in the sense that it contains all the possibilities of the Divine within it, but it has to evolve them and in its evolution it assumes the form of a developing psychic individual evolving in the manifestation the individual Prakriti and taking part in the evolution. It is the spark of the Divine Fire that grows behind the mind, vital and physical by means of the psychic being until it is able to transform the Prakriti of Ignorance into a Prakriti of Knowledge.

The soul is the witness, upholder, experiencer, but it is master only in theory, in fact it is not-master, anisa, so long as it consents to the Ignorance. For that is a general consent which implies that the Prakriti (Nature) gambols about with the Purusha (Soul) and does pretty well what she likes with him. When he wants to get back his mastery, make the theoretical practical, he needs a lot of tapasya to do it.

> In a vast of Truth and Consciousness and Light
> The soul looked out from its felicity.
> It felt the Spirit's interminable bliss,
> It knew itself deathless, timeless, spaceless, one,
> It saw the Eternal, lived in the Infinite.

The Soul's Liberation

The human soul's individual liberation and enjoyment of union with the Divine in spiritual being, consciousness and delight must always be the first object of the Yoga; its free enjoyment of the cosmic unity of the Divine becomes a second object; but out of that a third appears, the effectuation of the meaning of the divine unity with all beings by a sympathy and participation in the spiritual purpose of the Divine in humanity. The individual Yoga then turns from its separateness and becomes a part of the collective Yoga of the divine Nature in the human race. The liberated individual being, united with the Divine in self and spirit, becomes in his natural being a self-perfecting instrument for the perfect outflowering of the Divine in humanity.

The liberation of the individual soul is therefore the keynote of the definite divine action; it is the primary divine necessity and the pivot on which all else turns. It is the point of Light at which the intended complete self-manifestation in the Many begins to emerge. But the liberated soul extends its perception of unity horizontally as well as vertically. Its unity with the transcendent One is incomplete without its unity with the cosmic Many. And that lateral unity translates itself by a multiplication, a reproduction of its own liberated state at other points in the Multiplicity.

Therefore, whenever even a single soul is liberated, there is a tendency to an extension and even to an outburst of the same divine self-consciousness in other individual souls of our terrestrial humanity and, perhaps even beyond the terrestrial consciousness.

The Absolute, the Perfect, the Immune,
One who is in us as our secret self,
Our mask of imperfection has assumed,
He has made this tenement of flesh his own,
His image in the human measure cast
That to his divine measure we might rise.

Soul and Nature or Purusha and Prakriti

There are two elements in the existence of living beings, of human beings at least if not of all cosmos, — a dual being, Nature and the soul.

The Purusha is, says the Gita, witness, upholder, source of the sanction, knower, lord, enjoyer; Prakriti executes, it is the active principle and must have an operation corresponding to the attitude of the Purusha. The soul may assume, if it wishes, the poise of the pure witness, saksi; it may look on at the action of Nature as a thing from which it stands apart; it watches, but does not itself participate. We have seen the importance of this quietistic capacity; it is the basis of the movement of withdrawal by which we can say of everything, — body, life, mental action, thought, sensation, emotion, — "This is Prakriti working in the life, mind and body, it is not myself, it is not even mine," or "This is imposed on me, but really external to myself," and come to the soul's separation from these things and their quiescence.

As the pure Witness, the soul refuses the function of upholder or sustainer of Nature. The upholder, bhartā, is another, God or Force or Maya, but not the soul, which only admits the reflection of the natural action upon its watching consciousness, but not any responsibility for maintaining or continuing it. It does not say "All this is in me and maintained by me, an activity of my being," but at the most "This is imposed on me, but really external to myself." Unless there is a clear and real duality in existence, this cannot be the whole truth of the matter; the soul is the upholder also, it supports in its being the energy which unrolls the spectacle of the cosmos and which conducts its energies.

This status of an inner passivity and an outer action independent of each other is a state of entire spiritual freedom. The Yogin, as the Gita says, even in acting does no actions, for it is not he, but universal Nature directed by the Lord of Nature which is at work. He is not bound by his works, nor do they leave any after effects or consequences in his mind, nor cling to or leave any mark on his soul; they vanish and are dissolved by their very execution and

254

leave the immutable self unaffected and the soul unmodified. Therefore this would seem to be the poise the uplifted soul ought to take, if it has still to preserve any relations with human action in the world-existence, an unalterable silence, tranquillity, passivity within, an action without regulated by the universal Will and Wisdom which works, as the Gita says, without being involved in, bound by or ignorantly attached to its works. And certainly this poise of a perfect activity founded upon a perfect inner passivity is that which the Yogin has to possess...

This is the knot that ties together the stars:
The Two who are one are the secret of all power,
The Two who are one are the might and right in things.
His soul, silent, supports the world and her,
His acts are her commandment's registers.

Spirit

Our true being, of which we become aware when the higher self-knowledge comes. It presides over the individual and its developments; itself it is plunged in the Divine and one with the Eternal for ever.

We can indeed become aware of the true Self or Spirit in ourselves by turning our sense and vision inward; we can discover too the same Self or Spirit in the external world and its phenomena by plunging them there also inward through the veil of names and forms to that which dwells in these or else stands behind them. Our normal consciousness through this inward look may become by reflection aware of the infinite being, consciousness and delight of the Self and share in its passive or static infinity of these things.

The Jivatma or spirit is self-existent above the manifested or instrumental being — it is superior to birth and death, always the same, it is the individual Self or Atman; the eternal true being of the individual. The soul is a spark of the Divine in the heart of the living creatures of Nature. It is not seated above the manifested being; it enters into the manifestation of the self, consents to be a part It is necessary to understand clearly the difference between the evolving soul (psychic being) and the pure Atman, self or spirit. The pure self is unborn, does not pass through death or birth, is independent of birth or body, mind or life or this manifested Nature. It is not bound by these things, not limited, not affected, even though it assumes and supports them.

Spirit is the crown of universal existence; Matter is its basis; Mind is the link between the two. Spirit is that which is eternal; Mind and Matter are its workings. Spirit is that which is concealed and has to be revealed; mind and body are the means by which it seeks to reveal itself. Spirit is the image of the Lord of the Yoga; mind and body are the means He has provided for reproducing that image in phenomenal existence. All Nature is an attempt at a progressive revelation of the concealed Truth, a more and more successful reproduction of the divine image.

The Jivatman is for me the Unborn who presides over the individual being and its developments, associated with it but above it and them and who by the very nature of his existence knows himself as universal and transcendent no less than individual and feels the Divine to be his origin, the truth of his being, the master of his nature, the very stuff of his existence. He is plunged in the Divine and one with the Eternal for ever ...

All earth shall be the Spirit's manifest home,
Hidden no more by the body and the life,
Hidden no more by the mind's ignorance;
An unerring hand shall shape event and act.

Spiritual Experience

If the rift in the lid of mind is made, what happens is an opening of vision to something above us or a rising up towards it or a descent of its powers into our being. What we see by the opening of vision is an Infinity above us, an eternal Presence or an infinite Existence, an infinity of consciousness, an infinity of bliss, — a boundless Self, a boundless Light, a boundless Power, a boundless Ecstasy. It may be that for a long time all that is obtained is the occasional or frequent or constant vision of it and a longing and aspiration, but without anything further, because, although something in the mind, heart or other part of the being has opened to this experience, the lower nature as a whole is too heavy and obscure as yet for more.

A light descends and touches or envelops or penetrates the lower being, the mind, the life or the body; or a presence or a power or a stream of knowledge pours in waves or currents, or there is a flood of bliss or a sudden ecstasy; the contact with the superconscient has been established. For such experiences repeat themselves till they become normal, familiar and well-understood, revelatory of their contents and their significance which may have at first been involved and wrapped into secrecy by the figure of the covering experience. For a knowledge from above begins to descend, frequently, constantly, then uninterruptedly, and to manifest in the mind's quietude or silence; intuitions and inspirations, revelations born of a greater sight, a higher truth and wisdom, enter into the being, a luminous intuitive discrimination works which dispels all darkness of understanding or dazzling confusions, puts all in order; a new consciousness begins to form, the mind of a high wide self-existent thinking knowledge or an illumined or an intuitive or an overmental consciousness with new forces of thought or sight and a greater power of direct spiritual realisation which is more than thought or sight, a greater becoming in the spiritual substance of our present being; the heart and the sense become subtle, intense, large to embrace all existence, to see God, to feel and hear and touch the Eternal, to make a deeper and closer unity of self and the world in a transcendent realisation. Other decisive experiences, other changes of consciousness determine themselves which are corollaries and consequences of this fundamental change. No limit can be fixed to this revolution; for it is in its nature an invasion by the Infinite.

Experience is a word that covers almost all the happenings in yoga, only when something gets settled then it is no longer an experience but part of the siddhi.

The descent is that of the powers of the higher consciousness which is above the head. It usually descends from centre to centre till it has occupied the whole being. But at the beginning the action is very variable. It is only when the Peace from above has not only descended but established itself in the whole system that there is a continuous action. The descent comes in order to transform the consciousness but the transformation takes time. It is not done all in a moment.

On a height he stood that looked towards greater heights.
Our early approaches to the Infinite
Are sunrise splendours on a marvellous verge
While lingers yet unseen the glorious sun.

Spiritual Man

The spiritual man is one who has discovered his soul: he has found his self and lives in that, is conscious of it, has the joy of it; he needs nothing external for his completeness of existence.

He will have the cosmic consciousness, sense, feeling, by which all objective life will become part of his subjective existence and by which he will realise, perceive, feel, see, hear the Divine in all forms; all forms and movements will be realised, sensed, seen, heard, felt as if taking place within his vast self of being. The world will be connected not only with his outer but with his inner life. He will not meet the world only in its external form by an external contact; he will be inwardly in contact with the inner self of things and beings: he will meet consciously their inner as well as their outer reactions; he will be aware of that within them of which they themselves will not be aware, act upon all with an inner comprehension, encounter all with a perfect sympathy and sense of oneness but also an independence which is not overmastered by any contact.

In all spiritual living the inner life is the thing of first importance; the spiritual man lives always within, and in a world of the Ignorance that refuses to change he has to be in a certain sense separate from it and to guard his inner life against the intrusion and influence of the darker forces of the Ignorance: he is out of the world even when he is within it; if he acts upon it, it is from the fortress of his inner spiritual being where in the inmost sanctuary he is one with the Supreme Existence or the soul and God are alone together.

A mightier race shall inhabit the mortal's world.
On Nature's luminous tops, on the Spirit's ground,
The superman shall reign as king of life,
Make earth almost the mate and peer of heaven
And lead towards God and truth man's ignorant earth
And lift towards godhead his mortality.

260

Spiritual Mind

The spiritual mind is a mind which, in its fullness, is aware of the Self, reflecting the Divine, seeing and understanding the nature of the Self and its relations with the manifestation, living in that or in contact with it, calm, wide and awake to higher knowledge, not perturbed by the play of the forces. When it gets its full liberated movement, its central station is very usually felt above the head, though its influence can extend downward through all the being and outward through space.

The ordinary mind is at its highest the free intelligence, receiving perhaps intuitions and intimations from above which it intellectualises. It is on the surface and sees things from outside except in so far as it is helped by intuition and other powers to see a little deeper. When this ordinary mind opens within to inner mind and psychic and above to higher mind and higher consciousness generally, then it begins to be spiritualised and its highest ranges merge into the spiritual mind-consciousness of which this higher mind can be a beginning. This merging is part of the spiritual transformation.

The sage and seer live in the spiritual mind, their thought or their vision is governed and moulded by an inner or a greater divine light of knowledge; the devotee lives in the spiritual aspiration of the heart, its self-offering and its seeking; the saint is moved by the awakened psychic being in the inner heart grown powerful to govern the emotional and vital being; the others stand in the vital kinetic nature driven by a higher spiritual energy and turned by it towards an inspired action, a God given work or mission, the service of some divine Power, idea or ideal.

Once the inner being once thoroughly establishes its separateness, even oceans of inertia cannot prevent it from keeping it. It is the first thing to be done in order to have a secure basis in the yoga, to establish thoroughly this separateness. It comes most usually when the peace is thoroughly fixed in the inner parts, then the separateness also becomes fixed and permanent.

> All here was known by a spiritual sense.
> Thought was not there but a knowledge near and one
> Seized on all things by a moved identity,

A sympathy of self with other selves.
The touch of consciousness on consciousness
And being's look on being with inmost gaze
And heart laid bare to heart without walls of speech
And the unanimity of seeing minds
In myriad forms luminous with the one God.

Spiritual Sight

As soon as the sight, for example, becomes altered under the influence of the supramental seeing, the eye gets a new and transfigured vision of things and of the world around us. Itssight acquires an extraordinary totality and an immediate and embracing precision in which the whole and every detail stand out at once in the complete harmony and vividness of the significance meant by Nature in the object and its realisation of the idea in form, executed in a triumph of substantial being. It is as if the eye of the poet and artist had replaced the vague or trivial unseeing normal vision, but singularly spiritualised and glorified, — as if indeed it were the sight of the supreme divine Poet and Artist in which we were participating and there were given to us the full seeing of his truth and intention in his design of the universe and of each thing in the universe. There is an unlimited intensity which makes all that is seen a revelation of the glory of quality and idea and form and colour. The physical eye seems then to carry in itself a spirit and a consciousness which sees not only the physical aspect of the object but the soul of quality in it, the vibration of energy, the light and force and spiritual substance of which it is made. Thus there comes through the physical sense to the total sense consciousness within and behind the vision a revelation of the soul of the thing seen and of the universal Spirit that is expressing itself in this objective form of its own conscious being

> The high gods look on man and watch and choose
> Today's impossibles for the future's base.
> His transience trembles with the Eternal's touch,
> His barriers cede beneath the Infinite's tread;
> The Immortals have their entries in his life;
> The Ambassadors of the Unseen draw near.

Spiritualisation

One must first acquire an inner Yogic consciousness and replace by it our ordinary view of things, natural movements, motives of life; one must revolutionise the whole present build up of our being. Next we have to go still deeper discover our veiled psychic entity and in its light and under its government psychise our inner and outer parts, turn mind-nature, life-nature, body-nature and all our mental, vital, physical action and states and movements into a conscious instrumentation of the soul. Afterwards or concurrently we have to spiritualise the being in its entirety by a descent of a Divine Light, Force, Purity, Knowledge, freedom and wideness. It is necessary to break down the limits of the personal mind, life and physicality, dissolve the ego, enter into the cosmic consciousness, realise the self, acquire a spiritualised and universalised mind and heart, life-force, physical consciousness. Then only the passage into supramental consciousness begins to become possible, and even then there is a difficult ascent to make each stage of which is a separate arduous achievement.

The supramental change is a thing decreed and inevitable in the evolution of the earth's consciousness; for its upward ascent is not ended and mind is not its last summit.

On the pale shores of conscious foaming straits
That flow beneath a grey tormented sky
Two powers from one ecstasy born
Pace near, but parted in the life of man:
One leans to earth, the other yearns to the sky:
Heaven in its rapture dreams of perfect earth,
Earth in its sorrow dreams of perfect heaven.

Spirituality

Spirituality is in its essence an awakening to the inner reality of our being, to a spirit, self, soul which is other than our mind, life and body, an inner aspiration to know, to feel, to be that, to enter into contact with the greater Reality beyond and pervading the universe which inhabits also our own being, to be in communion with It and union with It, and a turning, a conversion, a transformation of our whole being as a result of the aspiration, the contact, the union, a growth or waking into a new becoming or new being, a new self, a new nature.

Spirituality can only come by opening of the mind, vital and physical to the inmost soul, to the higher Self, to the Divine, and their subordination to the spiritual forces and instrumentation as channels of the inner Light, the higher Knowledge and Power

It is spirituality when you begin to become aware of another consciousness than the ego and begin to live in it or under its influence more and more. It is that consciousness wide, infinite, self-existent, pure of ego etc. which is called Spirit (Self, Brahman, Divine), so this necessarily must be the meaning of spirituality.

Reason or no reason, desire, selfishness, jealousy, demand, anger, etc. have no place in the spiritual life.

You must always discourage desire and selfishness in you and all that comes from them such as jealousy, claim, anger etc. It is no use alleging that there are good reasons for their rising — even if all the alleged reasons were true, they would not justify your indulging them, for in a sadhak nothing can justify that.

> Even now hints of a luminous Truth like stars
> Arise in the mind-mooned splendour of Ignorance;
> Even now the deathless Lover's touch we feel:
> If the chamber's door is even a little ajar,
> What then can hinder God from stealing in
> Or who forbid his kiss on the sleeping soul?

Splendors

There can be the experience of a spiritual and boundless Ananda on the plane of matter, on the plane of life, on the plane of mind as well as on the gnostic truth-plane of knowledge and above it. And the Yogin who enters into these lesser realisations, may find them so complete and compelling that he will imagine there is nothing greater, nothing beyond it. For each of the divine principles contains in itself the whole potentiality of all the other six notes of our being; each plane of Nature can have its own perfection of these notes under its own conditions. But the integral perfection can come only by a mounting ascent of the lowest into the highest and an incessant descent of the highest into the lowest till all becomes one at once solid block and plastic sea-stuff of the Truth infinite and eternal.

> My dreadful hands laid on thy bosom shall force
> Thy being bathed in fiercest longings' streams.
> Thou shalt discover the one and quivering note
> And cry, the harp of all my melodies,
> And roll, my foaming wave in seas of love.

Sri Aurobindo

It is true that I want the supramental not for myself but for the earth and souls born on the earth, and certainly therefore I cannot object if anybody wants the supramental. But there are the conditions. He must want the divine Will first and the soul's surrender and spiritual realisation (through works, bhakti, knowledge, self-perfection) on the way.

My own life and my yoga have always been, since my coming to India, both this-worldly and other-worldly without any exclusiveness on either side. All human interests are, I suppose, this-worldly and most of them have entered into my mental field and some, like politics, into my life, but at the same time, since I set foot on the Indian soil on the Apollo Bunder in Bombay, I began to have spiritual experiences, but these were not divorced from this world but had an inner and infinite bearing on it, such as a feeling of the Infinite pervading material space and the Immanent inhabiting material objects and bodies. At the same time I found myself entering supraphysical worlds and planes with influences and an effect from them upon the material plane, so I could make no sharp divorce or irreconcilable opposition between what I have called the two ends of existence and all that lies between them. For me all is Brahman and I find the Divine everywhere. Everyone has the right to throw away this-worldliness and choose other-worldliness only, and if he finds peace by that choice he is greatly blessed. I, personally, have not found it necessary to do this in order to have peace. In my yoga also I found myself moved to include both worlds in my purview — the spiritual and the material — and to try to establish the Divine Consciousness and the Divine Power in men's hearts and earthly life, not for a personal salvation only but for a life divine here. This seems to me as spiritual an aim as any and the fact of this life taking up earthly pursuits and earthly things into its scope cannot, I believe, tarnish its spirituality or alter its Indian character. This at least has always been my view and experience of the reality and nature of the world and things and the Divine: it seemed to me as nearly as possible the integral truth about them and I have therefore spoken of the pursuit of it as the integral yoga. Everyone is, of course, free to reject and disbelieve in this kind of integrality or to believe in the spiritual necessity of an entire other-worldliness altogether, but that would make the exercise of my yoga impossible. My yoga can include indeed a full experience of the other worlds, the plane of the Supreme Spirit and the other planes in between and their possible effects upon our life and the material world; but it will be quite possible to insist only on the realisation of the Supreme Being or Ishwara even in one aspect, Shiva, Krishna as Lord of the world and Master of ourselves and our works or else the Universal Sachchidananda, and attain to the essential results of this yoga and afterwards to proceed from them to the integral results if one accepted the ideal of the divine life and this material world conquered by the Spirit. It is this view and experience of things and of the truth of existence that enabled me to write The Life Divine and Savitri. The realisation of the Supreme, the Ishwara, is certainly the essential thing; but to approach Him with love and devotion and bhakti, to serve Him with one's works and to know Him, not necessarily by the intellectual cognition, but in a spiritual experience, is also essential in the path of the integral yoga.

I know that I can lift man's soul to God,
I know that he can bring the Immortal down.
Our will labours permitted by thy will.

J believe that you are quite capable of attaining this and realising the Divine and I have never been able to share your constantly recurring doubts about your capacity and their persistent recurrence is not a valid ground for believing that they can never be overcome. Such a persistent recurrence has been a feature in the sadhana of many who have finally emerged and reached the goal; even the sadhana of very great yogis has not been exempt from such violent and constant recurrences, they have sometimes been special objects of such persistent assaults, as I have indeed indicated in Savitri in more places than one, and that was indeed founded on my own experience. In the nature of these recurrences there is usually a constant return of the same adverse experiences, the same adverse resistance, thoughts destructive of all belief and faith and confidence in the future of the sadhana, frustrating doubts of what one has known as the truth, urgings to abandonment of the yoga or to other disastrous counsels of déchéance. The course taken by the attacks is not indeed the same for all, but still they have strong

family resemblance. One can eventually overcome if one begins to realise the nature and source of these assaults and acquires the faculty of observing them, bearing, without being involved or absorbed into their gulf, finally becoming the witness of their phenomena and understanding them and refusing the mind's sanction even when the vital is still tossed in the whirl and the most outward physical mind still reflects the adverse suggestions. In the end, these attacks lose their power and fall away from the nature; the recurrence becomes feeble or has no power to last: even, if the detachment is strong enough, they can be cut out very soon or at once. The strongest attitude to take is to regard these things as what they really are: incursions of dark forces from outside taking advantage of certain openings in the physical mind or the vital part, but not a real part of oneself or spontaneous creation in one's own nature. To create a confusion and darkness in the physical mind and to throw into it or awake in it mistaken ideas, dark thoughts, false impressions is a favourite method of these assailants, and if they can get the support of this mind from over-confidence in its own correctness or the natural rightness of its impressions and inferences, then they can have a field-day until the true mind reasserts itself and blows the clouds away. Another device of theirs is to awake some hurt or rankling sense of grievance in the lower vital parts and keep them hurt or rankling as long as possible. In that case one has to discover these openings in one's nature and learn to close them permanently to such attacks or to throw out the intruders at once or as soon as possible. The recurrence is no proof of a fundamental incapacity; if one takes the right inner attitude, it can and will be overcome. One must have faith in the Master of our life and works, even if for a long time He conceals Himself, and then in His own right time He will reveal His Presence.

Subconscient

The subconscient is the Inconscient in the process of becoming conscious; it is a support and even a root of our inferior parts of being and their movements. It sustains and reinforces all in us that clings most and refuses to change, our mechanical recurrences of unintelligent thought, our persistent obstinacies of feeling, sensation, impulse, propensity, our uncontrolled fixities of character. The animal in us, — the infernal also, — has its lair of retreat in the dense jungle of the subconscience. To penetrate there, to bring in light and establish a control, is indispensable for the completeness of any higher life, for any integral transformation of the nature.

A decent into the subconscient would not help us to explore this region, for it would plunge us into incoherence or into sleep or a dull trance or a comatose torpor. A mental scrutiny or insight can give us some indirect and constructive idea of these hidden activities; but it is only by drawing back into the subliminal or by ascending into the superconscient and from there looking down or extending ourselves into these obscure depths that we can become directly and totally aware and in control of the secrets of our subconscient physical, vital and mental nature.

The subconscient lies between this Inconscient and the conscious mind, life and body. It contains the potentiality of all the primitive reactions to life which struggle out to the surface from the dull and inert strands of Matter and form by a constant development a slowly evolving and self-formulating consciousness; it contains them not as ideas, perceptions or conscious reactions but as the fluid substance of these things. But also all that is consciously experienced sinks down into the subconscient, not as precise though submerged memories but as obscure yet obstinate impressions of experience, and these can come up at any time as dreams, as mechanical repetitions of past thought, feelings, action, etc., as "complexes" exploding into action and event, etc., etc. The subconscient is the main cause why all things repeat themselves and nothing ever gets changed except in appearance. It is the cause why people say character cannot be changed, the cause also of the constant return of things one hoped to have got rid of for ever. All seeds are there and all Sanskaras of the mind, vital and body, — it is the main support of death and disease and the last fortress (seemingly impregnable) of the Ignorance. All too that is suppressed without being wholly got rid of sinks down there and remains as seed ready to surge up or sprout up at any moment.

The subconscient is only the lower basis of the Ignorance and affects mostly the lower vital and physical exterior consciousness and these again affect the higher parts of the nature. While it is well to see what it is and how it acts, one must not be too preoccupied with this dark side or this apparent aspect of the instrumental being. One should rather regard it as something not oneself, a mask of false nature imposed on the true being by the Ignorance. The true being is the inner with all its vast possibilities of reaching and expressing the Divine and especially the inmost, the soul, the psychic Purusha which is always in its essence pure, divine, turned to all that is good and true and beautiful. The exterior being has to be taken hold of by the inner being and turned into an instrument no longer of the upsurging of the ignorant subconscient Nature, but of the Divine.

Man harbours dangerous forces in his house.
The Titan and the Fury and the Djinn
Lie bound in the subconscient's cavern pit
And the Beast grovels in his antre den.

Subliminal

Behind our mind, our life, our conscious physical there is a larger subliminal consciousness, — there are inner mental, inner vital, inner more subtle physical reaches supported by an inmost psychic existence which is the connecting soul of all the rest; and in these hidden reaches too lie a mass of numerous pre-existent personalities which supply the material, the motive-forces, the impulsions of our developing surface existence. For in each one of us here there may be one central person, but also a multitude of subordinate personalities created by the past history of its manifestation or by expressions of it on these inner planes which support its present play in this external material cosmos. And while on our surface we are cut off from all around us except through an exterior mind and sense-contact which delivers but little of us to our world or of our world to us, in these inner reaches the barrier between us and the rest of existence is thin and easily broken; there we can feel at once — not merely infer from their results, but feel directly — the action of the secret world-forces, mind-forces, life-forces, subtle physical forces that constitute universal and individual existence; we shall even be able, if we will but train ourselves to it, to lay our hands on these world-forces that throw themselves on us or around us and more and more to control or at least strongly modify their action on us and others, their formations, their very movements. Yet again above our human mind are still greater reaches superconscient to it and from there secretly descend influences, powers, touches which are the original determinants of things here and, if they were called down in their fullness, could altogether alter the whole make and economy of life in the material universe. It is all this latent experience and knowledge that the Divine Force working upon us by our opening to it in the integral Yoga, progressively reveals to us, uses and works out the consequences as means and steps towards a transformation of our whole being and nature.

Messengers from our subliminal greatnesses,
Guests from the cavern of the secret soul.
Into dim spiritual somnolence they break
Or shed wide wonder on our waking self,
Ideas that haunt us with their radiant tread,
Dreams that are hints of unborn Reality.

Subtle Physical

The subtle physical is closest to the physical, and most like it. But yet the conditions are different and the thing too different. For instance, the subtle physical has a freedom, plasticity, intensity, power, colour, wide and manifold play (there are thousands of things there that are not here) of which, as yet, we have no possibility on earth. And yet there is something here, a potentiality of the Divine which the other, in spite of its greater liberties, has not, something which makes creation more difficult, but in the last result justifies the labour.

We can feel the symptoms of illness, fever or cold, for instance, in the subtle physical sheath before they are manifest in the gross body and destroy them there, preventing them from manifesting in the body. Take now the call for the Divine Power, Light, Ananda. If we live only in the outward physical consciousness, it may descend and work behind the veil, but we shall feel nothing and only see certain results after a long time. Or at most we feel a certain clarity and peace in the mind, a joy in the vital a happy state in the physical and infer the touch of the Divine. But if we are awake in the physical, we shall feel the light, power or Ananda flowing through the body, the limbs, nerves, blood, breath and, through the subtle body, affecting the most material cells and making them conscious and blissful and we shall sense directly the Divine Power and Presence. These are only two instances out of a thousand that are possible and can be constantly experienced by the sadhak.

They [mediums, clairvoyants, etc.] are most of them in contact with the vital-physical or subtle physical worlds and do not receive anything higher at all.

There are also beings who pick up the discarded feelings and memories of the dead and masquerade with them. There are a great number of beings who come to such seances only to play with the consciousness of men or exercise their powers through this contact with the earth and who dope the mediums and sitters with their falsehoods, tricks and illusions. (I am supposing, of course, the case of mediums who are not themselves tricksters.) A contact with such a plane of spirits can be harmful (most mediums become nervously or morally unbalanced) and spiritually dangerous. Of course, all pretended communications with the famous dead of long-past times are in their very nature deceptive and most of those with the recent ones also — that is evident from the character of these communications. Through conscientious mediums one may get sound results (in the matter of the dead), but even these are very ignorant of the nature of the forces they are handling and have no discrimination which can guard them against trickery from the other side of the veil.

The object of our yoga is to establish direct contact with the Divine above and bring down the divine Consciousness from above into all the centres. Occult powers belonging to the mental, vital and subtle physical planes are not our object. One can have contact with various Divine Forces and Personalities on the way, but there is no need to establish them in the centres, though sometimes that happens automatically (as with the four Personalities of the Mother) for a time in the course of the sadhana. But it is not a rule to do so. Our yoga is meant to be plastic and to allow all necessary workings of the Divine Power according to the nature, but these in their details may vary with each individual.

But only when we break through Matter's wall
In that spiritual vastness can we stand
Where we live the masters of our world,
And mind is only a means and body a tool.
For above the birth of body and of thought
Our spirit's truth lives in the naked self
And from that height, unbound, surveys the world.

Sunlit Path

That this way is difficult is a strange misconception; for it is on the contrary, the easiest and simplest and most direct way and anyone can do it, if he makes his mind and vital quiet. As for the Mother and myself, we had to try all ways, follow all methods, to surmount mountains of difficulties, a far heavier burden to bear than you or anybody else in the Ashram or outside; far more difficult conditions, battles to fight, wounds to endure, ways to cleave through impenetrable morass and desert and forest, hostile masses to conquer — a work such as I am certain none else had to do before us. It is because we have the complete experience that we can show a straighter and easier road to others — if they will only consent to take it. It is because of our experience won at a tremendous price that we can urge upon you and others, "Take the psychic attitude, follow the straight sunlit path, with the Divine openly or secretly upbearing you — if secretly, he will yet show himself in good time, do not insist on the hard, hampered, roundabout and difficult journey." When the psychic being comes out in its inherent power, its consecration, adoration, love of the Divine, self-giving, surrender and imposes these on the mind, vital and physical consciousness and compels them to turn all their movements Godward — the way is sunlit and a great joy and sweetness are the note of the whole sadhana.

He found the occult cave, the mystic door
Near to the well of vision in the soul,
And entered where the Wings of Glory brood
In the sunlit space where all is for ever known.

Supermind

In the supermind all is self-known self-luminously, there are no divisions, oppositions or separated aspects as in Mind whose principle is division of Knowledge into parts and setting each part against another.

In the supermind Knowledge and Will are one, Love and Force a single movement.

The utmost Ananda the body and life are now capable of is a brief excitement of the vital mind or the nerves or the cells which is limited, imperfect and soon passes: with the supramental change all the cells, nerves, vital forces, embodied mental forces can become filled with a thousandfold Ananda, capable of an intensity of bliss which passes description and which need not fade away.

All truths below the supramental (even that of the highest spiritual on the mental plane, which is the highest that has yet manifested) are either partial or relative or otherwise deficient and unable to transform the earthly life; they can only at most modify and influence it. The supermind is the vast Truth-Consciousness of which the ancient seers spoke; there have been glimpses of it till now, sometimes an indirect influence or pressure, but it has not been brought down into the consciousness of the earth and fixed there. To so bring it down is the aim of our yoga.

There the perfection born from Eternity
Calls to it the perfection born in Time,
The truth of God surprising human life,
The image of God overtaking finite shapes.
There is a world of everlasting Light,
In the realms of the Supermind.

Supramental

Above the human mind in the greater reaches, from where secretly descend influences, powers, touches which are original determinates of things here, if they were called down in their fullness, could altogether alter the whole make and economy of life in the material universe.

It is the supramental power which delivers man from his nature so that he becomes a free being and master of his mind, sense, life and body.

The Supramental Consciousness is not only a Knowledge, a Bliss, an intimate Love and Oneness, it is also a Will, a principle of Power and Force, and it cannot descend till the element of Will, of Power, of Force in this manifested Nature is sufficiently developed and sublimated to receive and bear it.

The mass of humanity evolves slowly, containing in itself all stages of the evolution from the material and the vital man to the mental man. A small minority has pushed beyond the barriers, opening the doors to occult and spiritual knowledge and preparing the ascent of the evolution beyond mental man into spiritual and supramental being. Sometimes this minority has exercised an enormous influence as in Vedic India, Egypt or, according to tradition, in Atlantis, and determined the civilisation of the race, giving it a strong stamp of the spiritual or the occult; sometimes they have stood apart in their secret schools or orders, not directly influencing a civilisation which was sunk in material ignorance or in chaos and darkness or in the hard external enlightenment which rejects spiritual knowledge.

The object of the yoga is to bring down the supramental consciousness on earth, to fix it there, to create a new race with the principle of the supramental consciousness governing the inner and outer individual and collective life.

It is first through the individuals that it [the supramental consciousness] becomes part of the earth-consciousness and afterwards it spreads from the first centers and takes up more and more of the global consciousness till it becomes an established force there.

It is ourselves that we have to transform and change the earth-consciousness by bringing in the supramental principle into the evolution there. Once there it will necessarily have a powerful influence in the whole earth-life — as mind has had through the evolution of men, but much greater.

It is the earth-consciousness, not the supramental world that has to gain by the descent of the supramental principle — that is sufficient reason for it to descend. The supramental worlds remain as they are and are in no way affected by the descent.

The supermind shall be his nature's fount,
The Eternal's truth shall mould his thoughts and acts,
The Eternal's truth shall be his light and guide.
All then shall change, a magic order come
Overtopping this mechanical universe.

Supraphysical Faculty

This faculty of sensing supraphysical things internally or externalising them, so to speak, so that they become visible, audible, sensible to the outward eye, ear, even touch, just as are gross physical objects, this power or gift is not a freak or an abnormality; it is a universal faculty present in all human beings, mostly latent, often near the surface sometimes but much more rarely already on the surface. If one practises tratak, — concentrating the vision on a single point or object — it is pretty certain to come out sooner or later. The first sign of its opening in the externalised way is very often that seeing of "sparkles" or small luminous dots, shapes etc. Develop this power of inner sense and all that it brings you. These first seeings are an outer fringe — behind lie whole worlds of experience which fill what seems to the natural man the gap between the earth-consciousness and the Eternal and the Infinite.

Aware of his occult omnipotent Source,
Allured by the omniscient Ecstasy,
A living centre of the Illimitable
Widened to equate with the world's circumference,
He turned to his immense spiritual fate.

Supraphysical Worlds

It is true that the glimpse of supraphysical realities acquired by methodical research has been imperfect and is yet ill-affirmed; for the methods used are still crude and defective. But subtle senses have atleast been found to be true witness to physical facts beyond the range of the corporeal organs.

The worlds beyond exist: they have their universal rhythm, their grand lines and formations, their self-existent laws and mighty energies, their just and luminous means of knowledge. And here on our physical existence and in our physical body they exercise their influences; here also they organise their means of manifestations and commission their messengers and their witnesses.

When the laws and forces of the supraphysical are studied with the right starting-point, the means will infallibly be found for Mind directly to seize on the physical energy and speed it accurately on its errand. There, once we begin ourselves to recognise it, lie the gates that open upon the enormous vistas of the future.

A Truth occult has made this mighty world:
The Eternal's wisdom and self-knowledge act
In ignorant Mind and in the body's steps.
The Inconscient is the Superconscient's sleep.

Supreme

The Divine being; the master and creator of the universe. He is Omnipotent, Omniscient, the controller of all energies, the conscious in all that is conscient or Inconscient, the Inhabitant of all souls and minds and hearts and bodies, the Ruler or Overruler of all works, the enjoyer of all delight, the Creator who has built all things in his own being, the All-Person of whom all beings are personalities, the Power from whom are all powers, the Self, the Spirit in all, by his being the Father of all that is, in his Consciousness-Force the Divine Mother, the Friend of all creatures, the All-blissful and All-beautiful of whom beauty and joy are the revelation, the All Beloved and All-Lover. He is supracosmic as well as intracosmic. He is that which exceeds and inhabits and supports all individuality.

> The superman shall wake in mortal man
> And manifest the hidden demi-god
> Or grow into the God-Light and God-Force
> Revealing the secret deity in the cave.
> Then shall the earth be touched by the Supreme

Supreme Personality

When he ascends above mind and life to the gnosis that the Purusha becomes the master of his own nature because subject only to supreme Nature. For there force or will is the exact counterpart, the perfect dynamis of the divine knowledge. And that knowledge is not merely the eye of the Witness, it is the immanent and compelling gaze of the Ishwara (Lord). Its luminous governing power, a power not to be hedged in or denied, imposes its self-expressive force on all the action and makes true and radiant and authentic and inevitable every movement and impulse.

The gnostic soul is the child, but the king-child; here is the royal and eternal childhood whose toys are the worlds and all universal Nature is the miraculous garden of the play that tires never.

The gnosis does not reject the realisations of the lower planes; for it is not an annihilation or extinction, not a Nirvana but a sublime fulfilment of our manifested Nature. It possesses the first realisations under its own conditions after it has transformed them and made them elements of a divine order. The gnostic soul is the child, but the king-child; (So Heraclitus, "The kingdom is of the child.") here is the royal and eternal childhood whose toys are the worlds and all universal Nature is the miraculous garden of the play that tires never.

A magician with the omnipotent wand of thought,
He builds the secret uncreated worlds.
Armed with the golden speech, the diamond eye,
His is the vision and the prophecy.

The Supreme Working

It is a tremendous work that is being done in you, the alteration of your whole human nature into a divine nature, the crowding of centuries of evolution into a few years. You ought not to grudge the time. There are other paths that offer more immediate results or at any rate by offering you some definite kriya you can work at yourself, give your ahankara (ego) the satisfaction of feeling that you are doing something, so many more pranayamas today, so much longer a time for the asana, so many more repetitions of the japa, so much done, so much definite progress marked. But once you have chosen this path, you must cleave to it. Those are human methods, not the way that the infinite Shakti works, which moves silently, sometimes imperceptibly to its goal, advances here, seems to pause there, then mightily and triumphantly reveals the grandiose thing that it has done. Artificial paths are like canals hewn by the intelligence of man; you travel easily, safely, surely, but from one given place to another. This path is the broad and trackless ocean by which you can travel widely to all parts of the world and are admitted to the freedom of the infinite. All that you need are the ship, the steering-wheel, the compass, the motive-power and a skilful captain. Your ship is the Brahmavidya, faith is your steering-wheel, self-surrender your compass, the motive-power is she who makes, directs and destroys the worlds at God's command and God himself is your captain. But he has his own way of working and his own time for everything. Watch his way and wait for his time. Understand also the importance of accepting the Shastra and submitting to the Guru and do not do like the Europeans who insist on the freedom of the individual intellect to follow its own fancies and preferences which it calls reasonings, even before it is trained to discern or fit to reason. It is much the fashion nowadays, to indulge in metaphysical discussions and philosophical subtleties about Maya and Adwaita and put them in the forefront, making them take the place of spiritual experience. Do not follow that fashion or confuse yourself and waste time on the way by questionings which will be amply and luminously answered when the divine knowledge of the vijnana awakes in you. Metaphysical knowledge has its place but as a handmaid to spiritual experience, showing it the way sometimes but much more dependent on it and living upon its bounty. By itself it is mere panditya, a dry and barren thing and more often a stumbling-block than a help. Having accepted this path, follow its Shastra without unnecessary doubt and questioning, keeping the mind plastic to the light of the higher knowledge, gripping firmly what is experienced, waiting for light where things are dark to you, taking without pride what help you can from the living guides who have already trod the path, always patient, never hastening to narrow conclusions, but waiting for a more complete experience and a fuller light, relying on the Jagadguru who helps you from within.

Even the most powerful Rajayogic samyama, the most developed pranayama, the most strenuous meditation, the most ecstatic Bhakti, the most self-denying action, mighty as they are and efficacious, are comparatively weak in their results when set beside this supreme working. For those are all limited to a certain extent by our capacity, but this is illimitable in potency because it is God's capacity. It is only limited by his will which knows what is best for the world and for each of us in the world and apart from it.

Men shall be lit with the Eternal's ray
And the glory of my sun-lift in their thoughts
And feel in their hearts the sweetness of my love
And in their acts my Power's miraculous drive.
My will shall be the meaning of their days;
Living for me, by me, in me they shall live.

Surrender

Surrender means to give up our little mind and its mental ideas and preferences into a divine Light and a greater Knowledge, our petty personal troubled blind stumbling will into a great, calm, tranquil luminous Will and Force, our little, restless, tormented feelings into a wide intense divine love and Ananda.

The surrender must be total and seize all the parts of the being. It must be self-made and free; the surrender of a living being, not of an inert automaton or mechanical tool. A glad and strong and helpful submission is demanded to the working of the Divine Force.

It is no doubt impossible for the human nature being mental in its basis to overcome the Ignorance and rise to or obtain the descent of the supermind by its own unaided effort, but by surrender to the Divine it can be done. One brings it down into the earth Nature through his own consciousness and so opens the way for the others, but the change has to be repeated in each consciousness to become individually effective.

The core of the inner surrender is trust and confidence in the Divine. One takes the attitude: "I want the Divine and nothing else. I want to give myself entirely to him and since my soul wants that, it cannot be but that I shall meet and realise him. I ask nothing but that and his action in me to bring me to him, his action secret or open, veiled or manifest. I do not insist on my own time and way; let him do all in his own time and way; I shall believe in him, accept his will, aspire steadily for his light and presence and joy, go through all difficulties and delays, relying on him and never giving up. Let my mind be quiet and trust him and let him open it to his light; let my vital be quiet and turn to him alone and let him open it to his calm and joy. All for him and myself for him. Whatever happens, I will keep to this aspiration and self-giving and go on in perfect reliance that it will be done."

That is the attitude into which one must grow; for certainly it cannot be made perfect at once — mental and vital movements come across — but if one keeps the will to it, it will grow in the being. The rest is a matter of obedience to the guidance when it makes itself manifest, not allowing one's mental and vital movements to interfere.

They reckon not our virtue and our sin,
They bend not to the voices that implore,
They hold no traffic with error and its reign:
They are guardians of the silence of the Truth,
They are keepers of the immutable decree.
A deep surrender is their source of might,
A still identity their way to know,
Motionless is their action like a sleep.

Tamas

Tamas is the Indian word for the principle of inertia of consciousness and force: a consciousness dull and sluggish and incompetent in its play is said to be tamasic; a force, a Life-energy that is indolent and limited in its capacity, bound to a narrow range of instinctive impulses, not developing, not seeking farther, not urged to a greater kinetic action or a more luminously conscious action, would be assigned to the same category.

All that makes in man the coarse, heavy and vulgar spirit.

Inertia comes usually from the ordinary physical consciousness, especially when the vital is actively not supporting the sadhana. These things can only be cured by a persistent bringing down of the higher spiritual consciousness into all the parts of the being.

The three modes of Nature are termed in the Indian books as qualities, gunas, and are given the names sattva, rajas, tamas. Sattwa is the force of equilibrium and translates in quality as good and harmony and happiness and light; Rajas is the force of kinesis and translates in quality as struggle and effort, passion and action; Tamas is the force of inconscience and inertia and translates in quality as obscurity and incapacity and inaction. Ordinarily used for psychological self-analysis, these distinctions are valid also in physical Nature. Each thing and every existence in the lower Prakriti contains them and its process and dynamic form are the result of the interaction of these qualitative powers.

Heaven's call is rare, rarer the heart that heeds;
The doors of light are sealed to common mind,
And earth's needs nail to earth the human mass,
Only in an uplifting hour of stress
Men answer to the touch of greater things.

The Temporal Manifestation

There is the unmanifest and there is the manifestation, but a manifestation of the Real must itself be real; there is the Timeless and there is the process of things in Time, but nothing can appear in Time unless it has a basis in the timeless Reality.

Instead of the original and ultimate Consciousness which sees reality as a whole, our consciousness sees a part and parts only of the Manifestation, — if manifestation it be, — and treats it or them as if they were separate entities; all our illusions and errors arise from a limited separative awareness which creates unrealities or misconceives the Real.

A miracle of the Absolute was born,
Infinity put on a finite soul,
All ocean lived within a wandering drop,
A time-made body housed the Illimitable.
To live this Mystery out our souls came here.

Thinking Mind

The mind proper is divided into three parts — (Thinking mind, dynamic mind, and externalising mind). The thinking mind is concerned with the ideas and knowledge in their own right. Its function is to reason from the perceptions of the mind and senses, to form conclusions and to put things in logical relation with each other.

A well-trained intellect is a good preparation of the mind for greater knowledge, but it cannot itself give the yogic knowledge or know the Divine — it can only have ideas about the Divine, but having ideas is not knowledge. Intellectual activities are not part of the inner being — it is the outer mind.

To see the Truth does not depend on a big intellect or small intelllect. It depends on being in contact with the Truth and the mind silent and quiet to receive it. The thinking mind with most men is, in matters of life, only an instrument of the vital.

An architect of knowledge, not its source.
This powerful bondslave of his instruments
Thinks his low station Nature's highest top.

Thoughts and Feelings

COMING FROM OUSIDE

It is becoming always clearer that not only does the capacity of our total consciousness far exceed that of our organs, the senses, the nerves, the brain, but that even for our ordinary thought and consciousness these organs are only their habitual instruments and not their generators.

Much more than half our thoughts and feelings are not our own in the sense that they take form out of ourselves; of hardly anything can it be said that it is truly original to our nature. A large part comes to us from others or from the environment, whether as raw material or as manufactured imports; but still more largely they come from universal Nature here or from other worlds and planes and their beings and powers and influences; for we are overtopped and environed by other planes of consciousness, mind planes, life planes, subtle matter planes, from which our life and action here are fed, or fed on, pressed, dominated, made use of for the manifestation of their forms and forces. The difficulty of our separate salvation is immensely increased by this complexity and manifold openness and subjection to the in-streaming energies of the universe. Of all this we have to take account, to deal with it, to know what is the secret stuff of our nature and its constituent and resultant motions and to create in it all a divine centre and a true harmony and luminous order.

Moreover, there is a stuff of mind in each man and the incoming thought uses that for shaping itself or translating itself (transcribing we usually call it), but the stuff is finer or coarser, stronger or weaker, etc., etc., in one mind than in another. Also, there is a mind-energy actual or potential in each which differs and this mind-energy in its recipience of the thought can be luminous or obscure with consequences that vary in each case.

Our errors are his steps upon the way;
He works through the fierce vicissitudes of our lives,
He works through the hard breath of battle and toil,
He works through our sins and sorrows and our tears,
His knowledge overrules our nescience.

Three Powers of the Eternal Manifestation

By knowing the eternal unity of these three powers of the eternal manifestation, God, Nature and the individual self, and their intimate necessity to each other, we come to understand existence itself and all that in the appearances of the world now puzzles our ignorance. Our self-knowledge abolishes none of these things, it abolishes only our ignorance and those circumstances proper to the ignorance which made us bound and subject to the egoistic determinations of our nature. When we get back to our true being, the ego falls away from us; its place is taken by our supreme and integral self, the true individuality. As this supreme self it makes itself one with all beings and sees all world and Nature in its own infinity. What we mean by this is simply that our sense of separate existence disappears into a consciousness of illimitable, undivided, infinite being in which we no longer feel bound to the name and form and the particular mental and physical determinations of our present birth and becoming and are no longer separate from anything or anyone in the universe. This was what the ancient thinkers called the Non-birth or the destruction of birth or Nirvana. At the same time we continue to live and act through our individual birth and becoming, but with a different knowledge and quite another kind of experience; the world also continues, but we see it in our own being and not as something external to it and other than ourselves. To be able to live permanently in this new consciousness of our real, our integral being is to attain liberation and enjoy immortality.

A Wisdom knows and guides the mysteried world;
A Truth-gaze shapes its beings and events;
A Word self-born upon creation's heights,
Voice of the Eternal in the temporal spheres,
Prophet of the seeings of the Absolute,
Sows the Idea's significance in Form
And from that seed the growths of Time arise.

Time Travel

A completer opening of the psychical consciousness leads us far beyond this faculty of vision by images and admits us not indeed to a new time consciousness, but to many ways of the triple time knowledge. The subliminal or psychic self can bring back or project itself into past states of consciousness and experience and anticipate or even, though this is less common, strongly project itself into future states of consciousness and experience. It does this by a temporary entering into or identification of its being or its power of experiencing knowledge with either permanences or representations of the past and the future that are maintained in an eternal time consciousness behind our mentality or thrown up by the eternity of supermind into an indivisible continuity of time vision.

Then kindling the gold tongue of sacrifice,
Calling the powers of a bright hemisphere,
We shall shed the discredit of our mortal state,
Make the abysm a road for Heaven's descent.
Acquaint our depths with the supernal Ray
And cleave the darkness with the mystic Fire.

Training for Intuition

We may train our mentality not to seize, as it does now, upon every separate flash of intuitive illumination for its own inferior purposes, not to precipitate our thought at once into a crystallising intellectual action around it; we can train it to think in a stream of successive and connected intuitions, to pour light upon light in a brilliant and triumphant series. We shall succeed in this difficult change in proportion as we purify the interfering intelligence, — if we can reduce in it the element of material thought enslaved to the external appearances of things, the element of vital thought enslaved to the wishes, desires, impulses of the lower nature, the element of intellectual thought enslaved to our preferred, already settled or congenial ideas, conceptions, opinions, fixed operations of intelligence, if, having reduced to a minimum those elements, we can replace them by an intuitive vision and sense of things, an intuitive insight into appearances, an intuitive will, an intuitive ideation.

> The knowledge of the thinker and the seer
> Saw the unseen and thought the unthinkable,
> Opened the enormous doors of the unknown,
> Rent Man's horizons into infinity.

Transcendental

The Transcendent, the Supracosmic is absolute and free in itself beyond Time and Space and beyond the conceptual opposites of finite and infinite. But in cosmos it uses its liberty of self-formulation, its Maya, to make a scheme of itself in the complementary terms of unity and multiplicity, and this multiple unity it establishes in the three conditions of the subconscient, the conscient and the superconscient.

The seat of the Transcendent Consciousness is above in an absoluteness of divine Existence — and there too is the absolute Power, Truth, Bliss of the Eternal — of which our mentality can form no conception and of which even our greatest spiritual experience is only a diminished reflection in the spiritualised mind and heart, a faint shadow, a thin derivate. Yet proceeding from it there is a sort of golden corona of Light, Power, Bliss and Truth — a divine Truth-Consciousness as the ancient mystics called it, a Supermind, a Gnosis, with which this world of a lesser consciousness proceeding by Ignorance is in secret relation and which alone maintains it and prevents it from falling into a disintegrated chaos.

I am the Mystery beyond reach of mind
I am the goal of the travail of the suns;
My fire and sweetness are the cause of life.

Transformation

I use transformation in a special sense, a change of consciousness radical and complete and of a certain specific kind which is so conceived as to bring about a strong and assured step forward in the spiritual evolution of the being of a greater and higher kind and of a larger sweep and completeness than what took place when a mentalised being first appeared in a vital and material animal world. If anything short of that takes place or at least if a real beginning is not made on that basis, a fundamental progress towards this fulfilment, then my object is not accomplished. A partial realisation, something mixed and inconclusive, does not meet the demand I make on life and yoga.

Mind, vital, physical are properly instruments for the soul and spirit; when they work for themselves then they produce ignorant and imperfect things — if they can be made into conscious instruments of the psychic and the spirit, then they get their own diviner fulfilment; that is the idea contained in what we call transformation in this yoga.

For a real transformation there must be a direct and unveiled intervention from above; there would be necessary too a total submission and surrender of the lower consciousness, a cessation of its insistence, a will in it for its separate law of action to be completely annulled by transformation and lose all rights over our being. If these two conditions can be achieved even now by a conscious call and will in the spirit and a participation of our whole manifested and inner being in its change and elevation, the evolution, the transformation can take place by a comparatively swift conscious change; the supramental Consciousness-Force from above and the evolving Consciousness-Force from behind the veil acting on the awakened awareness and will of the mental human being would accomplish by their united power the momentous transition. There would be no farther need of a slow evolution counting many millenniums for each step, the halting and difficult evolution operated by Nature in the past in the unconscious creatures of the Ignorance.

Nature shall live to manifest secret God,
The Spirit shall take up the human play
This earthly life become the life divine.

True Mind-Vital-Physical

"A state which was full of knowledge, calm serenity, strength and wide consciousness — all questions automatically solved — a continuous stream of power passed into the body through the forehead centre — extremely powerful, having undisturbed samatā, calm conviction, keen sight and knowledge." This was the consciousness of the true Purusha in you aware of his own supramental being and it is this which must become your normal consciousness and the basis of the supramental development. In order that it may so become, the mind has to be made calm and strong, the emotional and vital being purified and the physical consciousness so opened that the body can hold and retain the consciousness and power. The calm and strength will descend from above, what you have to do is to open yourself and receive it and at the same time reject all the movements of the lower nature which prevent it from remaining and which are ruled by desires and habits inconsistent with the true being, the true power and the true knowledge.

> But vain are human power and human love
> To break earth's seal of ignorance and death;
> His nature's might seemed now an infant's grasp;
> Heaven is too high for outstretched hands to seize.
> This Light comes not by struggle or by thought;
> In the mind's silence the Transcendental acts
> And the hushed heart hears the unuttered Word.

Truth

My truth is one that rejects ignorance and falsehood and moves to the knowledge, rejects darkness and moves to the light, rejects egoism and moves to the Divine Self, rejects imperfections and moves to perfection. My truth is not only the truth of Bhakti or of psychic development but also of knowledge, purity, divine strength and calm and of the raising of all these things from their mental, emotional and vital forms to their supramental reality.

Every being is in essence one with the Divine and in his individual being a portion of the Divine, so there is no insuperable bar to his becoming supramental.

If you call for the Truth and yet something in you chooses what is false, ignorant and undivine or even is unwilling to reject it altogether, then always you will be open to attack and the Grace will recede from you.

His truth in human thinking cannot dwell:
If thou desirest truth then still thy mind
For ever, slain by the dumb unseen Light.

Two Beings In Us

There are, we might say, two beings in us, one on the surface, our ordinary exterior mind, life, body consciousness, another behind the veil, an inner mind, an inner life, an inner physical consciousness constituting another or inner self. This inner self once awake opens in its turn to our true real eternal self. It opens inwardly to the soul, called in the language of this yoga the psychic being which supports our successive births and at each birth assumes a new mind, life and body. It opens above to the Self or Spirit which is unborn and by conscious recovery of it we transcend the changing personality and achieve freedom and full mastery over our nature.

Out of my curtained past his arms arrived;
They have touched me like the soft persuading wind,
They have plucked me like a glad and trembling flower,
And clasped me happily burned in ruthless flame.

Universal

All action, all mental, vital, physical activities in the world are the operation of the universal Energy, a conscious-Force which is the power of the Cosmic Spirit working out the cosmic and individual truth of things.

To be in the limitations of a small restricted ego is to exist, but it is an imperfect existence: in its very nature it is to live in an incomplete consciousness, an incomplete force and delight of existence. It is to be less than oneself and it brings an inevitable subjection to ignorance, weakness and suffering: or even if by some divine composition of the nature it could exclude these things, it would be to live in a limited scope of existence, a limited consciousness and power and joy of existence. All being is one and to be fully is to be all that is. To be in the being of all and to include all in one's being, to be conscious of the consciousness of all, to be integrated in force with the universal force, to carry all action and experience in oneself and feel it as one's own action and experience, to feel all selves as one's own self, to feel all delight of being as one's own delight of being is a necessary condition of the integral divine living.

In this tremendous universality
Not only his soul-nature and mind-sense
Included every soul and mind in his,
But even the life of flesh and nerve was changed

Universal Forces

Universal forces means all forces good or bad, favourable or hostile, of light and darkness that move in the cosmos.

The earth is the place of evolution in which all these forces meet and try to manifest and out of their working something has to develop. On the other planes (the mental, vital etc.) there is not the evolution — there each acts separately according to its own law.

All action, all mental, vital, physical activities in the world are the operation of a universal Energy, a Consciousness-Force which is the power of the Cosmic Spirit working out the cosmic and individual truth of things.

Each natural individual is a receptacle of these cosmic forces and a dynamo for their propagation; there passes from each to each a constant stream of mental and vital energies, and these run too in cosmic waves and currents no less than the forces of physical Nature. All this action is veiled from our surface mind's direct sense and knowledge, but it is known and felt by the inner being.

> Even should a hostile force cling to its reign
> And claim its right's perpetual sovereignty
> And man refuse his high spiritual fate,
> Yet shall the secret Truth in things prevail.
> For in the march of all-fulfilling Time
> The hour must come of the Transcendent's will.

Universal Love

A universal love we must have, calm and yet eternally intense beyond the brief vehemence of the most violent passion; a delight in things rooted in a delight in God that does not adhere to their forms but to that which they conceal in themselves and that embraces the universe without being caught in its meshes.

I have known even instances in which the perception of the Divine in all accompanied by an intense experience of universal love or a wide experience of an inner harmony had an extraordinary effect in making all around kind and helpful, even the most coarse and hard and cruel.

Universal love is not personal — it has to be held within as a condition of the consciousness which will have its effects according to the Divine Will or be used by that Will if necessary; but to run about expressing it for one's personal satisfaction or the satisfaction of others is only to spoil and lose it.

One can have a psychic feeling of love for someone, a universal love for all creatures, but one has to give oneself only to the Divine.

There was no more division's endless scroll;
One grew the Spirit's secret unity,
All nature felt again the single bliss;
There was no cleavage between soul and soul,
There was no barrier between world and God.

Unmanifest to Manifestation

Sachchidananda -- Unmanifest, making possible every kind of manifestation.

Sachchidananda in Manifestation

The Supreme Planes of Infinite Consciousness

1. Sat (implying Chit-Tapas and Ananda)

2. Chit (implying Sat and Ananda)

3. Ananda (implying Sat and Chit-Tapas)

The universe is dynamism, movement -- the essential experience of Sachchidananda apart from the dynamism and movement is static. The full dynamic truth of Sachchidananda and the universe and its consequence cannot be grasped by any other consciousness than the supermind, because the instrumentation in all other (lower) planes is inferior and there is therefore a disparity between the fullness of the static experience and the incompleteness of the dynamic power, knowledge, result of the inferior light and power of other planes. This is the reason why the consciousness of the other spiritual planes, even if it descends, can make no radical change in the earth-consciousness, it can only modify or enrich it. The radical transformation needs the descent of a supramental power and nature.

> The beauty and the ceaseless miracle
> Let in a glow of the Unmanifest:
> The formless Everlasting moved in it
> Seeking its own perfect form in souls and things.

302

Visions

Inner vision is vivid like actual sight, always precise and contains a truth in it. In mental vision the images are invented by the mind and are partly true, partly a play of possibilities.

Just as your physical eyes see things in the physical world, so the inner eyes see things and images that belong to the other worlds and subtle images of things of this physical world also.

The inner vision can see objects, but it can see instead the vibration of the forces which act through the object.

Vision is of value because it is often a first key to inner planes of one's own being and one's own consciousness as distinguished from worlds or planes of the cosmic consciousness. Yoga-experience often begins with some opening of the third eye in the forehead (the centre of vision in the brows) or with some kind of beginning and extension of subtle seeing which may seem unimportant at first but is the vestibule to deeper experience. Even when it is not that, — for one can go to experience direct, — it can come in afterwards as a powerful aid to experience; it can be full of indications which help to self-knowledge or knowledge of things or knowledge of people; it can be veridical and lead to prevision, premonition and other openings of less importance but very useful to a yogi. In short, vision is a great instrument though not absolutely indispensable.

The inner vision is an open door on higher planes of consciousness beyond the physical mind which gives room for a wider truth and experience to enter and act upon the mind. It is not the only or the most important door, but it is one which comes readiest to very many if not most and can be a very powerful help. It does not come as easily to intellectuals as it does to men with a strong life-power or the emotional and the imaginative.

People value visions for one thing because they are one key (there are others) to contact with the other worlds or with the inner worlds and all that is there and these are regions of immense riches which far surpass the physical plane as it is at present. One enters into a larger freer self and a larger more plastic world; of course individual visions only give a contact, not an actual entrance, but the power of vision accompanied with the power of other subtle senses (hearing, touch, etc.) as it expands does give this entrance.

Visions do not come from the spiritual plane — they come from the subtle physical, the vital, the mental, the psychic or from the planes above the Mind. What comes from the spiritual plane are experiences of the Divine, e.g. the experience of self everywhere, of the Divine in all, etc.

> The Presence chambered in lotus secrecy,
> Came down and held the centre in her brow
> Where the mind's Lord in his control-room sits;
> He opens that third mysterious eye in man,
> The Unseen's eye that looks at the unseen.

Vital

The vital is the Life-nature made up of desires, sensations, feelings, passions, energies of action, will of desire, reactions of the desire-soul in man and of all that play of possessive and other related instincts, anger, fear, greed, lust, etc., that belong to this field of nature. Mind and vital are mixed up on the surface of the consciousness, but they are quite separate forces in themselves and as soon as one gets behind the ordinary surface consciousness one sees them as separate, discovers their distinction and can with the aid of this knowledge analyse their surface mixtures. It is quite possible and even usual during a time shorter or longer, sometimes very long, for the mind to accept the Divine or the yogic ideal while the vital is unconvinced and unsurrendered and goes obstinately on its way of desire, passion and attraction to the ordinary life. Their division or their conflict is the cause of most of the more acute difficulties of the sadhana.

The vital being and the life-force in man are separated from the Divine Light and, so separated, they are an instrument for any power that can take hold of them, illumined or obscure, divine or undivine.

It is in the vital that thought is transformed into will and becomes a dynamism for action.

It is undesirable to make peace, joy or Ananda a condition for following the Yoga. If you do so, then the vital, not the psychic, takes the lead. When the vital takes the lead, then unrest, despondency, unhappiness can always come, since these things are the very nature of the vital — the vital can never remain constantly in joy and peace, for it needs their opposites in order to have the sense of the drama of life.

> This is the world in which thou mov'st, astray
> In the tangled pathways of the human mind,
> In the issueless circling of thy human life,
> Searching for thy soul and thinking God is here.
> But where is room for soul or place for God
> In the brute immensity of a machine?

Vital Mind

There is a part of the nature which I have called the vital mind; the function of this mind is not to think and reason, to perceive, consider and find out or value things, for that is the function of the thinking mind proper, buddhi, — but to plan or dream or imagine what can be done. It makes formations for the future which the will can try to carry out if opportunity and circumstances become favourable or even it can work to make them favourable. In men of action this faculty is prominent and a leader of their nature; great men of action always have it in a very high measure. But even if one is not a man of action or practical realisation or if circumstances are not favourable or one can do only small and ordinary things, this vital mind is there. It acts on them on a small scale, or if it needs some sense of largeness, what it does very often is to plan in the void, knowing that it cannot realise its plans or else to imagine big things, stories, adventures, great doing in which oneself is the hero or the creator. What you describe as happening in you is the rush of this vital mind or imagination making its formations; its action is not peculiar to you but works pretty much in the same way in most people — but in each according to his turn of fancy, interest, favourite ideas and desire. You have to become master of its action and not to allow it to seize your mind and carry it away when and where it wants. In sadhana when the experiences begin to come, it is exceedingly important not to allow this power to do what it likes with you; for it then creates false experiences according to its nature and persuades the sadhak that these experiences are true or it builds unreal formations and persuades him that this is what he has to do. Some have been taken away by this misleading force used by powers of Falsehood who persuaded them through it that they had a great spiritual, political or social work to do in the world and led them away to disappointment and failure.

Vital mind is a mind of dynamic will, action, desire — occupied with force and achievement and satisfaction and possession, enjoyment and suffering, giving and taking, growth, expansion, success and failure, good fortune and ill fortune, etc. day-dreaming, talking mentally to another person — are the actions of vital mind.

O man, the events that meet thee on thy road,
Though they smite the body and soul with joy and grief,
Are not thy fate; they touch thee awhile and pass;
Even death can cut not short thy spirit's walk:
Thy goal, the road thou choosest are thy fate.

Vital Physical

It is made more of automatic or habitual instincts, impulses, sensations and feelings than any thing else. If the mind stands back and judges and questions, the vital physical can only answer "I want", "I like", "I dislike", "I feel like that."

The cardinal defect, that which has been always standing in the way and is now isolated in an extreme prominence, is seated or at least is at present concentrated in the lower vital being. I mean that part of the vital-physical nature with its petty and obstinate egoism which actuates the external human personality, - that which supports its surface thoughts and dominates its habitual ways of feeling, character and action. I am not concerned here with the other parts of the being and I do not speak of anything in the higher mind, the psychic self or the higher and larger vital nature; for, when the lower vital rises, these are pushed into the background, if not covered over for the time, by the lower vital being and this external personality. Whatever there may be in these higher parts, aspiration to the Truth, devotion, or will to conquer the obstacles and the hostile forces, it cannot become integral, it cannot remain unmixed or unspoilt or continue to be effective so long as the lower vital and the external personality have not accepted the Light and consented to change.

Aroused from the darkness where they crouched in the depths,
Prisoned from the sight, they can be held no more
His nature's impulses are now his lords.

Vital Plane

As there is a poise of the relations of Soul with Nature in which Matter is the first determinant, a world of material existence, so there is another just above it in which Matter is not supreme, but rather Life-force takes its place as the first determinant. The vital worlds are original constructions, organised developments, native habitats of the universal Life-principle, acting in its own field and in its own nature. It is a much richer and more plastic field of consciousness than the physical. Without the vital plane there would be no art, poetry or literature — these things come through the vital before they can manifest here.

It seems even to be the fact that the vital worlds are the natural home of the Powers that most disturb human life; this is indeed logical, for it is through our vital being that they sway us and they must therefore be powers of a larger and more powerful life-existence.

You must remember that these worlds, which are different from the true or divine vital, are full of enchantments and illusions and they present appearances of beauty which allure only to mislead or destroy. They are worlds of 'Rakshasimaya' and their heavens are more dangerous than their hells. They have to be known and their powers met when need be but not accepted; our business is with the supramental and with the vital only when it is supramentalised and until then we have always to be on our guard against any lures from that other quarter.

> The world is other than we now think and see,
> Our lives a deeper mystery than we have dreamed;
> Our minds are starters in the race to God,
> Our souls deputed selves of the Supreme.

Voices

As there is an inner sight other than the physical, so there is an inner hearing other than that of the external ear, and it can listen to voices and sounds and words of other worlds, other times and places, or those which come from supraphysical beings. But here you must be careful. If conflicting voices try to tell you what to do or not to do, you should not listen to them or reply. It is only myself and the Mother who can tell you what you should or should not do or guide or advise you.

When the sadhana progresses, one almost always gets the power of vision; what one sees is true if one remains in the right consciousness. There are also wrong voices and experiences. The people who have gone mad, went mad because they were egoistic, began to think themselves great sadhaks and attach an exaggerated importance to themselves and their experiences; this made them get a wrong consciousness and wrong voices and visions and inspirations. They attached so much importance to them that they refused to listen to the Mother and finally became hostile to her because she told them they were in error and checked their delusions.

Not to listen to the hostile voices that suggest failure or to the voices of impatient, vital haste that echo them, not to believe that because great difficulties are there, there can be no success or that because the Divine has not yet shown himself he will never show himself, but to take the position that everyone takes when he fixes his mind on a great and difficult goal, "I will go on till I succeed — all difficulties notwithstanding." To which the believer in the Divine adds, "The Divine exists, my following after the Divine cannot fail. I will go on through everything till I find him."

You have only to set about resolutely slaying the Rakshasa and the doors will open to you as they have done to many others who were held up by their own mind or vital nature.

When naked of ego and mind it hears the Voice:
It looks through light to ever greater light
And sees Eternity ensphering Life.

The Way

First be sure of the call and of thy soul's answer. For if the call is not true, not the touch of God's powers or the voice of his messengers, but the lure of thy ego, the end of thy endeavour will be a poor spiritual fiasco or else a deep disaster.

And if not the soul's fervour, but only the mind's assent or interest replies to the divine summons or only the lower life's desires clutches at some side attraction of the fruits of Yoga-power or Yoga-pleasure or only a transient emotion leaps like an unsteady flame moved by the intensity of the Voice or its sweetness or grandeur, then too there can be little surety for thee in the difficult path of Yoga.

The outer instruments of mortal man have no force to carry him through the severe ardours of this spiritual journey and Titanic inner battle or to meet its terrible or subtle and formidable dangers. Only his spirit's august and steadfast will and the quenchless fire of his soul's invincible ardour are sufficient for this difficult transformation and this high improbable endeavour.

A call was on him from intangible heights;
Indifferent to the little outpost Mind,
He dwelt in the wideness of the Eternal's reign.
His being now exceeded thinkable Space,
His boundless thought was neighbour to cosmic sight:
A universal light was in his eyes,
A golden influx flowed through heart and brain;
A force came down into his mortal limbs,
A current from eternal seas of Bliss;
He felt the invasion and the nameless joy.

The Way – Its Ambushes

Imagine not the way is easy; the way is long, arduous, dangerous, difficult. At every step is an ambush, at every turn a pitfall. A thousand seen or unseen enemies will start up against thee, terrible in subtlety against thy ignorance, formidable in power against thy weakness. And when with pain thou hast destroyed them, other thousands will surge up to take their place. Hell will vomit its hordes to oppose thee and enring and wound and menace; Heaven will meet thee with its pitiless tests and its cold luminous denials.

Thou shalt find thyself alone in thy anguish, the demons furious in thy path, the Gods unwilling above thee. Ancient and powerful, cruel, unvanquished and close and innumerable are the dark and dreadful Powers that profit by the reign of Night and Ignorance and would have no change and are hostile. Aloof, slow to arrive, far-off and few and brief in their visits are the Bright Ones who are willing or permitted to succour.

> An inconsequence dogs every effort made,
> And chaos waits on every cosmos formed:
> In each success a seed of failure lurks.
> He saw the doubtfulness of all things here,
> The incertitude of man's proud confident thought,
> The transience of the achievements of his force.

The Way – Its Battles

Each step forward is a battle. There are precipitous descents, there are unending ascensions and ever higher peaks upon peaks to conquer. Each plateau climbed is but a stage on the way and reveals endless heights beyond it. Each victory thou thinkest the last triumphant struggle proves to be but the prelude to a hundred fierce and perilous battles...

But thou sayest God's hand will be with me and the Divine Mother near with her gracious smile of succour? And thou knowest not then that God's Grace is more difficult to have or to keep than the nectar of the Immortals or Kuvera's priceless treasures? Ask of His chosen and they will tell thee how often the Eternal has covered his face from them, how often he has withdrawn from them behind his mysterious veil and they have found themselves alone in the grip of Hell, solitary in the horror of the darkness, naked and defenceless in the anguish of the battle.

> Pierced through his back by Evil's poignant stake.
> So might one fall on the Eternal's road
> Forfeiting the spirit's lonely chance in Time
> And no news of him reach the waiting gods,
> Marked "missing" in the register of souls,
> His name the index of a falling hope,
> The position of a dead remembered star.

The Way - Immortality

And if his presence is felt behind the veil, yet is it like the winter sun behind clouds and saves not from the rain and snow and the calamitous storm and the harsh wind and the bitter cold and the grey of a sorrowful atmosphere and the dun weary dullness. Doubtless the help is there even when it seems to be withdrawn, but still is there the appearance of total night with no sun to come and no star of hope to pierce the blackness.

Beautiful is the face of the Divine Mother, but she too can be hard and terrible. Nay, then, is immortality a plaything to be given lightly to a child or the divine life a prize without effort or the crown for a weakling? Strive rightly and thou shalt have; trust and thy trust shall in the end be justified; but the dread Law of the Way is there and none can change it.

To meet its luminous self of Truth and Bliss.
It pears at the Real through the apparent form;
It labours in our mortal mind and sense;
Amid the figures of the Ignorance,
In the symbol pictures drawn by word and thought,
It seeks the truth to which all figures point.

Will

Our human will is misled and wandering ray that has parted from the supreme Puissance. The period of slow emergence out of this lower working into a higher light and purer force is the valley of the shadow of death for the striver after perfection; it is a dreadful passage full of trials, sufferings, sorrows, obscurations, stumblings, errors, pitfalls. To bridge and alleviate this ordeal or to penetrate with the divine light faith is necessary, an increasing surrender of the mind to the knowledge that imposes itself from within and, above all, a true aspiration and a right and unfaltering and sincere practice. When the individual soul is entirely at one in its being and knowledge with the Lord and directly in touch with the original Shakti, the transcendent Mother, the supreme Will can then arise in us too in the high divine manner as a thing that must be and is achieved by the spontaneous action of Nature. There is then no desire, no responsibility, no reaction; all takes place in the peace, calm, light, power of the supporting and enveloping and inhabiting Divine.

> Amid the trivial sounds, the unchanging scene
> Her soul arose confronting Time and Fate,
> Immobile in herself, she gathered force.

Wisdom

If the truth of our being is an infinite unity in which alone there is perfect wideness, light, knowledge, power, bliss, and if all our subjection to darkness, ignorance, weakness, sorrow, limitation comes of our viewing existence as a clash of infinitely multiple separate existences, then obviously it is the most practical and concrete and utilitarian as well as the most lofty and philosophical wisdom to find a means by which we can get away from the error and learn to live in the truth. So also, if that One is in its nature a freedom from bondage to this play of qualities which constitute our psychology and if from subjection to that play are born the struggle and discord in which we live, floundering eternally between the two poles of good and evil, virtue and sin, satisfaction and failure, joy and grief, pleasure and pain, then to get beyond the qualities and take our foundation in the settled peace of that which is always beyond them is the only practical wisdom. If attachment to mutable personality is the cause of our self-ignorance, of our discord and quarrel with ourself and with life and with others, and if there is an impersonal One in which no such discord and ignorance and vain and noisy effort exist because it is in eternal identity and harmony with itself, then to arrive in our souls at that impersonality and untroubled oneness of being is the one line and object of human effort to which our reason can consent to give the name of practicality.

> Awakened to the meaning of my heart,
> That to feel love and oneness is to live
> And this the magic of our golden change
> Is all the truth I know or seek, O sage.

Withdrawl

There is not and cannot be any ascetic or contemplative or mystic abandonment of works and life altogether, any gospel of an absorbed meditation and inactivity, any cutting away or condemnation of the Life-Force and its activities, any rejection of the manifestation in the Earth-nature. It may be necessary for the seeker at any period to withdraw into himself, to remain plunged in his inner being, to shut out from himself the noise and turmoil of the life of the Ignorance until a certain inner change has been accomplished or something achieved without which a further effective action on life has become difficult or impossible. But this can only be a period or an episode, a temporary necessity or a preparatory spiritual manoeuvre; it cannot be the rule of his Yoga or its principle.

> No helper had she save the Strength within;
> There was no witness of terrestrial eyes;
> The Gods above and Nature sole below
> Were the spectators of that mighty strife.

The Work

Our nature is not only mistaken in will and ignorant in knowledge but weak in power; but the Divine Force is there and will lead us if we trust in it and will use our deficiencies and our powers for the divine purpose. If we fail in our immediate aim, it is because he has intended the failure; often our failure or ill-result is the right road to a truer issue than an immediate and complete success would have put in our reach. If we suffer, it is because something in us has to be prepared for a rarer possibility of delight. If we stumble, it is to learn in the end the secret of a more perfect walking. Let us not be in too furious a haste to acquire even peace, purity and perfection. Peace must be ours, but not the peace of an empty or devastated nature or of slain or mutilated capacities incapable of unrest because we have made them incapable of intensity and fire and force. Purity must be our aim, but not the purity of a void or of a bleak and rigid coldness. Perfection is demanded of us, but not the perfection that can exist only by confining its scope within narrow limits or putting an arbitrary full stop to the ever self-extending scroll of the Infinite. Our object is to change into the divine nature, but the divine nature is not a mental or moral but a spiritual condition, difficult to achieve, difficult even to conceive by our intelligence. The Master of our work and our Yoga knows the thing to be done, and we must allow him to do it in us by his own means and in his own manner.

The movement of the Ignorance is egoistic at its core and nothing is more difficult for us than to get rid of egoism while yet we admit personality and adhere to action in the half-light and half-force of our unfinished nature. It is easier to starve the ego by renouncing the impulse to act or to kill it by cutting away from us all movement of personality. It is easier to exalt it into self-forgetfulness immersed in a trance of peace or an ecstasy of divine Love. But our more difficult problem is to liberate the true Person and attain to a divine manhood which shall be the pure vessel of a divine force and the perfect instrument of a divine action. Step after step has to be firmly taken; difficulty after difficulty has to be entirely experienced and entirely mastered. Only the Divine Wisdom and Power can do this for us and it will do all if we yield to it in an entire faith and follow and assent to its workings with a constant courage and patience.

The first step on this long path is to consecrate all our works as a sacrifice to the Divine in us and in the world; this is an attitude of the mind and heart, not too difficult to initiate, but very difficult to make absolutely sincere and all-pervasive. The second step is to renounce attachment to the fruit of our works; for the only true, inevitable and utterly desirable fruit of sacrifice — the one thing needful — is the Divine Presence and the Divine Consciousness and Power in us, and if that is gained, all else will be added. This is a transformation of the egoistic will in our vital being, our desire-soul and desire-nature, and it is far more difficult than the other. The third step is to get rid of the central egoism and even the ego-sense of the worker. That is the most difficult transformation of all and cannot be perfectly done if the first two steps have not been taken; but these first steps too cannot be completed unless the third comes in to crown the movement and, by the extinction of egoism, eradicates the very origin of desire. Only when the small ego-sense is rooted out from the nature can the seeker know his true person that stands above as a portion and power of the Divine and renounce all motive-force other than the will of the Divine Shakti.

A few shall see what none yet understands;
God shall grow up while the wise men talk and sleep;
For man shall not know the coming till its hour
And belief shall be not till the work is done.

The Working

The Shakti, the power of the Infinite and the Eternal descends within us, works, breaks up our present psychological formations, shatters every wall, widens, liberates, presents us with always newer and greater powers of vision, ideation, perception and newer and greater life-motives, enlarges and new-models increasingly the soul and its instruments, confronts us with every imperfection in order to convict and destroy it, opens to greater perfection, does in a brief period the work of many lives or ages, so that new births and new vistas open constantly within us. Expansive in her action, she frees the consciousness from confinement in the body; it can go out in trance or sleep or even waking and enter into worlds or other regions of this world and act there or carry back its experience. It spreads out, feeling the body only as a small part of itself, and begins to contain what before contained it; it achieves the cosmic consciousness and extends itself to be commensurate with the universe. It begins to know inwardly and directly and not merely by external observation and contact the forces at play in the world, feels their movement, distinguishes their functioning and can operate immediately upon them as the scientist operates upon physical forces, accept their action and results in our mind, life, body or reject them or modify, change, reshape, create immense new powers and movements in place of the old small functionings of the nature. We begin to perceive the working of the forces of universal Mind and to know how our thoughts are created by that working, separate from within the truth and falsehood of our perceptions, enlarge their field, extend and illumine their significance, become master of our own minds and action and capable and active to shape the movements of Mind in the world around us. We begin to perceive the flow and surge of the universal Life-forces, detect the origin and law of our feelings, emotions, sensations, passions, are free to accept, reject, new-create, open to wider, rise to higher planes of Life-Power. We begin to perceive too the key to the enigma of Matter, follow the interplay of Mind and Life and Consciousness upon it, discover more and more its instrumental and resultant function and detect ultimately the last secret of Matter as a form not merely of Energy but of involved and arrested or instably fixed and restricted consciousness and begin to see too the possibility of its liberation and plasticity of response to higher Powers, its possibilities for the conscious and no longer the more than half-inconscient incarnation and self-expression of the Spirit. All this and more becomes more and more possible as the working of the Divine Shakti increases in us and, against much resistance or labour to respond of our obscure consciousness, through much struggle and movement of progress and regression and renewed progress necessitated by the work of intensive transformation of a half-inconscient into a conscious substance, moves to a greater purity, truth, height, range. All depends on the psychic awakening in us, the completeness of our response to her and our growing surrender.

The full transformation can come only by the ascent of the sacrifice to the furthest heights and its action upon life with the power and light and beatitude of the divine supramental Gnosis.

Let a greater being then arise from man,
The superhuman with the Eternal mate
And the Immortal shine through earthly forms.

Worlds

Man, the microcosm, has all these planes in his own being, ranged from his subconscient to his superconscient existence. By a developing power of Yoga he can become aware of these concealed worlds hidden from his physical, materialised mind and senses which know only the material world, and then he becomes aware that his material existence is not a thing apart and self-existent, as the material universe in which he lives is also not a thing apart and self-existent, but is in constant relation to the higher planes and acted on by their powers and beings. He can open up and increase the action of these higher planes in himself and enjoy some sort of participation in the life of the other worlds, — which, for the rest, are or can be his dwelling-place, that is to say, the station of his awareness, dhāma, after death or between death and rebirth in a material body. But his most important capacity is that of developing the powers of the higher principles in himself, a greater power of life, a purer light of mind, the illumination of supermind, the infinite being, consciousness and delight of spirit. By an ascending movement he can develop his human imperfection towards that greater perfection.

A playing-ground and dwelling-house of God
Who hides himself in bird and beast and man
Sweetly to find himself again by love,
By oneness. His presence leads the rhythms of life
That seek for mutual joy inspite of pain.

World's Laws

The laws of this world as it is are the laws of the Ignorance and the Divine in the world maintains them so long as there is the Ignorance; if he did not, the universe would crumble to pieces — utsïdeyur ime lokãh, as the Gita puts it. There are also, very naturally, conditions for getting out of the Ignorance into the Light. One of them is that the mind of the sadhak should co-operate with the Truth and that his will should co-operate with the Divine Power which, however slow its action may seem to the vital or to the physical mind, is uplifting the nature towards the Light; when that co-operation is complete, the progress can be rapid enough. But the sadhak should not grudge the time and labour needed to make the co-operation fully possible to the blindness and weakness of human nature and effective.

As for your fitness or unfitness for the yoga, it is not a question on which your physical mind can be a judge — it judges by the immediate appearance of things and has no knowledge of the laws that govern consciousness or the powers that act in yoga. In fact, the question is not of fitness or unfitness but of the acceptance of Grace. There is no human being whose physical outer consciousness — the part of yourself in which you are now living — is fit for the yoga. It is by Grace and a light from above that it can become capable and for that the necessity is to be persevering and open it to the Light.

The Divine is there, but He does not ignore the conditions, the laws, the circumstances of Nature; it is under these conditions that He does all His work, His work in the world and in man and consequently also in the sadhak, the aspirant, even in the God-knower and God-lover; even the saint and the sage continue to have difficulties and to be limited by their human nature. A complete liberation and a complete perfection or the complete possession of the Divine and possession by the Divine is possible, but it does not usually happen by an easy miracle or a series of miracles. The miracle can and does happen but only when there is the full call and complete self-giving of the soul and the entire widest opening of the nature.

The outward and the immediate are our field,
The dead past is our background and our support;

Mind keeps the soul prisoner, we are slaves to our acts;
We cannot free our gaze to reach wisdom's sun.

Yoga

Yoga means union with the Divine — a union either transcendental (above the universe) or cosmic (universal) or individual or, as in our yoga, all three together. Or it means getting into a consciousness in which one is no longer limited by the small ego, personal mind, personal vital and body but is in union with the supreme Self or with the universal (cosmic) consciousness or with some deeper consciousness within in which one is aware of one's own soul, one's own inner being and of the real truth of existence. In the yogic consciousness one is not only aware of things, but of forces, not only of forces, but of the conscious being behind the forces. One is aware of all this not only in oneself but in the universe.

All life is a Yoga of Nature seeking to manifest God within itself. Yoga marks the stage at which this effort becomes capable of self-awareness and therefore of right completion in the individual. It is a gathering up and concentration of the movements dispersed and loosely combined in the lower evolution.

What Nature aims at for the mass in a slow evolution, Yoga effects for the individual by a rapid revolution. It works by a quickening of all her energies, a sublimation of all her faculties. While she develops the spiritual life with difficulty and has constantly to fall back from it for the sake of her lower realisations, the sublimated force, the concentrated method of Yoga can attain directly and carry with it the perfection of the mind and even, if she will, the perfection of the body. Nature seeks the Divine in her own symbols: Yoga goes beyond Nature to the Lord of Nature, beyond universe to the Transcendent and can return with the transcendent light and power, with the fiat of the Omnipotent.

Our purpose in Yoga is to exile the limited outward-looking ego and to enthrone God in its place as the ruling Inhabitant of the nature. And this means, first, to disinherit desire and no longer accept the enjoyment of desire as the ruling human motive. The spiritual life will draw its sustenance not from desire but from a pure and selfless spiritual delight of essential existence. And not only the vital nature in us whose stamp is desire, but the mental being too must undergo a new birth and a transfiguring change.

Yoga has four powers and objects, purity, liberty, beatitude and perfection. Whosoever has consummated these four mightinesses in the being of the transcendental, universal, lilamãya and individual God is the complete and absolute Yogin.

In Yoga also it is the Divine who is the Sadhaka and the Sadhana; it is her Shakti with her light, power, knowledge, consciousness, Ananda, acting upon the Adhara, pouring into it these divine forces that make the Sadhana possible. But so long as the lower nature is active, the personal effort of the Sadhaka remains necessary.

A divine force shall flow through tissue and cell
And take the charge of breath and speech and act
And the thoughts shall be a glow of suns
And every feeling a celestial thrill.

Yoga and its Stages

Yoga is a rapid and concentrated conscious evolution of the being, but however rapid, even though it may effect in a single life what in an instrumental Nature might take centuries and millenniums or many hundreds of lives, still all evolution must move by stages; even the greatest rapidity and concentration of the movement cannot swallow up all the stages or reverse natural process and bring the end near to the beginning. A hasty and ignorant mind, a too eager force easily forget this necessity; they rush forward to make the supermind an immediate aim and expect to pull it down with a pitchfork from its highest heights in the Infinite. This is not only an absurd expectation but full of danger. For the vital desire may very well bring in an action of dark or vehement vital powers which hold out before it a promise of immediate fulfilment of its impossible longing; the consequence is likely to be a plunge into many kinds of self-deception, a yielding to the falsehoods and temptations of the forces of darkness, a hunt for supernormal powers, a turning away from the Divine to the Asuric nature, a fatal self-inflation into an unnatural unhuman and undivine bigness of magnified ego. If the being is small, the nature weak and incapable, there is not this large-scale disaster; but a loss of balance, a mental unhinging and fall into unreason or a vital unhinging and consequent moral aberration or a deviation into some kind of morbid abnormality of the nature may be the untoward consequence. This is not a Yoga in which abnormality of any kind, even if it be an exalted abnormality, can be admitted as a way to self-fulfilment or spiritual realisation.

The aim of the yoga is to open the consciousness to the Divine and to live in the inner consciousness more and more while acting from it on the external life, to bring the inmost psychic into the front and by the power of the psychic to purify and change the being so that it may become ready for transformation and be in union with the Divine Knowledge, Will and Love. Secondly, to develop the yogic consciousness, i.e., to universalise the being in all the planes, become aware of the cosmic being and cosmic forces and be in union with the Divine on all the planes up to the overmind. Thirdly, to come into contact with the transcendent Divine beyond the overmind through the supramental consciousness, supramentalise the consciousness and the nature and make oneself an instrument for the realisation of the dynamic Divine Truth and its transforming descent into the earth-nature.

> None was apart, none lived for himself alone,
> Each lived for God in him and God in all,
> Each soleness inexpressibly held the whole.
> There Oneness was not tied to monotone;
> It showed a thousand aspects of itself
> Its luminous immutable stability
> Upbore on a changeless ground for ever safe.

Yoga of Nature and The Integral Yoga

All life is a secret Yoga, an obscure growth of Nature towards the discovery and fulfilment of the divine principle hidden in her.

So long as there is only an intellectual, ethical and other self-training for the now normal purposes of life which does not travel beyond the ordinary circle of working of mind, life and body, we are still only in the obscure and yet unillumined preparatory Yoga of Nature; we are still in pursuit of only an ordinary human perfection.

A Yoga of integral perfection regards man as a divine spiritual being involved in mind, life and body; it aims therefore at a liberation and a perfection of his divine nature. It seeks to make an inner living in the perfectly developed spiritual being his constant intrinsic living and the spiritualised action of mind, life and body only its outward human expression. In order that this spiritual being may not be something vague and indefinable or else but imperfectly realised and dependent on the mental support and the mental limitations, it seeks to go beyond mind to the supramental knowledge, will, sense, feeling, intuition, dynamic initiation of vital and physical action, all that makes the native working of the spiritual being. It accepts human life, but takes account of the large supraterrestrial action behind the earthly material living, and it joins itself to the divine Being from whom the supreme origination of all these partial and lower states proceeds so that the whole of life may become aware of its divine source and feel in each action of knowledge, of will, of feeling, sense and body the divine originating impulse. It rejects nothing that is essential in the mundane aim, but enlarges it, finds and lives in its greater and its truer meaning now hidden from it, transfigures it from a limited, earthly and mortal thing to a figure of intimate, divine and immortal values.

On a dizzy verge where all disguises fail
And human mind must abdicate in Light
Or die like a moth in the naked blaze of Truth,
He stood compelled to a tremendous choice.
All he had been and all towards which he grew
Must now be left behind or else transform
Into a self of That which has no name.

Yogi

The yogi is one who is already established in realisation — the sadhak is one who is getting or still trying to get realisation.

The Yogin's distinction from other men is this that he lives in a higher and vaster spiritual consciousness; all his work of knowledge or creation must then spring from there: it must not be made in the mind, - for it is a greater truth and vision than mental man's that he has to express or rather that presses to express itself through him and mould his works, not for his personal satisfaction, but for a divine purpose.

At the same time the Yogin who knows the Supreme is not subject to any need or compulsion in these activities; for to him they are neither a duty nor a necessary occupation for the mind nor a high amusement, nor imposed even by the loftiest human purpose. He is not attached, bound and limited by any nor has he any personal motive of fame, greatness or personal satisfaction in these works; he can leave or pursue them as the Divine in him wills, but he need not otherwise abandon them in his pursuit of the higher integral knowledge. He will do these things just as the supreme Power acts and creates, for a certain spiritual joy in creation and expression or to help in the holding together and right ordering or leading of this world of God's workings.

In matter shall be lit the spirit's glow,
In body and body kindled the sacred birth;
Night shall awake to the anthem of the stars,
The days become a happy pilgrim march,
Our will a force of the Eternal's power,
And thought the rays of a spiritual sun.

Yogic Experiences in Sleep

These things take place either in sleep or in an indrawn meditation and not in the waking state. There is a twofold reason. First, that usually in yoga these things begin in an indrawn state and not in the waking condition — it is only if or when the waking mind is ready that they come as readily in the waking state.

It is through the inner consciousness and primarily through the inner mind that these things come; so, if there is not a clear passage from the inner to the outer, it must be in the inner states that they first appear. If the waking mind is subject or surrendered to the inner consciousness and willing to become its instrument, then even from the beginning these openings can come through the waking consciousness.

There are experiences that help or lead towards the realisation of things spiritual or divine or bring openings or progressions in the sadhana or are supports on the way, — experiences of a symbolic character, visions, contacts of one kind or another with the Divine or with the workings of higher Truth, things like the waking of the Kundalini, the opening of the Chakras, messages, intuitions, openings of the inner powers, etc. The one thing that one has to be careful about is to see that they are genuine and sincere and that depends on one's own sincerity — for if one is not sincere, if one is more concerned with the ego or being a big yogi or becoming a superman than with meeting the Divine or getting the Divine consciousness which enables one to live in or with the Divine, then a flood of pseudos or mixtures comes in, one is led into the mazes of the intermediate zone or spins in the grooves of one's own formations.

A dream disclosed to her the cosmic past,
The crypt-seed and the mystic origins,
The shadowy beginnings of world-fate:
A lamp of symbol lighting hidden truth
Imaged to her the world's significance.

Your Psychic

There is within you a psychic being which is divine, directly a part of the Mother, pure of all these defects. It is covered and concealed by the ordinary consciousness and nature, but when it is unveiled and able to come forward and govern the being, then it changes the ordinary consciousness, throws all these undivine things out and changes the outer nature altogether. That is why we want the sadhaks to concentrate, to open this concealed consciousness — it is by concentration of whatever kind and the experiences it brings that one opens and becomes aware within and the new consciousness and nature begin to grow and come out. Of course we want them also to use their will and reject the desires and wrong movements of the vital, for by doing that the emergence of the true consciousness becomes possible. But rejection alone cannot succeed; it is by rejection and by inner experience and growth that it is done.

The psychic is the soul or spark of the Divine Fire supporting the individual evolution on the earth and the psychic being is the soul-consciousness developing itself or rather its manifestation from life to life with the mind, vital and body as its instruments until all is ready for the union with the Divine.

O human copy and disguise of God
Who seekst the deity thou keepest hid
And livest by the Truth thou hast not known,
Follow the world's winding highway to its source.
There in the silence few have ever reached,
Thou shalt see the Fire burning on the bare stone
And the deep cavern of thy secret soul.

To Your Success

One may practice yoga and get illuminations in the mind and the reason; one may conquer power and luxuriate in all kinds of experiences in the vital; one may establish even surprising physical Siddhis; but if the true soul-power behind does not manifest, if the psychic nature does not come into the front, nothing genuine has been done. In this yoga the psychic is that which opens the rest of the nature to the true supramental light and finally to the supreme Ananda.

If the inmost soul is awakened, if there is a new birth out of the mere mental, vital and physical into the psychic consciousness, then this yoga can be done; otherwise (by the sole power of the mind or any other part) it is impossible... If there is refusal of the psychic new birth, a refusal to become the child new born from the Mother, owing to attachment to intellectual knowledge or mental ideas or to some vital desire, then there will be failure in the sadhana.

> At last he wakes into spiritual mind;
> A high liberty begins and luminous room:
> He glimpses eternity, touches the infinite,
> He meets the gods in great sudden hours,
> He feels the universe as his larger self,
> Makes Space and Time his opportunity
> To join the heights and depths of being in light,
> In the heart's cave speaks secretly with God.

Sri Aurobindo's Biobiography

EARLY LIFE AND CAREER

SRI AUROBINDO was born in Calcutta on August 15, 1872. At the age of five he was sent along with his two elder brothers, Benoybhushan and Manmohan, to the Loretto Convent School at Darjeeling. After two years, in 1879, he was taken with his elder brothers to England for education. Sri Aurobindo lived in England for fourteen years. He was brought up at first in an English family (the Drewett family) at Manchester. While his two brothers, Benoybhushan and Manmohan went to the Manchester Grammar School, Sri Aurobindo was privately educated by Mr. and Mrs. Drewett. Mr. Drewett was an accomplished Latin scholar; he taught Sri Aurobindo Latin so well that when the latter had joined St. Paul's School in London in 1885, the Headmaster himself took up Sri Aurobindo personally to ground him in Greek and then pushed him rapidly through the higher classes of the School. Towards the end of 1889 he went from St. Paul's with a senior classical scholarship to King's College, Cambridge, where he studied for two years. Sri Aurobindo gave much attention to the classics at Manchester and at Saint Paul's; but in his last three years at St. Paul's he paid less attention to these subjects, taking them only casually, and spent all his time outside school in general reading, especially English poetry, literature and fiction, French literature and the history of ancient, mediaeval and modern Europe. He spent some time also over learning Italian, some German and a little Spanish. He spent much time too in writing poetry. The school studies during this period engaged very little of his time; he was already at ease in them and did not think it necessary to labour over them any longer. All the same he was able to win all the prizes in King's College in one year for Greek and Latin verse At Cambridge Sri Aurobindo passed high in the First Part of the Tripos (first class); it was on passing this First Part that the degree of B.A. is usually given; but as he had only two years at his disposal, he had to pass it in his second year at Cambridge, and the First Part gives the degree only if it is taken in the third year; if one takes it in the second year one has to appear for the second part of the Tripos in the fourth year to qualify for the degree. He might have got the degree if he had made an application for it, but he did not care to do so. A degree in England is valuable only if one wants to take up an academical career

In 1890 he passed the open competition for the Indian Civil Service, but he neglected his lessons in riding and failed in the last riding test. He was, as is often done, given another chance to pass, but avoided presenting himself in time for the test. He was on this pretext disqualified for the Service, although in similar cases successful probationers have been given a further chance to qualify themselves in India itself. He felt no call for the I.C.S. and was seeking some way to escape from that bondage. He thus deliberately disqualified himself without himself rejecting the Service, which his family would not have allowed him to do.

At the age of eleven Sri Aurobindo had already received strongly the impression that a period of general upheaval and great revolutionary changes was coming in the world and he himself was destined to play part in it. His father in his letters had bitterly complained of the mechanical character and heartlessness of the British Government in India. He also sent him Indian newspapers marking for attention news items relating to maltreatment of Indians by Englishmen in that country. This and other circumstances raised a feeling of resentment against the subjection of India to a foreign rule. But the decision to take part himself in some action directed towards the liberation of the country took shape only after some years. At Cambridge as a member of the Indian Majlis of which latterly he became the secretary, he delivered many revolutionary speeches which, as he afterwards learnt, had their part in determining the authorities to exclude him from the Indian Civil Service. Among the Indians in London he and his brothers formed a part of a small revolutionary group who rebelled habitually against the leadership of Dadabhai Naoroji and his moderate politics. During the last days of his stay in England he attended a private meeting of Indians in London at which there was formed a secret society with the romantic name of the "Lotus and Dagger" in which all the members took the vow to adopt each some chosen part which would help in leading to the overthrow of foreign rule. But the society was still-born and its members dispersed without meeting again; some however kept individually to their vow and one of these was Sri Aurobindo.

When Sri Aurobindo was disqualified for the Indian Civil Service, the Gaekwar of Baroda was in London. Sri Aurobindo was introduced to him by the brother of Sir Henry Cotton and obtained an appointment in the Baroda service and left England in February, 1893.

Sri Aurobindo passed thirteen years, from 1893 to 1906, in the Baroda service, first in the Settlement and Revenue Department and in secretariate work for the Maharaja, afterwards as Professor of English and, finally, Vice-Principal in the Baroda College. These were years of self-culture, of literary activity-for much of the poetry afterwards published from Pondicherry was written at this time-and of preparation for his future work. In England he had received, according to his father's express instructions, an entirely occidental education without any contact with the culture of India and the East. At Baroda he made up the deficiency, learned Sanskrit and several modern Indian languages, especially Marathi and Gujarati, the two official languages of the Baroda State. He learnt Bengali very quickly and for the most part all by himself.* A great part of the last years of this period was spent on leave in silent political activity, for he was barred from public action by his position at Baroda. The outbreak of the agitation against the partition of Bengal in 1905 gave him the opportunity to give up the Baroda service and join openly in the political movement. He left Baroda in 1906 and went to Calcutta as Principal of the newly-founded Bengal National College.

Footnote: *Dinendra Kumar Roy lived with Sri Aurobindo in Baroda as a companion and his work was rather to help him to correct and perfect his knowledge of the language and to accustom him to conversation in Bengali than any regular teaching.

Political Life

There were three sides to Sri Aurobindo's political ideas and activities. First, there was the action with which he started, a secret revolutionary propaganda and organisation of which the central object was the preparation of an armed insurrection. Secondly, there was a public propaganda intended to convert the whole nation to the ideal of independence which was regarded, when he entered into politics, by the vast majority of Indians as unpractical and impossible, an almost insane chimera. It was thought that the British Empire was too powerful and India too weak, effectively disarmed and impotent even to dream of the success of such an endeavour. Thirdly, there was the organisation of the people to carry on a public and united opposition and undermining of the foreign rule through an increasing non-cooperation and passive resistance.

At that time the military organisation of the great empires and their means of military action were not so overwhelming and apparently irresistible as they now are: the rifle was still the decisive weapon, air power had not developed and the force of artillery was not so devastating as it afterwards became. India was disarmed, but Sri Aurobindo thought that with proper organisation and help from outside this difficulty might be overcome and in so vast a country as India and with the smallness of the regular British armies, even a guerrilla warfare accompanied by general resistance and revolt might be effective. There was also the possibility of a great revolt in the Indian army. At the same time he had studied the temperament and characteristics of the British people and the turn of their political instincts, and he believed that although they would resist any attempt at self-deliberation by the Indian people and would at the most only concede very slowly such reforms as would not weaken their imperial control, still they were not of the kind which would be ruthlessly adamantine to the end: if they found resistance and revolt becoming general and persistent they would in the end try to arrive at an accommodation to save what they could of their empire or in an extremity prefer to grant independence rather than have it forcefully wrested from their hands.

In some quarters there is the idea that Sri Aurobindo's political standpoint was entirely pacifist, that he was opposed in principle and in practice to all violence and that he denounced terrorism, insurrection etc. as entirely forbidden by the spirit and letter of the Hindu religion. It is even suggested that he was a forerunner of the gospel of Ahimsa. This is quite incorrect. Sri Aurobindo is neither an impotent moralist nor a weak pacifist.

The rule of confining political action to passive resistance was adopted as the best policy for the National Movement at that stage and not as a part of a gospel of Non-violence or pacific idealism. Peace is a part of the highest ideal, but it must be spiritual or at the very least psychological in its basis; without a change in human nature it cannot come with any finality. If it is attempted on any other basis (moral principle or gospel of Ahimsa or any other) it will fail, and even may leave things worse than before. He is in favour of an attempt to put down war by international agreement and international force, what is now contemplated in the "New Order", if that proves possible, but that would not be Ahimsa, it would be a putting down of anarchic force by legal force, and even then one cannot be sure that it would be permanent. Within nations this sort of peace has been secured, but it does not prevent occasional civil wars and revolutions and political outbreaks and repressions, sometimes of a sanguinary character. The same might happen to a similar world-peace. Sri Aurobindo has never concealed his opinion that a nation is entitled to attain its freedom by violence, if it can do so or if there is no other way; whether it should do so or not, depends on what is the best policy, not on ethical considerations. Sri Aurobindo's position and practice in this matter was the same as Tilak's and that of other Nationalist leaders who were by no means Pacifists or worshippers of Ahimsa.

For the first few years in India, Sri Aurobindo abstained from any political activity (except the writing of the articles in the Induprakash) and studied the conditions in the country so that he might be able to judge more maturely what could be done. Then he made his first move when he sent a young Bengali soldier of the Baroda army, Jatin Banerji, as his lieutenant to Bengal with a programme of preparation and action which he thought might occupy a period of 30 years before fruition could become possible. As a matter of fact it has taken 50 years for the movement of liberation to arrive at fruition and the beginning of complete success. The idea was to establish secretly or, as far as visible action could be taken, under various pretexts and covers, revolutionary propaganda and recruiting throughout Bengal. This was to be done among the youth of the country while sympathy and support and financial and other assistance were to be obtained from the older men who had advanced views or could be won over to them. Centres were to be established in every town and eventually in every village. Societies of young men were to be established with various ostensible objects, cultural, intellectual or moral and those already existing were to be won over for revolutionary use. Young men were to be trained in activities which might be helpful for ultimate military action, such as riding, physical training, athletics of various kinds, drill and organized movement. As soon as the idea was sown it attainted a rapid prosperity; already existing small groups and associations of young men who had not yet the clear idea or any settled programme of revolution began to turn in this direction and a few who had already the revolutionary aim were contacted and soon developed activity on organised lines; the few rapidly became many. Meanwhile Sri Aurobindo had met a member of the Secret Society in Western India, and taken the oath of the Society and had been introduced to the Council in Bombay. His future action was not pursued under any directions by this Council, but he took up on his own responsibility the task of generalising support for its objects in Bengal where as yet it had no membership or following. He spoke of the Society and its aim to P. Mitter and other leading men of the revolutionary group in Bengal and they took the oath of the Society and agreed to carry out its objects on the lines suggested by Sri Aurobindo. The special cover used by Mitter's group was association for lathi play which had already been popularised to some extent by Sarala Ghoshal in Bengal among the young men; but other groups used other ostensible covers. Sri Aurobindo's attempt at a close organisation of the whole movement did not succeed, but the movement itself did not suffer by that, for the general idea was taken up and activity of many separate groups led to a greater and more widespread diffusion of the revolutionary drive and its action. Afterwards there came the partition of Bengal and a general outburst of revolt which favoured the rise of the extremist party and the great nationalist movement. Sri Aurobindo's activities were then turned more and more in this direction and the secret action became a secondary and subordinate element. He took advantage, however, of the Swadeshi movement to popularise the idea of violent revolt in the future. At Barin's suggestion he agreed to the starting of a paper, yugantar, which was to preach open revolt and the absolute denial of the British rule and include such items as a series of articles containing instructions for guerrilla warfare. Sri Aurobindo himself wrote some of the opening articles in the early numbers and he always exercised a general control; when a member of the sub-editorial staff, Swami Vivekananda's brother, presented himself on his own motion to the police in a search as the editor of the paper and, was prosecuted, the Yugantar under Sri Aurobindo's orders adopted the policy of refusing to defend itself in a British Court on the ground that it did not recognise the foreign Government and this immensely increased the prestige and influence of the paper. It had as its chief writers and directors three of the ablest younger writers in Bengal, and it at once acquired an immense influence throughout Bengal. It may be noted that the Secret Society did not include terrorism in its programme but this element grew up in Bengal as a result of the strong repression and the reaction to it in that province.

The public activity of Sri Aurobindo began with the writing of the articles in the Induprakash. These seven articles written at the instance of K. G. Deshpande, editor of the paper and Sri Aurobindo's Cambridge friend, under the caption 'New Lamps for Old' vehemently denounced the then congress policy of pray, petition and protest and called for a dynamic leadership based upon self-help and fearlessness. But this outspoken and irrefutable criticism was checked by the action of a Moderate leader who frightened the editor and thus prevented any full development of his ideas in the paper; he had to turn aside to generalities such as the necessity of extending the activities of the Congress beyond the circle of the bourgeois or middle class and calling into it the masses. Finally, Sri Aurobindo suspended all public activity of this kind and worked only in secret till 1905, but he contacted Tilak whom he regarded as the one possible leader for a revolutionary party and met him at the Ahmedabad Congress; there Tilak took him out of the pandal and talked to him for an hour in the grounds expressing his contempt for the Reformist movement and explaining his own line of action in Maharashtra.

Sri Aurobindo included in the scope of his revolutionary work one kind of activity which afterwards became an important item in the public programme of the Nationalist party. He encouraged the young men in the centres of work to propagate the Swadeshi idea which at that time was only in its infancy and hardly more than a fad of the few. One of the ablest men in these revolutionary groups was a Mahratta named Sakharam Ganesh Deuskar who was an able writer in Bengali (his family had been long domiciled in Bengal) and who had written a popular life of Shivaji in Bengali in which he first brought in the name of – Swaraj afterwards adopted by the Nationalists as their word for independence, – Swaraj became one item of the fourfold Nationalist programme. He published a book entitled Desher Katha describing in exhaustive detail the British commercial and industrial exploitation of India. This book had an immense repercussion in Bengal, captured the mind of young Bengal and assisted more than anything else in the preparation of the Swadeshi movement. Sri Aurobindo himself had always considered the shaking off of this economic yoke and the development of India trade and industry as a necessary concomitant of the revolutionary endeavour.

As long as he was in the Baroda service, Sri Aurobindo could not take part publicly in politics. Apart from that, he preferred to remain and act and even to lead from behind the scenes without his name being known in public; it was the Government's action in prosecuting him as editor of the Bande Mataram that forced him into public view. And from that time forward he became openly, what he had been for sometime already, a prominent leader of the Nationalist party, its principal leader in action in Bengal and the organiser there of its policy and strategy. He had decided in his mind the lines on which he wanted the country's action to run: what he planned was very much the same as was developed afterwards in Ireland as the Sinn Fein movement; but Sri Aurobindo did not derive his ideas, as some have represented, from Ireland, for the Irish movement became prominent later and he knew nothing of it till after he had withdrawn to Pondicherry. There was moreover a capital difference between India and Ireland which made his work much more difficult; for all its past history had accustomed the Irish people to rebellion against British rule and this history might be even described as a constant struggle for independence intermittent in its action but permanently there in principle; there was nothing of this kind in India. Sri Aurobindo had to establish and generalise the idea of independence in the mind of the Indian people and at the same time to push first a party and then the whole nation into an intense and organised political activity which would lead to the accomplishment of that ideal. His idea was to capture the Congress and to make it an instrument for revolutionary action instead of a centre of a timid constitutional agitation which would only talk and pass resolutions and recommendations to the foreign Government; if the Congress could not be captured, then a central revolutionary body would have to be created which could do this work. It was to be a sort of State within the State giving its directions to the people and creating organised bodies and institutions which would be its means of action; there must be an increasing non-cooperation and passive resistance which would render the administration of the country by a foreign Government difficult or finally impossible, a universal unrest which would wear down repression and finally, if need be, an open revolt all over the country. This plan included a boycott of British trade, the substitution of national schools for the Government institutions, the creation of arbitration courts to which the people could resort instead of depending on the ordinary courts of law, the creation of volunteer forces which would be the nucleus of an army of open revolt, and all other action that could make the programme complete. The part Sri Aurobindo took publicly in Indian politics was of brief duration, for he turned aside from it in 1910 and withdrew to Pondicherry; much of his programme lapsed in his absence, but enough had been done to change the whole face of Indian politics and the whole spirit of the Indian people, to make independence its aim and non-cooperation and resistance its method, and even an imperfect application of this policy heightening into sporadic periods of revolt has been sufficient to bring about the victory. The course of subsequent events followed largely the line of Sri Aurobindo's idea. The Congress was finally captured by the Nationalist party, declared independence its aim, organised itself for action, took almost the whole nation minus a majority of the Mohammedans and a minority of the depressed classes into acceptance of its leadership and eventually formed the first national, though not as yet an independent, Government in India and secured from Britain acceptance of independence for India.

At first Sri Aurobindo took part in Congress politics only from behind the scenes as he had not yet decided to leave the Baroda service; but he took long leave without pay in which, besides carrying on personally the secret revolutionary work, he attended the Barisal Conference broken up by the police and toured East Bengal along with Bepin Pal and associated himself closely with the forward group in the Congress. It was during this period that he joined Bepin Pal in the editing of the Bande Mataram, founded the new political party in Bengal and attended the Congress session at Calcutta at which the Extremists, though still a minority, succeeded under the leadership of Tilak in imposing part of their political programme on the Congress. The founding of the Bengal National College gave him the opportunity he needed and enabled him to resign his position in the Baroda service and join the college as its Principal. Subodh Mullick, one of Sri Aurobindo's collaborators in his secret action and afterwards also in Congress politics, in whose house he usually lived when he was in Calcutta, had given a lakh of rupees for this foundation and had stipulated that Sri Aurobindo should be given a post of professor in the college with a salary of Rs.150; so he was now free to give his whole time to the service of the country. Bepin Pal, who had been long expounding a policy of self-help and non-cooperation in his weekly journal, now started a daily with the name of Bande Mataram, but it was likely to be a brief adventure since he began with only Rs.500 in his pocket and no firm assurance of financial assistance in the future. He asked Sri Aurobindo to join him in this venture to which a ready consent was given, for now Sri Aurobindo saw his opportunity for starting the public propaganda necessary for his revolutionary purpose. He called a meeting of the forward group of young men in the Congress and decided then to organise themselves openly as a new political party joining hands with the corresponding group in Maharashtra under the proclaimed leadership of Tilak and to join battle with the Moderate party which was done at the Calcutta session. He also persuaded them to take up the Bande Mataram daily as their party organ and a Bande Mataram Company was started to finance the paper, whose direction Sri Aurobindo undertook during the absence of Bepin Pal who was sent on a tour in the districts to proclaim the purpose and programme of the new party. The new party was at once successful and the Bande Mataram paper began to circulate throughout India. On its staff were not only Bepin Pal and Sri Aurobindo but some other very able writers, Shyam Sundar Chakravarty, Hemendra Prasad Ghose and Bejoy Chatterjee. Shyam Sundar and Bejoy were masters of the English language, each with a style of his own; Shyam Sundar caught up something like Sri Aurobindo's way of writing and later on many took his articles for Sri Aurobindo's. But after a time dissensions arose between Bepin Pal on one side and the other contributors and the directors of the Company because of temperamental incompatibility and differences of political view especially with regard to the secret revolutionary action with which others sympathised but to which Bepin Pal was opposed. This ended soon in Bepin Pal's separation from the journal. Sri Aurobindo would not have consented to this departure, for he regarded the qualities of Pal as a great asset to the Bande Mataram, since Pal, though not a man of action or capable of political leadership, was perhaps the best and most original political thinker in the country, an excellent writer and a magnificent orator: but the separation was effected behind Sri Aurobindo's back when he was convalescing from a dangerous attack of fever. His name was even announced without his consent in Bande Mataram as editor but for one day only, as he immediately put a stop to it since he was still formally in the Baroda service and in no way eager to have his name brought forward in public. Henceforward, however, he controlled the policy of the Bande Mataram along with that of the party in Bengal. Bepin Pal had stated the aim of the new party as complete self-government free from British control but this could have meant or at least included the Moderate aim of colonial self-government and Dadabhai Naoroji as President of the Calcutta session of the Congress had actually tried to capture the name of Swaraj, the Extremists' term for independence, for this colonial self-government. Sri Aurobindo's first preoccupation was to declare openly for complete and absolute independence as the aim of political action in India and to insist on this persistently in the pages of the journal; he was the first politician in India who had the courage to do this in public and he was immediately successful. The party took up the word Swaraj to express its own ideal of independence and it soon spread everywhere; but it was taken up as the ideal of the Congress much later on at the Karachi session of that body when it had been reconstituted and renovated under Nationalist leadership. The journal declared and developed a new political programme for the country as the programme of the Nationalist Party, non-cooperation, passive resistance, Swadeshi, Boycott, national education, settlement of disputes in law by popular arbitration and other items of Sri Aurobindo's plan. Sri Aurobindo published in the paper a series of articles on passive resistance, another developing a political philosophy of revolution and wrote many leaders aimed at destroying the shibboleths and superstitions of the Moderate Party such as the belief in British justice and benefits bestowed by foreign government in India, faith in British law courts and in the adequacy of the education given in schools and universities in India and stressed more strongly and persistently than had been done the emasculation, stagnation or slow progress, poverty, economic dependence, absence of a rich industrial activity and all other evil results of a foreign government; he insisted especially that even if an alien rule were benevolent and beneficent, that could not be a substitute for a free and healthy national life. Assisted by this publicity the ideas of the Nationalists gained ground everywhere especially in the Punjab which had before been predominantly moderate. The Bande Mataram was almost unique in journalistic history in the influence it exercised in converting the mind of a people and preparing it for revolution. But its weakness was on the financial side; for the Extremists were still a poor man's party. So long as Sri Aurobindo was there in active control, he managed with great difficulty to secure sufficient public support for running the paper, but not for expanding it as he wanted, and when he was arrested and held in jail for a year, the economic situation of Bande Mataram became desperate: finally, it was decided that the journal should die a glorious death rather than perish by starvation and Bejoy Chatterji was commissioned to write an article for which the Government would certainly stop the publication of the paper. Sri Aurobindo had always taken care to give no handle in the editorial articles of the Bande Mataram either for a prosecution for sedition or any other drastic action fatal to its existence; an editor of the Statesman complained that the paper reeked with sedition patently visible between every line but it was so skillfully written that no legal action could be taken. The manoeuvre succeeded and the life of the Bande Mataram came to an end in Sri Aurobindo's absence.

The Nationalist programme could only achieve a partial beginning before it was temporarily broken by severe government repression. Its most important practical item was Swadeshi plus Boycott; for Swadeshi much was done to make the idea general and a few beginnings were made but the greater results showed themselves only afterwards in the course of time. Sri Aurobindo was anxious that this part of the movement should be not only propagated in idea but given a practical organisation and an effective force. He wrote from Baroda asking whether it would not be possible to bring in the industrialists and manufacturers and gain the financial support of landed magnates and create an organisation in which men of industrial and commercial ability and experience and not politicians alone could direct operations and devise means of carrying out the policy; but he was told that it was impossible, the industrialists and the landed magnates were too timid to join in the movement, and the big commercial men were all interested in the import of British goods and therefore on the side of the status quo: so he had to abandon his idea of the organisation of Swadeshi and Boycott. Both Tilak and Sri Aurobindo were in favour of an effective boycott of British goods - but of British goods only; for there was little in the country to replace foreign articles: so they recommended the substitution for the British of foreign goods from Germany and Austria and America so that the fullest pressure might be brought upon England. They wanted the Boycott to be a political weapon and not merely an aid to Swadeshi; the total boycott of all foreign goods was an impracticable idea and the very limited application of it recommended in Congress resolutions was too small to be politically effective. They were for national self-sufficiency in key industries, the production of necessities and of all manufactures of which India had the natural means, but complete self-sufficiency or autarchy did not seem practicable or even desirable since a free India would need to export goods as well as supply them for internal consumption and for that she must import as well and maintain an international exchange. But the sudden enthusiasm for the boycott of all foreign goods was wide and sweeping and the leaders had to conform to this popular cry and be content with the impulse it gave to the Swadeshi idea. National education was another item to which Sri Aurobindo attached much importance. He had been disgusted with the education given by the British system in the schools and colleges and universities, a system of which as a professor in the Baroda College he had full experience. He felt that it tended to dull and impoverish and tie up the naturally quick and brilliant and supple Indian intelligence, to teach it bad intellectual habits and spoil by narrow information and mechanical instruction its originality and productivity. The movement began well and many national schools were established in Bengal and many able men became teachers, but still the development was insufficient and the economical position of the schools precarious. Sri Aurobindo had decided to take up the movement personally and see whether it could not be given a greater expansion and a stronger foundation, but his departure from Bengal cut short this plan. In the repression and the general depression caused by it, most of the schools failed to survive. The idea lived on and it may be hoped that it will one day find an adequate form and body. The idea of people's courts was taken up and worked in some districts not without success, but this too perished in the storm. The idea of volunteer groupings had a stronger vitality; it lived on, took shape, multiplied its formations and its workers were the spearhead of the movement of direct action which broke out from time to time in the struggle for freedom. The purely political elements of the Nationalist programme and activities were those which lasted and after each wave of repression and depression renewed the thread of the life of the movement for liberation and kept it recognisably one throughout nearly fifty years of its struggle. But the greatest thing done in those years was the creation of a new spirit in the country. In the enthusiasm that swept surging everywhere with the cry of Bande Mataram ringing on all sides men felt it glorious to be alive and dare and act together and hope; the old apathy and timidity were broken and a force created which nothing could destroy and which rose again and again in wave after wave till it carried India to the beginning of a complete victory.

After the Bande Mataram case, Sri Aurobindo became the recognised leader of Nationalism in Bengal. He led the party at the session of the Bengal Provincial Conference at Midnapore where there was a vehement clash between the two parties. He now for the first time became a speaker on the public platform, addressed large meetings at Surat and presided over the Nationalist conference there. He stopped at several places on his way back to Calcutta and was the speaker at large meetings called to hear him. He led the party again at the session of the Provincial Conference at Hooghly. There it became evident for the first time that Nationalism was gaining the ascendant, for it commanded a majority among the delegates and in the Subjects Committee Sri Aurobindo was able to defeat the Moderates' resolution welcoming the Reforms and pass his own resolution stigmatising them as utterly inadequate and unreal and rejecting them. But the Moderate leaders threatened to secede if this was maintained and to avoid a scission he consented to allow the Moderate resolution to pass but spoke at the public session explaining his decision and asking the Nationalists to acquiesce in it in spite of their victory so as to keep some unity in the political forces of Bengal. The Nationalist delegates, at first triumphant and clamorous, accepted the decision and left the hall quietly at Sri Aurobindo's order so that they might not have to vote either for or against the Moderate resolution. This caused much amazement and discomfiture in the minds of the Moderate leaders who complained that the people had refused to listen to their old and tried leaders and clamoured against them, but at the bidding of a young man new to politics they had obeyed in disciplined silence as if a single body.

About this period Sri Aurobindo had decided to take up charge of a Bengali daily, Nava Shakti, and had moved from his rented house in Scott's Lane, where he had been living with his wife and sister, to rooms in the office of this newspaper, and there, before he could begin this new venture, early one morning while he was still sleeping, the police charged up the stairs, revolver in hand, and arrested him. He was taken to the police station and hence to Alipore Jail where he remained for a year during the magistrate's investigation and the trial in the Sessions Court at Alipore. At first he was lodged for some time in a solitary cell but afterwards transferred to a large section of the jail where he lived in one huge room with the other prisoners in the case; subsequently, after the assassination of the approver in the jail, all the prisoners were confined in contiguous but separate cells and met only in the court or in the daily exercise where they could not speak to each other. It was in the second period that Sri Aurobindo made the acquaintance of most of his fellow–accused. In the jail he spent almost all his time in reading the Gita and the Upanishads and in intensive meditation and the practice of Yoga. This he pursued even in the second interval when he had no opportunity of being alone and had to accustom himself to meditation amid general talk and laughter, the playing of games and much noise and disturbance; in the first and third periods he had full opportunity and used it to the full. In the Sessions Court the accused were confined in a large prisoners' cage and here during the whole day he remained absorbed in his meditation attending little to the trial and hardly listening to the evidence. C. R. Das, one of his Nationalist collaborators and a famous lawyer, had put aside his large practice and devoted himself for months to the defence of Sri Aurobindo who left the case entirely to him and troubled no more about it; for he had been assured from within and knew that he would be acquitted. During this period his view of life was radically changed; he had taken up Yoga with the original idea of acquiring spiritual force and energy and divine guidance for his work in life. But now the inner spiritual life and realisation which had continually been increasing in magnitude and universality and assuming a larger place took him up entirely and his work became apart and result of it and besides far exceeded the service and liberation of the country and fixed itself in an aim, previously only glimpsed, which was world-wide in its bearing and concerned with the whole future of humanity.

When he came out from jail, Sri Aurobindo found the whole political aspect of the country altered; most of the Nationalist leaders were in jail or in self-imposed exile and there was a general discouragement and depression, though the feeling in the country had not ceased but was only suppressed and was growing by its suppression. He determined to continue the struggle; he held weekly meetings in Calcutta, but the attendance which had numbered formerly thousands full of enthusiasm, was now only of hundreds and had no longer the same force and life. He also went to places in the districts to speak and at one of these delivered his speech at Uttarpara in which for the first time he spoke publicly of his Yoga and his spiritual experiences. He started also two weeklies, one in English and one in Bengali, the Karmayogin and Dharma, which had a fairly large circulation and were, unlike the Bande Mataram, easily self-supporting. He attended and spoke at the Provincial Conference at Barisal in 1909: for in Bengal owing to the compromise at Hooghly the two parties had not split altogether apart and both joined in the Conference, though there could be no representatives of the Nationalist party at the meeting of the Central Moderate Body which had taken the place of the Congress. Surendra Nath Banerji had indeed called a private conference attended by Sri Aurobindo and one or two other leaders of the Nationalists to discuss a project of uniting the two parties at the session in Benares and giving a joint fight to the dominant right wing of the Moderates; for he had always dreamt of becoming again the leader of a united Bengal with the Extremist party as his strong right arm : but that would have necessitated the Nationalists being appointed as delegates by the Bengal Moderates and accepting the constitution imposed at Surat. This Sri Aurobindo refused to do; he demanded a change in that constitution enabling newly formed associations to elect delegates so that the Nationalists might independently send their representatives to the All-India session and on this point the negotiations broke down. Sri Aurobindo began however to consider how to revive the national movement under the changed circumstances. He glanced at the possibility of falling back on a Home Rule movement which the Government could not repress, but this, which was actually realised by Mrs. Besant later on, would have meant a postponement and a falling back from the ideal of independence. He looked also at the possibility of an intense and organised passive resistance movement in the manner afterwards adopted by Gandhi. He saw however that he himself could not be the leader of such a movement.

At no time did he consent to have anything to do with the sham Reforms which were all the Government at that period cared to offer. He held up always the slogan of 'no compromise' or, as he now put it in his Open Letter to his countrymen published in the Kamzayogin,'no co-operation without control' It was only if real political, administrative and financial control were given to popular ministers in an elected Assembly that he would have anything to do with offers from the British Government. Of this he saw no sign until the proposal of the Montagu Reforms in which first something of the kind seemed to appear. He foresaw that the British Government would have to begin trying to meet the national aspiration half-way, but he would not anticipate that moment before it actually came. The Montagu Reforms came nine years after Sri Aurobindo had retired to Pondicherry and by that time he had abandoned all outward and public political activity in order to devote himself to his spiritual work, acting only by his spiritual force on the movement in India, until his prevision of real negotiations between the British Government and the Indian leaders was fulfilled by the Cripps' proposal and the events that came after.

Meanwhile the Government were determined to get rid of Sri Aurobindo as the only considerable obstacle left to the success of their repressive policy. As they could not send him to the Andamans they decided to deport him. This came to the knowledge of Sister Nivedita and she informed Sri Aurobindo and asked him to leave British India and work from outside, so that his work would not be stopped or totally interrupted. Sri Aurobindo contented himself with publishing in the Karmayogin a signed article in which he spoke of the project of deportation and left the country what he called his last will and testament; he felt sure that this would kill the idea of deportation and in fact it so turned out. Deportation left aside, the Government could only wait for some opportunity for prosecution for sedition and this chance came to them when Sri Aurobindo published in the same paper another signed article reviewing the political situation. The article was sufficiently moderate in its tone and later on the High Court refused to regard it as seditious and acquitted the printer. Sri Aurobindo one night at the Karmayogin office received information of the Government's intention to search the office and arrest him. While considering what should be his attitude, he received a sudden command from above to go to Chandernagore in French India. He obeyed the command at once, for it was now his rule to move only as he was moved by the divine guidance and never to resist and depart from it; he did not stay to consult with anyone but in ten minutes was at the river ghat and in a boat plying on the Ganges, in a few hours he was at Chandernagore where he went into secret residence. He sent a message to Sister Nivedita asking her to take up the editing of the Karmayogin in his absence. This was the end of his active connection with his two journals. At Chandernagore he plunged entirely into solitary meditation and ceased all other activity. Then there came to him a call to proceed to Pondicherry. A boat manned by some young revolutionaries of Uttarpara took him to Calcutta; there he boarded the Dupleix and reached Pondicherry on April 4, 1910.

At Pondicherry from this time onwards Sri Aurobindo's practice of Yoga became more and more absorbing. He dropped all participation in any public political activity, refused more than one request to preside at sessions of the restored Indian National Congress and made a rule of abstention from any public utterance of any kind not connected with his spiritual activities or any contribution of writings or articles except what he wrote afterwards in the Arya. For some years he kept up some private communication with the revolutionary forces he had led through one or two individuals, but this also he dropped after a time and his abstention from any kind of participation in politics became complete. As his vision of the future grew clearer, he saw that the eventual independence of India was assured by the march of Forces of which he became aware, that Britain would be compelled by the pressure of Indian resistance and by the pressure of international events to concede independence and that she was already moving towards that eventuality with whatever opposition and reluctance. He felt that there would be no need of armed insurrection and that the secret preparation for it could be dropped without injury to the nationalist cause, although the revolutionary spirit had to be maintained and would be maintained intact. His own personal intervention in politics would therefore be no longer indispensable. Apart from all this, the magnitude of the spiritual work set before him became more and more clear to him, and he saw that the concentration of all his energies on it was necessary. Accordingly, when the Ashram came into existence, he kept it free from all political connections or action; even when he intervened in politics twice afterwards on special occasions, this intervention was purely personal and the Ashram was not concerned in it. The British Government and numbers of people besides could not believe that Sri Aurobindo had ceased from all political action and it was supposed by them that he was secretly participating in revolutionary activities and even creating a secret organisation in the security of French India. But all this was pure imagination and rumour and there was nothing of the kind. His retirement from political activity was complete, just as was his personal retirement into solitude in 1910.

But this did not mean, as most people supposed, that he had retired into some height of spiritual experience devoid of any further interest in the world or in the fate of India. It could not mean that, for the very principle of his Yoga was not only to realise the Divine and attain to a complete spiritual consciousness, but also to take all life and all world activity into the scope of this spiritual consciousness and action and to base life on the Spirit and give it a spiritual meaning. In his retirement Sri Aurobindo kept a close watch on all that was happening in the world and in India and actively intervened whenever necessary, but solely with a spiritual force and silent spiritual action; for it is part of the experience of those who have advanced far in Yoga that besides the ordinary forces and activities of the mind and life and body in Matter, there are other forces and powers that can act and do act from behind and from above; there is also a spiritual dynamic power which can be possessed by those who are advanced in the spiritual consciousness, though all do not care to possess or, possessing, to use it, and this power is greater than any other and more effective. It was this force which, as soon as he had attained to it, he used, at first only in a limited field of personal work, but afterwards in a constant action upon the world forces. He had no reason to be dissatisfied with the results or to feel the necessity of any other kind of action. Twice however he found it advisable to take in addition other action of a public kind. The first was in relation to the Second World War. At the beginning he did not actively concern himself with it, but when it appeared as if Hitler would crush all the forces opposed to him and Nazism dominate the world, he began to intervene. He declared himself publicly on the side of the Allies, made some financial contributions in answer to the appeal for funds and encouraged those who sought his advice to enter the army or share in the war effort. Inwardly, he put his spiritual force behind the Allies from the moment of Dunkirk when everybody was expecting the immediate fall of England and the definite triumph of Hitler, and he had the satisfaction of seeing the rush of German victory almost immediately arrested and the tide of war begin to turn in the opposite direction. This he did, because he saw that behind Hitler and Nazism were dark Asuric forces and that their success would mean the enslavement of mankind to the tyranny of evil, and a set-back to the course of evolution and especially to the spiritual evolution of mankind: it would lead also to the enslavement not only of Europe but of Asia, and in it India, an enslavement far more terrible than any this country had ever endured, and the undoing of all the work that had been done for her liberation. It was this reason also that induced him to support publicly the Cripps' offer and to press the Congress leaders to accept it. He had not, for various reasons, intervened with his spiritual force against the Japanese aggression until it became evident that Japan intended to attack and even invade and conquer India. He allowed certain letters he had written in support of the war affirming his views of the Asuric nature and inevitable outcome of Hitlerism to become public. He supported the Cripps' offer because by its acceptance India and Britain could stand united against the Asuric forces and the solution of Cripps could be used as a step towards independence. When negotiations failed, Sri Aurobindo returned to his reliance on the use of spiritual force alone against the aggressor and had the satisfaction of seeing the tide of Japanese victory, which had till then swept everything before it, changed immediately into a tide of rapid, crushing and finally immense and over-whelming defeat. He had also after a time the satisfaction of seeing his previsions about the future of India justify themselves so that she stands independent with whatever internal difficulties.

Spiritual Life

Sri Aurobindo began his Yoga in 1904. Even before this he had already some spiritual experiences and that before he knew anything about Yoga or even what Yoga was. For example, a vast calm descended upon him at the moment when he stepped first on Indian soil after his long absence, in fact with his first step on the Apollo Bunder in Bombay. This calm surrounded him and remained for long months afterwards. There was also a realisation of the vacant Infinite while walking on the ridge of the Takht-i-Suleman in Kashmir, the living presence of Kali in a shrine on the banks of the Narmada, the vision of the Godhead surging up from within when in danger of a carriage accident in Baroda in the first year of his stay etc. But these were inner experiences coming of themselves and with a sudden unexpectedness, not part of a sadhana. He started Yoga by himself without a Guru getting the rule from a friend, a disciple of Brahmananda of Ganga Matt; it was confined at first to assiduous practice of Pranayam (at one time for six or more hours a day). There was no conflict or wavering between Yoga and politics; when he started Yoga, he carried on both without any idea of opposition between them. He wanted however to find a Guru. He met a Naga Sannyasi, one of the heads, in the course of this search, but did not accept him as Guru, but was confirmed by him in a belief in Yoga-power when he saw him cure Barin in almost a moment of a violent and clinging hill fever by merely cutting through a glassful of water crosswise with a knife while he repeated a silent mantra. Barin drank and was cured. Sri Aurobindo also met Brahmananda and was greatly impressed by him; but he had no helper or Guru in Yoga till he met Lele in Baroda and that was only for a short time. Meditating only for three days with Lele, he followed his instructions for silencing the mind and freeing it from the constant pressure of thought; he entered into an absolute and complete silence of the mind and indeed of the whole consciousness and in that silence had suddenly the enduring realisation of the indefinable Brahman, Tat, in which the whole universe seemed to be unreal and only That existed. This silence he kept for several months and it remained always within him; for when activity returned, it proceeded on the surface and within him all was calm. But at the time there was not the slightest activity of any kind even on the surface; there was only a still motionless perception spiritual and mental in its character . But this was not what Lele wanted, for he wanted the silence only in order that the inner voice of the heart might be heard without any thought interference; so he did his best to get him out of this Advaitic condition. A meeting was to be held in Bombay to hear Sri Aurobindo speak and he asked Lele how he was to speak when not even the shadow of a passing thought could arise in him. Lele told him to make namaskar before delivering a speech to the audience and wait and speech would come to him from another source than the mind. So in fact, when he was about to address the meeting, speech came. It should be noted however that Sri Aurobindo was not at any time in trance and something saw all that happened and spoke and acted according to need without the necessity of any conceptual thought or personal volition. Ever since all the mental activities, speech, writing, thought, will and other kindred activities have so come to him from the same source above the brain-mind; he had entered into the spiritual mind and what he afterwards called the overhead consciousness. This was his first major and fundamental Yogic realisation and experience and the true beginning and foundation of his Yoga.

Sri Aurobindo himself once wrote in a letter about his practice of Yoga: "I began my Yoga in 1904 without a Guru; in 1908 I received important help from a Mahratta Yogi and discovered the foundations of my sadhana; but from that time till the Mother came to India I received no spiritual help from anyone else. My sadhana before and afterwards was not founded upon books but upon personal experiences that crowded on me from within. But in the jail I had the Gita and the Upanishads with me, practised the yoga of the Gita and meditated with the help of the Upanishads, these were the only books from which I found guidance; the Veda which I first began to read long afterwards in Pondicherry rather confirmed what experiences I already had than was any guide to my sadhana. I sometimes turned to the Gita for light when there was a question or a difficulty and usually received help or an answer from it. It is a fact that I was hearing constantly the voice of Vivekananda speaking to me for a fortnight in the jail in my solitary meditation and felt his presence. The voice spoke only on a special and limited but very important field of spiritual experience and it ceased as soon as it had finished saying all that it had to say on that subject."

Before coming to Pondicherry Sri Aurobindo had already realised in full two of the four great realisations on which his Yoga and his spiritual philosophy are founded. The first he had gained while meditating with the Maharashtrian Yogi, Vishnu Bhaskar Lele, at Baroda in January 1908; it was the realisation of the silent spaceless and timeless Brahman gained after a complete and abiding stillness of the whole consciousness and attended at first by the overwhelming feeling and perception of the total unreality of the world, though this feeling disappeared after his second realisation which was that of the cosmic consciousness and of the Divine as all beings and all that is, which happened in the Alipore Jail. To the other two realisations, that of the supreme Reality with the static and dynamic Brahman as its two aspects and that of the higher planes of consciousness leading up to the Supermind, he was already on his way in his meditations in the Alipore Jail. Moreover, he had accepted from Lele as the principle of his sadhana to rely wholly on the Divine and his guidance alone both for his sadhana and his outward actions.

Thus gathering the essential elements of spiritual experience that are gained by the path of divine communion and spiritual realisation followed till now in India, he passed on in his Pondicherry life in search of a more complete experience uniting and harmonising the two ends of existence, Spirit and Matter. Most ways of Yoga are paths to the Beyond leading to the Spirit and in the end, away from life; Sri Aurobindo's rises to the Spirit to redescend with its gains bringing the light and power and bliss of the Spirit into life to transform it. Man's present existence in the material world is in this view or vision of things a life in the Ignorance with the Inconscient at its base, but even in its darkness and nescience there are involved the presence and possibilities of the Divine. The created world is not

358

a mistake or a vanity and illusion to be cast aside by the soul returning to heaven or Nirvana, but the scene of a spiritual evolution by which out of this material inconscience is to be manifested progressively the Divine Consciousness in things. Mind is the highest term yet reached in the evolution, but it is not the highest of which it is capable. There is above it a Supermind or etemal Truth-Consciousness which is in its nature the self-aware and self-determining light and power of Divine Knowledge. Mind is an ignorance seeking after Truth, but this is a self-existent Knowledge harmoniously manifesting the play of its forms and forces. It is only by the descent of this Supermind that the perfection dreamed of by all that is highest in humanity can come. It is possible by opening to a greater divine consciousness to rise to this power of light and bliss, discover one's true self, remain in constant union with the Divine and bring down the supramental Force for the transformation of mind and life and body. To realise this possibility has been the dynamic aim of Sri Aurobindo's Yoga.

During all his stay at Pondicherry from 1910 to the present moment he has remained more and more exclusively devoted to his spiritual work and his sadhana. In 1914 after four years of silent Yoga he began the publication of a philosophical monthly, the Arya. Most of his more important works, those published since in book form, the Isha Upanishad, the Essays on the Gita, The Life Divine and the Synthesis of Yoga (only the first part of the last title has since been published) appeared serially in the Arya. These works embodied much of the inner knowledge that had come to him in his practice of Yoga. Others were concerned with the spirit and significance of Indian civilisation and culture, the true meaning of the Vedas, the progress of human society, the nature and evolution of poetry, the possibility of the unification of the human race. At this time also he began to publish his poems, both those written in England and at Baroda and those, fewer in number, added during his period of political activity and in the first years of his residence at Pondicherry. The Arya ceased publication in 1921 after six years and a half of uninterrupted appearance.

Sri Aurobindo lived at first in retirement at Pondicherry with four or five companions. Afterwards more and yet more began to come to him to follow his spiritual path and the number became so large that a community of sadhaks had to be formed for the maintenance and collective guidance of those who had left everything behind for the sake of a higher life. This was the foundation of the Sri Aurobindo Ashram which has less been created than grown around him as its centre.

It may be pointed out in this connection that Sannyas was never accepted by Sri Aurobindo as part of his yoga. His Ashram at Pondicherry is a glaring contradiction to this popular idea of Sannyas connected with the name of an Ashram. Members of his Ashram are not Sannyasis, they do not wear the ochre garb or practise complete asceticism but are sadhaks of a life based on spiritual realisation, the ideal being the attainment of the life divine here on this earth and in the earthly existence.

Sri Aurobindo Ashram and The Teaching

The Ashram

An Ashram means the house or houses of a Teacher or Master of spiritual philosophy in which he receives and lodges those who come to him for the teaching and practice. An Ashram is not an association or a religious body or a monastery-it is only what has been indicated above and nothing more.

Everything in the Ashram belongs to the Teacher; the sadhaks (those who practise under him) have no claim, right or choice in any matter. They remain or go according to his will. Whatever money he receives is his property and not that of a public body. It is not a trust or a fund; for there is no public institution. Such Ashrams have existed in India since many centuries before Christ and still exist in large numbers. All depends on the Teacher and ends with his lifetime, unless there is another Teacher who can take his place.

The Ashram in Pondicherry came into being in this way. Sri Aurobindo at first lived in Pondicherry with a few inmates in his house; afterwards a few more joined him. Later on after the Mother joined him in 1920, the numbers began so much to increase that it was thought necessary to make an arrangement for lodging those who came, and houses were bought and rented according to need for the purpose. Arrangements had also to be made for the maintenance, repair, rebuilding of houses, for the service of food and for decent living and hygiene. All these were private rules made by the Mother and entirely at her discretion to increase, modify or alter there is nothing in them of a public character.

All houses of the Ashram are owned either by Sri Aurobindo or by the Mother. All the money spent belongs either to Sri Aurobindo or the Mother. Money is given by many to help in Sri Aurobindo's work. Some who are here give their earnings, but it is given to Sri Aurobindo or the Mother and not to the Ashram as a public body, for there is no such body.

The Ashram is not an association; there is no constituted body, no officials, no common property owned by an association, no governing council or committee, no activity undertaken of a public character.

The Ashram is not a political institution; all association with political activities is renounced by those who live here. All propaganda - religious, political or social-has to be eschewed by the inmates.

The Ashram is not a religious association. Those who are here come from all religions and some are of no religion. There is no creed or set of dogmas, no governing religious body; there are only the teachings of Sri Aurobindo and certain psychological practices of concentration and meditation etc. for the enlarging of the consciousness, receptivity to the Truth, mastery over the desires, the discovery of the divine Self and Consciousness concealed within each human being, a higher evolution of the nature.

The Teaching

The teaching of Sri Aurobindo starts from that of the ancient sages of India that behind the appearances of the universe there is the Reality of a Being and Consciousness, a Self of all things, one and eternal. All beings are united in that One Self and Spirit but divided by a certain separativity of consciousness, an ignorance of their true Self and Reality in the mind, life and body. It is possible by a certain psychological discipline to remove this veil of separative consciousness and become aware of the true Self, the Divinity within us and all.

Sri Aurobindo's teaching states that this One Being and Consciousness is involved here in Matter. Evolution is the method by which it liberates itself; consciousness appears in what seems to be inconscient and once having appeared is self-impelled to grow higher and higher and at the same time to enlarge and develop towards a greater and greater perfection. Life is the first step of this release of consciousness; mind is the second; but the evolution does not finish with mind, it awaits a release into something greater, a consciousness which is spiritual and supramental. The next step of the evolution must be towards the development of Supermind and Spirit as the dominant power in the conscious being. For only then will the involved Divinity in things release self entirely and it become possible for life to manifest perfection.

But while the former steps in evolution were taken by Nature without a conscious will in the plant and animal life, in man Nature becomes able to evolve by a conscious will in the instrument. It is not, however, by the mental will in man that this can be wholly done, for the mind goes only to a certain point and after that can only move in a circle. A conversion has to be made, a turning of the consciousness by which mind has to change into the higher principle. This method is to be found through the ancient psychological discipline and practice of Yoga. In the past, it has been attempted by a drawing away from the world and a disappearance into the height of the Self or Spirit. Sri Aurobindo teaches that a descent of the higher principle is possible which will not merely release the spiritual Self out of the world, but release it in the world, replace the mind's ignorance or its very limited knowledge by a supramental Truth- Consciousness which will be a sufficient instrument of the inner Self and make it possible for the human being to find himself dynamically as well as inwardly and grow out of his still animal humanity into a diviner race. The psychological discipline of Yoga can be used to that end by opening all the parts of the being to a conversion or transformation through the descent and working of the higher still concealed supramental principle.

This however cannot be done at once or in a short time or by any rapid or miraculous transformation. Many steps have to be taken by the seeker before the supramental descent is possible. Man lives mostly in his surface mind, life and body, but there is an inner being within him with greater possibilities to which he has to awake - for it is only a very restricted influence from it that he receives now and that pushes him to a constant pursuit or a greater beauty, harmony, power and knowledge. The first process of Yoga is therefore to open the ranges of this inner being and to live from there outward, governing his outward life by an inner light and force. In doing so he discovers in himself his true soul which is not this outer mixture of mental, vital and physical elements but something of the Reality behind them, a spark from the one Divine Fire. He has to learn to live in his soul and purify and orientate by its drive towards the Truth the rest of the nature. There can follow afterwards an opening upward and descent or a higher principle of the Being. But even then it is not at once the full supramental Light and Force. For there are several ranges of consciousness between the ordinary human mind and the supramental Truth-Consciousness. These intervening ranges have to be opened up and their power brought down into the mind, life and body. Only afterwards can the full power of the Truth-Consciousness work in the nature. The process of this self-discipline or sadhana is therefore long and difficult, but even a little of it is so much gained because it makes the ultimate release and perfection more possible.

There are many things belonging to older systems that are necessary on the way-an opening of the mind to a greater wideness and to the sense of the Self and the Infinite, an emergence into what has been called the cosmic consciousness, mastery over the desires and passions; an outward asceticism is not essential, but the conquest of desire and attachment and a control over the body and its needs, greeds and instincts are indispensable. There is a combination of the principles of the old systems, the way of knowledge through the mind's discernment between Reality and the appearance, the heart's way of devotion, love and surrender and the way of works turning the will away from motives of self-interest to the Truth and the service of a greater Reality than the ego. For the whole being has to be trained so that it can respond and be transformed when it is possible for that greater Light and Force to work in the nature.

In this discipline the inspiration of the Master, and in the difficult stages his control and his presence, are indispensable-for it would be impossible otherwise to go through it without much stumbling and error which would prevent all chance of success. The Master is one who has risen to a higher consciousness and being and he is often regarded as its manifestation or representative. He not only helps by his teaching and still more by his influence and example but by a power to communicate his own experience to others.

This is Sri Aurobindo's teaching and method of practice. It is not his object to develop any one religion or to amalgamate the older religions or to found any new religion-for any of these things would lead away from his central purpose. The one aim of his Yoga is an inner self-development by which each one who follows it can in time discover the One Self in all and evolve a higher consciousness than the mental, a spiritual and supramental consciousness which will transform and divinise human nature.

The Mother's Symbol

It is the symbolic design of the white Lotus of Supreme Consciousness. The central circle represents the Divine Consciousness or the Supreme Mother.

The four petals represent the four powers (or Aspects) of the Mother.

The twelve petals represent the twelve powers of the Mother manifested for Her work.

Sri Aurobindo's Symbol

The descending triangle represents Sat - Chit - Ananda.

The ascending triangle represents the aspiring answer from matter under the form of life, light and love.

The junction of both — the central square — is the perfect manifestation having at its centre the Avatar of the Supreme — the Lotus.

The water — inside the square — represents the multiplicity, the creation.

Glossary

Adhara – vehicle (vessel, support); that in which the consciousness is now contained, mind-life-body.

Adwaita – One-Existence.

Adya Shakti – original power; the supreme divine Consciousness and Power above the worlds; the Transcendental Mother.

Ahankara – ego-sense; ego-idea; the divisional principle of ego-formation; the seperative ego-sense which makes each being conceive of itself as an independent personality.

Anisa – not-lord; subject.

Aparãrdha – lower half of (world existence); the lower hemisphere.

Attahãsya – the laughter that makes light of defeat and death and the powers of the ignorance.

Avatara – Incarnation; the descent into form; the revelation of the Godhead in humanity; the Divine manifest in human appearance.

Bhakti – love for the Divine, devotion to the Divine.

Bhoga – enjoyment, possesson.

Bhadram – good, happy; anything good, auspicious, happy.

Brahma – the power of the Divine which creates the world by the word.

Brahman – the Supreme is brahman, the one Reality which is not only the spiritual, material and conscious substance of all the ideas and forces and forms of the universe, but their origin, support and possessor, the cosmic and supracosmic Spirit.

Brahmavidya – the knowledge of Brahman.

Brahmarandhra – in yoga: the opening at the top of the skull.

Buddhi – intelligence-will; understanding; intellect; reason; thinking mind; the discriminating principle, at once intelligence and will.

Daityas – demons.

Dhãma – placing, status, position, foundation; the placing of the law in a founded harmony which creates for us our plane of living and the character of our consciousness, action and thought.

Gita – "the Song of the Blessed Lord", a celebrated scripture in the form of a dialogue between Krsna (Bhagavan) and Arjuna spoken on the battlefield of Kuruksetra, which occurs as an episode in Mahabharata.

Jagadguru – the World-Teacher.

Janaka – a famous king and sage the father of Sita.

Japa – repetition of a mantra or the name of God.

Jiva – living creature.

Karma – action is greater than inaction.

Kriya – effective practice (of yoga); every practice which helps the gaining of higher knowledge.

Kshatriya – men of power and action who have abandoned their life (for a cause).

Kuvera – The god of riches.

Lila – play, game, the cosmic play. play of the divine Delight

Lilamãya – playful.

Manomaya purusa – the mental Being, leader of the life and body.

Mantra – sacred syllable, name or mystic formula; the intuitive and inspired rhythmic utterance; any of the verses of the Veda, revealed verses of power not of ordinary but of a divine inspiration and source.

Mantric – relating to mantra

Mayavada – the doctrine which holds that the world is maya, i.e. an illusion.

Mukti – liberation.

Mülãdhãra – root vessel or chamber; the physical consciousness centre.

Namajapa – the constant calling to the Divine, the Lord or the Divine Mother by using the name. In this yoga the name of the Mother or Sri Aurobindo or of both is used i.e. Om namo bhagvate Sri Aurobindaya; Mother Sri Aurobindo is my refuge; Om Mother Sri Aurobindo.

Nadis – the nerve channels.

Nigraha – repression, suppression.

Prakriti – "working out"; Nature; Nature Force; Nature-Soul; executive or working force.

Pishachas – demons; (hostile) beings of the lower vital.

Prana – life-energy; life; the breath of life.

Pranayama – the government and control of the respiration; regulated direction and arrestation by exercises of breathing of the vital currents of energy of the body.

Purusha – Person; Conscious Being; Conscious Soul; Soul; essential being supporting the play of Prakriti; a Consciousness - or a Conscient – behind, that is the lord, witness, knower, enjoyer, upholder and source of sanction for Nature's works.

Rajas – the force of kenesis translates in quality as struggle and effort, passion and action. Rajas one of the three gunas, the mode of action, desire amd passion.

Rajasic – one who is dominated by rajas.

Rajayoga – (a particular system of yoga), the use of mental askesis for the opening up of the divine life on all its planes.

Rakshasa – giant, giant power of darkness, a (hostile) being of the middle vital plane.

Rakshasai Maya – illusion of the powers of darkness.

Rama – popular short form for Ramachandra, a celebrated avatara of Vishnu.

Ravana – King of the rakshasas; (the chief of the rakshasas who abducted Sita and was slain by her husband Rama).

Rig Veda – the most ancient of the sacred books of India, composed of metrical hymns arranged in ten books.

Rtam – the Right, truth of divine being regulating right activity both of mind and body, truth of knowledge and action; Truth; truth-Consciousness.

Rudra – "fierce, violent" ;(Ved); the Divine as master of our evolution by violence and battle, the deva or Deity ascending in the cosmos; the Terrible one, the God of might and wrath, a member of the divine Triad, expressive of the destructive process in the cosmos

Sadhak – one who is getting or trying to get realisation; one who seeks siddhi by the practice of sadhana.

Sadhana – the practice of yoga; the practice by which perfection (siddhi) is attained; spiritual self-training and exercise.

Samadhi – Yogic trance (in which the mind acquires the capacity of withdrawing from its limited waking activities into freer and higher states of consciousness; [in the Gita]; calm desireless, griefless fixity of the buddhi in self-poise and self-knowledge.

Samatã – equality, equanimity.

Sãmrãjya – empire; perfect empire without; mastery of one's environment and consciousness.

Samyama – 1. self-control, rejection or self-dissociation. 2. Concentration, directing or dwelling of the consciousness (by which one becomes aware of all that is in an object).

Sannyasin – an ascetic; (one who practises) laying aside; renunciation (of life and action).

Sankhyas – the analysis, the enumerative and discriminative setting forth of the principles of our being; the abstract and analytical realisation of truth.

Sanskaras – association, impression, fixed notion, habitual reaction formed by one's past.

Sãnti – calm, peace, spiritual peace.

Sarvam brahma – The All Brahma.

Satya Yuga – [the first of the four Ages]. The Age of the Truth; the Golden Age.

Sattwic – of Sattwa, one of the three gunas; the mode of light and poise and peace; the force of equilibrium (translates in quality as good and harmony and happiness and light).

Shakti – Energy, Force, Strength, Will,, Power; the self-existent, self-effective Power of the Lord which expresses itself in the working of prakriti.

Shastra – any systematised teaching and science; the moral and social code; the science and art of right knowledge, right works, right living; [in yoga]; the knowledge of the truths, principles, powers and and processes that govern the realisation.

Siddhi – 1.perfection, fulfilment, accomplishment of the aims of self-discipline by yoga. 2. An extraordinary or occult power.

Tamas – darkness, obscurity; [one of the three gunas] ; the mode of ignorance and inertia, the force of inconscient (translates in quality as incapacity and inaction).

Tamasic – One who is dominated by tamas.

Tantra – a yogic system which is in its nature synthetical and starts from a great central principle of Nature, a great dynamic force of Nature; in the Vedic method of yoga the lord of the yoga is the purusa, the Conscious-Soul, but in tantra it is rather prakriti the Nature-Soul, the Energy, the Will-in-Power executive in the universe; it was by learning and applying the secrets of the Will-in-Power, its methods, its tantra, that the tantrika yogin pursued the aim of his discipline – mastery, perfection, liberation, beautitude; the method of tantrika disciplines is to raise Nature in man into manifest powers of spirit.

Tantric – one who practices tantra.

Tapasya – effort, energism, austerity of the personal will, ascetic force, arkesis; concentration of the will and energy to control the mind, vital and physical and to change them or bring down the higher consciousness or for any other yogic purpose or high purpose.

Turiya – the fourth, the fourth plane of our consciousness, the superconscient; the Absolute

Vedanta – a system of philosophy based on the Upanishads teaching the culminating knowledge of the Absolute.

Vedantins – those who follow Vedanta.

Vijnana – the free spiritual or divine intelligence; causal Idea; Truth; gnosis; supermind; the comprehensive aspect of the true unifying knowledge; the large embracing consciousness, especially characteristic of the supramental energy, which takes into itself the truth and idea and object of knowledge and sees them all at once in their essence, totality and parts or aspects.

Yoga – joining, union; the union of the soul with the immortal being and consciousness and delight of the Divine; a methodical effort towards self-perfection by the expression of the potentialities latent in the being and union of the human individual with the universal and transcendent existence.

Yogadrishti – (power of) vision.

HEADINGS	PAGE NO.

HEADINGS	PAGE NO.

HEADINGS	PAGE NO.

HEADINGS	PAGE NO.

Sri Aurobindo's Biography

www.sriaurobindo.ca

www.sriaurobindo.us

CPSIA information can be obtained at www.ICGtesting.com
Printed in the USA
LVOW071534260613

340384LV00005B/138/P